THE CRITICAL IMAGINATION IN AFRICAN LITERATURE

THE Critical Imagination IN African Literature

ESSAYS IN HONOR OF Michael J. C. Echeruo

Edited by Maik Nwosu
and Obiwu

Syracuse University Press

First Edition 2015
15 16 17 18 19 20 6 5 4 3 2 1

∞ The paper used in this publication meets the minimum requirements of the American National Standard for Information Sciences—Permanence of Paper for Printed Library Materials, ANSI Z39.48-1992.

For a listing of books published and distributed by Syracuse University Press, visit www.SyracuseUniversityPress.syr.edu.

ISBN: 978-0-8156-3387-7 (pbk.) 978-0-8156-5310-3 (e-book)

Library of Congress Cataloging-in-Publication Data
The critical imagination in African literature : essays in honor of Michael J.C. Echeruo / edited by Maik Nwosu and Obiwu. — First edition.
pages cm
Includes bibliographical references and index.
ISBN 978-0-8156-3387-7 (pbk. : alk. paper) — ISBN 978-0-8156-5310-3 (e-book)
1. African literature (English)—20th century—History and criticism. 2. African literature (English)—21st century—History and criticism. 3. Africa—Intellectual life. I. Nwosu, Maik, editor. II. Obiwu, editor. III. Echeruo, Michael J. C., honouree.
PR9340.C745 2015
820.9'96—dc23 2015010779

Manufactured in the United States of America

Contents

Preface

MAIK NWOSU

In 2010, Professor Michael Joseph Chukwudalu Echeruo, the William Safire Professor of Modern Letters in the Department of English and Textual Studies at Syracuse University, retired from the academy. His career had spanned forty-five years, beginning in 1965 when he earned his doctoral degree from Cornell University. He taught at various universities (including the University of Nigeria, Nsukka, and the University of Ibadan) and served as the pioneer vice-chancellor at Abia State University, Uturu (formerly Imo State University). Echeruo defined himself through his work as a creative writer and a literary critic committed to the varied exploration and interrogation of diverse kinds of experience or systems of thought. The core of his concern remained the African experience and imagination, but its entire circumference included a spectrum of global imaginaries. The range of his writings encompassed poetry collections, particularly *Mortality* (1968); an interrogation of colonial literature in such works as *Joyce Cary and the Novel of Africa* (1973) and *The Conditioned Imagination from Shakespeare to Conrad* (1978); a study of nineteenth-century Lagos, *Victorian Lagos: Aspects of Nineteenth-Century Lagos Life* (1977); practical lexicography, the *Igbo-English Dictionary: A Comprehensive Dictionary of the Igbo Language* (1998); *A Concordance to the Poems of Christopher Okigbo* (2008); a key lecture on identity and continuity; a disputation on Jacques Derrida, language games, and theory; a treatise on diasporic ontology; a discourse on modernism, blackface, and the postcolonial condition; and much more. As important as it obviously was, it was not so much a concentration on an area of scholarship that defined Echeruo as it was the sort of rigorous intellectualism that he applied to different focal concerns. In African studies, where he is particularly celebrated, the "Echeruoan ideal" is understood as an intervention or intellectual engagement characterized by a broadness of vision as well as a depth of analysis. It is this ideal—this mode of thoughtful, Africa-centered scholarship—that this critical anthology projectively celebrates.

The essays collected here contextually honor Echeruo's scholarship and contributions to the African intellectual tradition. Most of the essays are not about Echeruo or his work. The range of interest evident in *The Critical Imagination in African Literature* is extensive. The critical anthology is divided into four parts. Although this division points up different aspects of African literature or its associated critical imagination (including interpretive possibilities), it is applied more for organizational convenience than as an inflexible lense for the apprehension of African literature. The first, African Literature and Global Imaginaries, looks at some significant aspects of African literature in relation to international dis/connections of people and ideas. My essay, "The Figuration of the *Un*: Between African and World Literature," examines the figuration of the *un* (the generative transformation or presential application of the *un*seen, the *un*done, the *un*known, and other pertinent *uns*) that luminously explains both African and world literature. I argue that an examination of the multidimensionality of African literature translates into (or can be translated into) a further appreciation of "world literature." In "The Vortex of the Expulsion: The Search for an Asian African Imaginary," Rashna Singh focuses on the 1972 expulsion of Asians who were not Ugandan citizens and the effect of that "historical moment" on Ugandan writers of Indian descent since then. The texts that she connectively examines include Peter Nazareth's *The General Is Up*, Jameela Siddiqi's *The Feast of the Nine Virgins*, and Mira Nair's film *Mississippi Masala* (scripted by Sooni Taraporevala).

The second part of the anthology, African Literature and Consciousness, interprets instances of (as well as trends in) African literature from different perspectives as manifestations of human consciousness grounded in particular sociohistorical or psychoanalytical contexts. Obiwu's essay, "Jacques Lacan in Africa: Travel, Moroccan Cemetery, Egyptian Hieroglyphics, and Other Passions of Theory," references Lacan's essays, seminars, interviews, and correspondences as it explores Lacan's African visitations as well as how the continent possibly and actually contributed to the shaping of Lacanian psychoanalytic theory. "(Re)Defining the Self through Trauma in West African Postcolonial Short Fiction" by Bojana Coulibaly demonstrates that West African short fiction evidences signs of traumas attributable to dynamic existential realities. Coulibaly's analysis of short narratives by Ama Ata Aidoo, Chinua Achebe, Flora Nwapa, Chris Abani, and Chimamanda Ngozi Adichie instantiates her thesis. In "African Postcolonial Imagination and the Moral Challenges of Our Times," Chielozona Eze interrogates the tendency in African literature and literary criticism toward counter-discourse. New generation African writers, he contends, have moved away from the earlier generations' "anti-imperialist rhetoric" and turned instead to "introspectionism," which he describes as "the simple act of self-observation, or the cultural act of looking inward with the goal of critiquing oneself in order to better relate to others."

African Literature and Feminist Perspectives, the third segment of the anthology, is constituted by three essays that particularly project the feminine/feminist point of view. Glen Bush's "Survivalist Autobiographies: The Struggles of African Muslim Women" discusses autobiographies by African Muslim women, which he describes as "narratives of escape and re-invention" that highlight "the daily abuses common in the African Muslim world." The autobiographies that he scrutinizes include *Desert Flower: The Extraordinary Life of a Desert Nomad* (1998) by Waris Dirie, *Slave* (2003) by Mende Nazer, *Infidel* (2007) by Ayaan Hirsi Ali, and *Tears of the Desert: A Memoir of Survival in Darfur* (2008) by Halima Bashir. In Kanchana Ugbabe's "Rebellion as a Narrative Strategy in Southern African Women's Writing," she discusses the creative ways in which Bessie Head, Miriam Tlali, and Tsitsi Dangarembga use rebellion and protest in their novels and short stories. She argues that the "feminine text" is not only "subversive in its narrative point of view [but also] undermines and demystifies patriarchal ideologies. The writer ventures into uncharted territories with a newness of vision and a zeal to tell a story. She is a metaphoric exile looking from the outside and trying to make sense of an inside world." Heather Hewett's "Rewriting Human Rights: Gender,

Violence, and Freedom in the Fiction of Chimamanda Ngozi Adichie" points out that much Anglophone African diasporic literature has been pro-human rights from its origins and has remained so. "Rather than jettisoning the system of human rights altogether," she remarks, "many feminists and women's rights activists have claimed human rights ideals for women at the same time that they have critiqued the human rights regime for its inattention to gender as well as other intersectional components of identity." She contextualizes contemporary African Anglophone "witness literature" in her analysis of Adichie's fiction.

The fourth section of the anthology, African Literature and Cultural Aesthetics, includes readings of African literature that centralize cultural or cross-cultural characteristics, concerns, and correspondences (especially with reference to narratives of power and redemption). Sule Egya's "Dialogism, African Poetics, and Contemporary Nigerian Poetry in English," utilizes both Mikhail M. Bakhtin's theory of dialogism and African oral performance theory in its study of Nigerian poetry under repressive military regimes between the 1980s and the 1990s. His exploration leads to the conclusion that "the contemporary poets, following the interventionist role of the oral artist, still see themselves as oracles that must speak up in the face of socio-political difficulties, and in doing so they *intentionally* set out to address characters and issues." Dul Johnson connects African and African American literature in "Confronting Politics Through History: A Reading of the Historical Novels of Ayi Kwei Armah and John Edgar Wideman." Arguing that history and politics are inseparable and that the invocation of history has always been an important part of African and African American life and literature, he demonstrates the validity of his argument by an arterial examination of the works of Ayi Kwei Armah and John Edgar Wideman.

Besides the ten essays in the four sections, there is also a special focus essay and a report. The essay, "Cultural Icon: Michael J. C. Echeruo and the African Academy" by Obiwu, discusses Professor Echeruo as an African intellectual and a humanist by analyzing some of his major works and other contributions. The report is a pertinent account of the Michael J. C. Echeruo Valedictory Symposium, which was held at Syracuse University,

New York, on October 15, 2010. The event convoked scholars (mostly Africanists) and provided an opportunity for responses to old questions and the articulation of new ones.

The concerns in *The Critical Imagination in African Literature* are indeed varied, as are the modes of inquiry, but a common quality is that many of the essays point up new theoretical directions in the continuing debate or discourse that has characterized modern African literature. These essays do not constitute the beginning of African literary history or theory, but many of them further a fuller text/context appreciation of modern African literature and criticism from both a distinctive and a relational perspective. Many of them belong to—and extend—the sphere of African intellectual thought pioneered by scholars such as Echeruo. It is this *extension,* in terms of insightfully contributing to an ongoing discourse and significantly highlighting or initiating new analytical possibilities, that constitutes the thrust of this critical anthology.

Our aim is a dual singularity, as paradoxical as this might seem—to further the culture of vigorous discourse on African literature and to salute an iconic figure that has incarnated that culture in the past fifty years, approximately. The breadth of Echeruo's scholarship is almost staggering—important contributions to intellectual debates on Igbo, African, African diaspora, European, and American literatures and literary theories; on nations and narratives; on global modernism; on structuralism and meaning; et cetera. A major aspect of that scholarship is methodological rigor. Echeruo's reputation mainly lies not in the fact that he has a subject or a list of subjects that he regularly returns to, as many scholars do, but that after he initiates or enters a conversation the intellectual tone is remarkably elevated. Not one to flounder in foggy or pseudo-intellectual atmospherics, Echeruo's scholarship is marked by the necessary historicization of relatable significancies in philosophical and literary thought. In part, that is why he matters, so much so that we feel it is only proper to honor him by producing a volume of essays that have been inspired by this sort of scholarship, essays that could collectively impact the discourse on African literature in the way that Echeruo has done over the years. These reflective essays may therefore be said to belong to an Echeruoan tradition of Africa-focused scholarship, intellectual curiosity, global imagination, and critical rigor. And, in a manner characteristic of this tradition, the essays do more than just invoke or gesture toward an ethos that is part of a global or human cognitive map. They often tend toward the expansion or reinvention of that tradition.

Denver, Colorado, 2014

THE CRITICAL IMAGINATION IN AFRICAN LITERATURE

1

Special Focus

Cultural Icon: Michael J. C. Echeruo and the African Academy

OBIWU

In 1979, Adiele Afigbo placed Echeruo in the front rank of the small group of professors whom Bertrand Russell identified as "whole-heartedly and enthusiastically" admired by inquiring minds (Afigbo 1979, 5). In his fiftieth birthday essay tribute to Echeruo in 1994, "The Dignity of Intellectual Labor," Isidore Okpewho positioned Echeruo as "the undisputed guru" of Africa's critical pantheon. According to Okpewho, "In any roll call of literary scholars today in Nigeria (if not Africa), his name is usually the first" (1994, 192). During his lecture visit to Syracuse University in 2000, the eminent critic Ben Obumselu spoke of Echeruo's unrivaled devotion to scholarship and his painstaking pursuit of critical excellence exemplified in his close attention to textual analysis and the archival excavation of background material.[1] Above all, noted Obumselu, Echeruo demonstrates a superior understanding of discourse and control of language that are not only the envy of his peers but have also set too high a standard for generations of Nigerian English scholars after him.

The foregoing encomiums on Echeruo beg the question: When his colleagues hail him in spite of his habitual defiance of the pomp of vanity

1. Conversations with Professor Obumselu during his month-long lecture visit on the invitation of the Syracuse University Student Union, the African Student Union, and the Center for International Services. His lecture was entitled "African Myths: Beyond the Killing Field."

and recognition (what Afigbo describes as "his unboastful character"), what exactly are they talking about? What is the substance of Echeruo's intellectual authority? The answer, though complex, would be traced partly to his stellar student antecedents and partly to his equally illustrious career. Echeruo graduated at the top of his class at the reputable Stella Maris High School, Port Harcourt, Nigeria. He was College Scholar and best graduating student at the University College, Ibadan, Nigeria, where he was a classmate of the respected African critic Abiola Irele. He completed his graduate studies at Cornell University with prestigious laurels, including Hoyt Scholar of the university, Phi Kappa Phi (social sciences), and Phi Beta Kappa (humanities). Today, the *Igbo-English Dictionary* is one of the select faculty texts in prominent display on the third floor of the Hall of Languages at Syracuse University, where Echeruo was the distinguished William Safire Professor of Modern Letters and now serves as professor emeritus.

As "a trained academic," Echeruo is not only concerned with the "intellectual history" of Africa, but even more with the "cosmopolitan black ethos" (Killam 1981, 126–29). As a public intellectual, Echeruo is committed to the epical quality of the regenerative human spirit. That is why he speaks of love as "no longer love in the young sense of the word, but love as a different and adult reality," terrible and filled with suffering. The pangs of love may be ecstatic, but the elation is of a higher order (Lindfors 1974, 7). This is the sensibility that is captured in the haunting imagery of the poem "Debut" in his first poetry collection, *Mortality* (1968): "A thing of beauty/ is a thing of sorrow, for ever" (3). For Echeruo, the "gladness" of beauty will "not pass away" and "catharsis is the prelude to a birth."

The postcolonial vision of Echeruo's poet-speaker is consciously juxtaposed against the untrammeled romanticism of John Keats's persona in "Endymion." Echeruo counteracts the mediated opening of Keats's song of innocence with the unpretentious harsh lights of his own song of experience because, he insists, "Things do not begin as they end." For Echeruo, therefore, the scholar is necessarily an intellectual who is always in the service of the community and whose experience is his or her inalienable inheritance. For the Echeruoan scholar, knowledge is uncircumscribed and service is without borders. The second stanza of "Debut" offers an eternal truth that the world is a marble canvas and language is the agency for the search, the discovery, and the redemption: "till we saw the palm-nuts again/ by which we were to live?"

It is natural that poetry would foreground a discussion of Echeruo's writing and his love of language, since poetry marked his early advent into the African continental literary landscape. Echeruo won first prize at the 1963 All Africa Poetry Competition, beating out Dennis Brutus and K. A. Nortje to second and third places, respectively ("South African, Nigerian Win" 1963, 4). That event was the pioneer literary contest for African writers in English organized by the Mbari Club and the International Congress for Cultural Freedom, and the judges were Langston Hughes, Ulli Beier, and Ezekiel Mphahlele. Five years later, Echeruo published *Mortality*, a collection of thirty poems arranged in five sections. Section 1, "Debut," contains eleven poems; section 2, "Mortal Songs," and section 3, "Defections," each have seven poems; the final sections 4, "Poems to God and O'Brien," and 5, "Daedalus," are comprised of four poems and one poem, respectively. The themes of *Mortality* range from spiritual quest and the spring of life to stultifying rainstorms that represent the 1966 Nigerian military coups and subsequent genocide against the Igbo ethnic group in Northern Nigeria and other parts of the country. Echeruo draws on the grim "specters of songs" ("Rain," 33), "wiser buds" of "June" ("Come, Come Spring," 34), and the "inheritance" of "June" ("Fanfare for June," 36) to explore the failure, perversion, and ruination of memory.

The appearance and success of *Mortality* in the middle of the Biafran War was followed by the publication of *Distanced* (1975), a collection of eighteen poems. Echeruo takes time to note in its three-sentence "Preface" that only one poem, "Their Finest Hour," was written in Biafra in June 1968. "All the other poems were written in Nigeria in the six months following the end of the War" (4). The haunting specter of June, which is encountered in the morbidity of *Mortality*, pervades the lyricism of the three sections of *Distanced* like a bestial, macabre dance. The first section ("Requiem") comprises six poems, and the second ("Prospect") and third ("My Fatherland!") comprise one and eleven poems, respectively. In five brief lines, the first poem of the collection eschews all pretensions to literary aesthetics in its stark and incisive depiction of the poet's path into a postmodern and postcolonial wasteland.

"Requiem"

They shot him down
    His first night out;
We buried him
    The very next day

A morning sun, proud, over him. (7)

In like manner the persona of the last poem of the collection, "Their Finest Hour," recoils from the tragic image of the "ravaged land" (33). In the metaphor of the "little ewes and the small kids," which are recognized by the bulging udders, the poet portrays bounties of the "known" past ("I have known"), in contrast with the devastation of kwashiorkor in the "unknown" present ("Now, I do not know").

Do I now know
the hearth from the fires that consume,
with this roaring wind in the air
and the fires still, still coming
the wind fanning the embers to death?

Unfortunately, Echeruo's poetic intensity suffered a hiatus after the publication of *Distanced*. He had famously informed the scholar-critic Bernth Lindfors in 1974 that he considered himself more of a critic than a poet. The sudden appearance of the poem "Dedication (After Chris Okigbo, friend)," as an epigraphic tribute to his landmark Okigbo *Concordance* in 2008 was therefore a surprise. Originally written in 2007, "Dedication" seeks to accentuate the interview with Lindfors by, on the one hand, mourning the demise of the late poet Christopher Okigbo in Biafra and, on the other hand, signing the epitaph heralding both the end of poetry and his own symbolic exit from the praxis of the genre. Broken into four stanzas of eleven, ten, six, and one line, the poem's second stanza suggests that the tragedy that inspires poetic invention also marks its impotency.

Too late now to be a poet
Too late now to learn
To say nothing that hastens a sunrise
When the southwesterly winds fan the waters
Into eddies of triumphant orgy
And the heart bleeds blood
And the eyes shed salt in pail-loads
And mourn the never-heaving,
    never urging ardor
    of a tired yard.

These poems prove what Okechukwu Umeh describes as Echeruo's "unique and unorthodox" perception as a religiously conscious poet far beyond the gaze of his Nigerian peers Pol Ndu, Okigbo, Okogbule Wonodi, and Wole Soyinka (1988, 204). They also clearly situate Adrian Roscoe's conjecture that Echeruo "did not seem as anxious as Gabriel Okara and Wole Soyinka to fashion" his art from traditional African material (1971, 63). Yet the perceptive observations on his craft have not endeared Echeruo to some critics whose shafts have latched onto the classical-cum-modernist pedigrees and Latinate phraseology of such early poems of *Mortality* as "Sophia" (4), "They . . ." (5), "Cross-roads" (6), and "Easter Penitence" (12) to assault the depth and language of his creative practice.

In such books as *Toward the Decolonization of African Literature* (Chinweizu, Jemie, and Madubuike 1985) and *The West and the Rest of Us* (Chinweizu 1975), Echeruo's poetry has been assailed for its obscurantism. I suspect, however, that much of Echeruo's earlier writing (particularly those published in the seventeen years between 1962 and 1979) could have drawn the ire of his intemperate critics.[2] Given his academic background, it is understandable that aesthetic consideration should rank high in his literary taste. Having come from the generation after Echeruo, the self-proclaimed "bolekaja" troika neither shared his orientation nor understood

2. I have provided a chronological list of Echeruo's primary texts below, including other titles I have not mentioned or fully discussed in the essay.

his mission. They found his poetry alienating and his discourse elitist. Violent resistance expressed in aggressive terms has proved to be the natural recourse of the psychotic subject. Branding Echeruo (along with J. P. Clark-Bekederemo, Okigbo, and Soyinka) as a "Euromodernist" (Chinweizu, Jemie, and Madubuike 1980, 147–238) and "Europhiliac" (Chinweizu 1975, 295–321), and ignoring the full extent of his contributions to the development of African scholarship, have only exposed the dangers of hasty criticism.[3]

Echeruo's composition in "Debut" points to his shared heritage with Chinua Achebe, who asserts in his novel *Things Fall Apart* (1958) that "Proverbs are the palm-oil with which words are eaten" (7). Further still, Echeruo and Achebe demonstrate their common inheritance of the great tradition of Olaudah Equiano, who posits in his pioneer slave narrative, *The Interesting Narrative of the Life of Olaudah Equiano, or Gustavus Vassa, the African, Written by Himself* (1789), that "we never polluted the name of the object of our adoration" (2003, 41). As in the writing of Equiano and Achebe, the discipline and devotion of Echeruo's scholarship that Obumselu and others vouchsafe is founded on the Igbo cultural ethic that celebrates the beauty and sanctity of discourse. That is why Echeruo insists, in his essay "Derrida, Language Games, and Theory" (1995), on the quality of language as "both a means and a condition for communication and consciousness" (102). He argues that language expresses us and by extension could be species specific. Language defines, defies, and denies. Being elastic, language constructs, deconstructs, and reconstructs. As much as any other African writer and scholar, Echeruo has for the past fifty years consistently demonstrated the integrity of language to accommodate any legitimate games its speakers care to play with it. This is the basis of his taking Jacques Derrida to task for blindsiding language, which Echeruo sees as "a continuous process of re-construction which, in hindsight, *looks*

3. Soyinka's responses in several essays in *Art, Dialogue, and Outrage* (1994), clearly demonstrate the enormous gap between the Echeruo generation and that of its successor-antagonists.

(must look) like deconstruction" (102). This is also the foundation of his odyssey in literature, public administration, and writing.

Echeruo's challenge to the critical imagination is central to language mainly as it relates to locution and the isolation of codes in communication. His originality lies in the discovery that the validity of Igbo as a complete system of signs depends on the functional location of the postcolonial subject as a speaking subject. This is the crux of Kay Williamson's invitation of native Igbo speakers to participate in the work of Igbo linguistics. For the postcolonial African scholar, the symbolic invention of colonial imperialism and globalization makes the task inevitable. For the Igbo scholar, the task is doubled by the subject of Biafra as the last historical determinism in the temporal breaks of a chiasmatic universal machine. According to Echeruo, "We are a people who should have disappeared from the face of the earth a long time ago from a multiplicity of vicissitudes but have miraculously avoided doing so (from famine as Achebe shows in *Things Fall Apart*; from slavery, as Equiano shows in *Interesting Narrative*; and from genocide, as Echeruo shows in *Distanced*)" (*A Matter of Identity* 1979, 7). That is why the analyst Jacques Lacan notes that "language is completely burdened with our history, it is as contingent as this sign, and what is more it is ambiguous." Lacan avers that in the game of diverse intersubjectivities, the world of language is possible insofar as we have our place in it anywhere. It is in this world that "each man has to recognize a calling, a vocation, which happens to be revealed to him" (Lacan 1991b, 277–87).

As much as his poetry, Echeruo's prose writing and critical literature enhance both his aesthetic vision and his linguistic mission. His *Victorian Lagos* (1977; the original draft was lost in the Biafran War, 1967–70) is a pioneer in the study of African modernism. *The Conditioned Imagination from Shakespeare to Conrad* (1978) is a precursor of emergent postcolonial studies. "Concert and Theater in Late Nineteenth-Century Lagos" (1981) is a foundational work in Nigerian theater studies, preceding Soyinka's "Towards a True Theater," J. P. Clark-Bekederemo's "Poetry of the Urhobo Dance Udje," Oyin Ogunba's "Theater in Nigeria," and J. A. Adedeji's "The Place of Drama in Yoruba Religious Observance." Onuora Nzekwu's

"Carnival in Opobo" and "Masquerade" may be the earliest published studies by a Nigerian before it.[4]

In *The Conditioned Imagination*, Echeruo discovers that the persistent schema of the "great" Euro-American literature of Africa and the Orient is a signification of the "tribal image of an alien creature" (Wren 1979, 459). Since great literature desires great prejudice to sustain it, "serious literature is essentially the statement and justification of human prejudice at the highest and most personal level"! It is in order to answer to what Wren calls Echeruo's own "challenge to the critical imagination" that Echeruo proposes a new concept in African critical tradition, "the conditioned imagination." This unique awareness of the ethnic and racial politics of language, evident in Western inventions of Africa, is responsible for the adventurous thrusts of Echeruo's middle writing in postcolonial discourse and theory in the seventeen years from 1980 to 1997. Included in this phase of polemical essays are such shorter pieces as "After Derrida," "From Transition to Transition," "'Theologizing Underneath the Tree': An African Topos in Ukawsaw Gronniosaw, William Blake, and William Cole," "Edward W. Blyden, W. E. B. DuBois, and the 'Color Complex,'" "Tennyson and 'Victorian' West Africa," "Negritude and History: Senghor's Argument with Frobenius," "Post-Negritude: The Odor of Grandfathers," "Derrida, Language Games, and Theory," "Modernism, Blackface, and the Postcolonial Condition," "Joyce's 'Epical Equidistance,'" and "An African Diaspora: The Ontological Project." Archival, exploratory, theoretical, and often provocative, these shaftlike essays have more than made up for the missing sixth chapter that Wren suggests would extend the concept of the conditioned imagination.

As has been noted earlier, Echeruo also distinguishes himself in public administration. Not much has been written about Echeruo's pioneering role as the first university graduate to serve in the Nigerian Customs and Immigration Service. That was his first postcollege job before he

4. See Ogunbiyi's *Drama and Theater in Nigeria* (1981), Okpewho's *Epic in Africa* (1979), and Uka's "Creation and Creativity" (2002) for more details on the development of the Nigerian theater.

proceeded to the United States for graduate studies. As director of the Biafran War Information Bureau, Echeruo and his colleagues led what has been acknowledged as one of the greatest propaganda operations in the history of modern warfare. Much of the credit for Biafra's successes in the civil war with Nigeria and the daunting resilience of the young republic in the face of the treachery of Britain and the Arab League have been attributed to the effort of the Bureau. For Echeruo and his peers, Biafra was the culmination of the noble ideas of the early twentieth-century responsible scholar and the late twentieth-century public intellectual. The leading minds of his generation, including Achebe ("The African Writer and the Biafran Cause" 1975), Obumselu (Ogbaa, "An African Critic on African Literary Criticism" 1989), and Soyinka ("The Writer in a Modern African State" 1975), have made those themes the cornerstone of their scholarship.[5]

Neither the anxiety of absence from the birth of his first child in the middle of the war nor the difficulty of tracking his young family's various hideouts could deter Echeruo's total commitment to the collective will of his people. This is despite the fact that all male members of his larger family were fully involved in the war effort. His younger brother, Emeka Patrick Echeruo (late senator of Nigeria's Second Republic and ambassador to Germany), an explosives engineer, was the director of engineering services at Biafra's Land Army and a staff member of the famed Research and Production department (RAP). His youngest brother, Kevin Echeruo (poet and painter), had his paintings on the haunting images of the war exhibited in Europe posthumously. In *There Was a Country*, Chinua Achebe notes the role of Echeruo's father, Eze J. M. Echeruo (Nigeria's First Republic minister and traditional ruler), as a member of the fifteen-man Council of State of Biafra and part of the delegation that signed the article of surrender at the end of the war (Achebe 2012, 91).[6] In addition to managing

5. My essay "Ben Obumselu: The Responsible Critic" (1993) explores the theme of the responsible critic in the twentieth-century academy. Achebe's great memoir, *There Was a Country* (2012), gives a good account of the role of Biafran and other Nigerian intellectuals of Echeruo's generation in the task of nation building. Echeruo is referenced on page 28.

6. See also my essay "Emeka Echeruo: Even the Stars . . . !" (2002) for further account of the Echeruo family's contribution to the Nigerian public life.

war communication needs, documentation, and storage, Echeruo himself also played a part in the preparation of the Biafran revolutionary handbook *Ahiara Declaration* and the writing of the speeches of the Head of State, General Chukwuemeka Odumegwu-Ojukwu.

The intellectual as a public administrator did not end with Biafra. Echeruo was part of the committee that went round Nigeria in 1970 to drum up support for the reestablishment of the University of Nigeria following the devastation of the erstwhile University of Biafra. The immediate education of millions of Igbo children who had been holed up in bushes and trenches for the three-year duration of the war was uppermost on the scale of every Igbo leader. The survival and subsequent triumph of the University of Nigeria as one of the country's best institutions of higher learning (National Universities Commission rating, 2002) is a testimony to the distinguishing qualities of perseverance, industry, and excellence for which the Igbo are legendary. These distinctions are nowhere more evident than in the fortitude with which Echeruo and other Igbo leaders stared down the inhumane odds against them, including the seizure of Igbo estates in the city of Port Harcourt by various ethnic groups under the infamous policy of "Abandoned Property" and the freezing of Igbo accounts in Nigerian banks by the federal government of the military dictator Yakubu Gowon and his finance minister, Obafemi Awolowo. The mischief against the academic reconstruction of Igboland betrayed the insipient fears of many of their former compatriots on the federal side who, in spite of the defeat of Biafra, still fretted over the imaginary threat of the former Biafrans. All these would buttress the case of genocide that Achebe makes against Nigeria's leaders in *There Was a Country* (2012, 226–36).

Apart from academic marginalization, Echeruo understood that nothing could be worse than the genocide against the Igbo and the military siege that claimed over two million lives from 1966 to 1970. The success of rebuilding the University of Nigeria, therefore, inspired him to jump at the next opportunity, on the invitation of the then Imo State governor, Sam Mbakwe, to construct a new state-owned university from scratch. In initiating the establishment of the state university, Governor Mbakwe proactively sought to assuage the social injustice of the marginalizing policies of "Federal Character" and "Catchment Area" that were consistently used to deny university admission to Igbo applicants. Prior to 1979, all Nigerian universities were owned and run by the federal government of Nigeria. Of the existing thirteen federal universities, only one, the University of Nigeria at Nsukka, was in the central Igboland area of the present Southeast region.[7] As the sole catchment area university of the Igbo, the University of Nigeria, therefore, proved grossly inadequate because of its limited size and funding to fulfill the emergency academic needs of millions of Igbo families whose children had been languishing in the devastated Biafran war zone in the thirteen years beginning with the pogroms in Northern Nigeria (1966), through the civil war (1967–70), and the postwar years of near-total social and economic inertia (1970–79). The Abia State University (originally Imo State University), therefore, quickly took off with the massive moral and financial support of excitable Igbo parents across the tristate of the current Imo, Abia, and Ebonyi states.[8] It was the second individual state government-funded, as opposed to federal government-funded, university in the history of Nigeria at its inception in 1981, having been preceded by the Enugu State University of Science and Technology

7. Those thirteen federal universities were: University of Ibadan (1948); University of Nigeria, Nsukka (1960); Ahmadu Bello University, Zaria (1962); Obafemi Awolowo University, Ife (1962); University of Lagos (1962); University of Benin (1970); University of Calabar (1975); University of Ilorin (1975); University of Jos (1975); University of Maiduguri (1975); University of Port Harcourt (1975); Usmanu Danfodiyo University, Sokoto (1975); and Bayero University, Kano (1977).

8. The Imo State University was founded in 1981 with a main campus at the rural Etiti community and a satellite campus at the commercial city of Aba. The two campuses were combined in 1986 when the university was relocated to the expansive cashew terrain of Uturu. When the new Abia State was carved out of the old Imo State in 1991, the university fell to the ceded geographical locale of the new state and its name was accordingly changed to Abia State University. With the management, employment, and student admission catchment falling to the new state, the old Imo State government and people clamored for another university of their own. Thus, a new Imo State University was created at Owerri, the state capital. Today, both the renamed Abia State University at Uturu and the new Imo State University at Owerri claim 1981 as their year of founding. I am a second-set alumnus of the first Imo State University that began at the Etiti campus.

(formerly Anambra State University of Science and Technology) that was founded in 1979. It was an instant success mainly because it raised a new hope for millions of college-aged children (including multitudes of much older former Biafran war veterans) who had despaired that they would miss out on university education.

Again, before 1981 the University of Nigeria was an exception to the prevalent British academic curriculum that had dominated tertiary education policy in Nigeria. In his autobiography, *My Odyssey*, its founder and Nigeria's first president Dr. Nnamdi Azikiwe details how the university was modeled after the American Wilberforce University, in Wilberforce, Ohio. As the founding president (vice-chancellor) of the Abia State University, Echeruo, who had studied at Cornell University and had previously taught at the University of Nigeria, expanded the American college curriculum in Nigeria.[9] The novelty of a state university, the emphasis on pragmatic curricula especially tailored to specific local needs, the American-oriented collegial programs and credit-scoring formula, among others, were all innovations in the Nigerian university system for which Echeruo deserves credit as an experimental scholar and intellectual pioneer. The Abia State University, Uturu, and its offshoot, the Imo State University, Owerri (rated first among all state-owned universities by the National Universities Commission, 2002), are bearers of Echeruo's dreams in the physical development of university education in Africa.

The foregoing achievements, however, must not becloud his profound successes in the development of indigenous curricula in an otherwise Eurocentric academy that had produced his generation. As senior faculty in English at the University of Nigeria, Echeruo and his colleagues initiated the African Studies Program beginning with Afro-centric staff development. As the foremost African chair of English and dean of the Faculty of Arts, University of Ibadan, Echeruo and his colleagues pioneered the same program. Many of the second generation of Nigerian university-educated scholars were beneficiaries of that commendable foresight. As

9. Echeruo is perhaps the first African from the continent to earn a PhD in English from the United States.

a young lecturer at the University of Jos, the late Ayo Mamudu informed me that Echeruo recruited him and M. A. Adekunle to become the founding faculty of the English program at the then Middle Belt campus of the University of Ibadan.

As president of the Abia State University, Echeruo saw to the establishment of the Department of Linguistics and Igbo, a pioneer degree program in a Nigerian university. Beyond Nigeria, Echeruo has served as graduate adviser to many universities across Africa, from Ghana, Kenya, Malawi, and South Africa to Zambia. It is for these activities that the University of Nebraska included him in its 130 years honorary degree list as Doctor of Humane Letters in 1991. In addition to awarding him an honorary doctoral degree, the Abia State University named its College of Arts and Sciences after Echeruo. Following on the lead of the above colleges, the Imo State University also honored him with another Doctor of Letters on April 13, 2002. *The Gong and the Flute: African Development and Celebration,* edited by Kalu Ogbaa, was compiled in honor of Echeruo's accomplishments in Africana studies. According to Ogbaa, Echeruo's accomplishments as university professor and scholar has enhanced not only his development of African literature in both curricula and content, but also his training of students who have developed themselves professionally to become university professors and administrators. "They, like their mentor, have joined in the business of training other persons as well as developing and celebrating African culture and civilization through its literature" (Ogbaa 1994, xii–xiii).

The point should be made, however, that Echeruo's foundational work in the postcolonial African university foregrounds a principal task he appears to have set for himself from the very beginning of his career. His excursions in poetry, criticism, theory, and community service have always been directed toward the reconstruction of the three-dimensional black African personality, what Werner Sollors calls "a well-rounded cosmopolitan" in reference to Equiano (2001, xv). In the deliberate manner of the *ijele* masquerade, Echeruo had been engaged in an enormous work of cultural redemption completely subversive of the flat-dimensional "blackface" constructions of Euro-American speculative historians of the sixteenth through nineteenth centuries. It is the same language that

Hegel and company exploit for their adverse representation of the African image that Echeruo employs in his professorial undertaking. In fact, Echeruo announces this shift from Occidentalism and the Roman alphabet to "Igbo resurgence" and how the culture relates to "the larger world" in his 1987 interview with Chukwuma Azuonye (Azuonye 1987, 173). In his essay "The African Roots of Michael Echeruo's Poetry" (2010), Azuonye rightly observes that "Echeruo's scholarship also follows more or less the same trajectory as his poetry" (5). The undercurrent of all these is Echeruo's realization that although a French traveler of the nineteenth century saw the Igbo as the embodiment of true liberty, he was quick to insist that the Igbo name "was not inscribed on any monument" (*A Matter of Identity* 1979, 12).

Echeruo notes (citing the European chronicler Fyfe) that most of the African slaves who wrote on behalf of their fellow slaves were themselves Igbo (*A Matter of Identity* 1979, 13). He is dismayed that, from their homeland in the Bight of Biafra (now "Bight of Benin") to elsewhere in the diaspora (including Belize, England, Haiti, Jamaica, Martinique, Sierra Leone, and the United States), no particular honor was bestowed on the Igbo (variously spelt "Ibo," "Ebo," "Eboe," "Egbo," "Heebo"), though their presence had been felt since the eighteenth century.[10] The people seemed to lack either coherence or identity. Echeruo recognizes the Igbo reverence for the word as universally evident in their leadership in black writing from the diaspora to the continent. There was Olaudah Equiano, the British American Igbo, who published his *Interesting Narrative* as an abolitionist instrument in 1789; William Henry Pratt, the British Igbo, who testified before the Parliamentary Committee investigating the slave trade in 1848; Archibald John Monteith ("Aneaso"), the Igbo assistant to the Jamaican Mission at New Carmel, who recorded his impression of Igbo life in 1853; and Edward Wilmot Blyden, the Liberian Igbo, tireless campaigner of

10. For Igbo intellectual tradition in the diaspora, see Obiwu, *Igbos of Northern Nigeria* (1996) and "The Pan-African Brotherhood" (2007); Chambers, *Murder at Montpelier* (2005) and *The Igbo Diaspora* (2014); and Chuku, *The Igbo Intellectual Tradition* (2013).

black resurgence, pioneer African educationist, and a most prolific writer with over a hundred major publications.

There was Dr. James Beale Africanus Horton, the Sierra Leonean Igbo medical graduate of surgery, physiology, and comparative anatomy from King's College, London, and Edinburgh, admitted to the Royal College of Surgeons of England in 1858, whose many publications include *The Medical Topography of the West Coast of Africa, with Sketches of Its Botany* (doctoral dissertation, Edinburgh University, 1859), *Physical and Medical Climate and Meteorology of the West Coast of Africa, with Valuable Hints to Europeans for the Preservation of Health in the Tropics* (1867), *Guinea Worm, or Dracunculus: Its Symptoms and Progress, Causes, Pathological Anatomy, Results, and Radical Cure* (1868), and *The Diseases of Tropical Climates and Their Treatment, with Hints for the Preservation of Health in the Tropics* (1874).[11] Horton's greatest impact, however, lies in his work of political activism, *West African Countries and Peoples* (1868). Horton reputedly influenced the decolonization project of the Fanti Confederation, the National Society of the Liberated Africans and Their Descendants, into producing one of the earliest constitutions of the modern world (Echeruo 1979, 13). There was David Cekparabietoa Pepple, sold into slavery at Bonny, who recorded his Isuama Igbo life in 1869; and Christian Cole, grandson of an Igbo ex-slave, who was the first African Bachelor of Arts graduate from Oxford's University College in 1876. These were all pathbreakers who charted the black intellectual tradition, of which Echeruo is a deserving inheritor.

Echeruo enthused as the inaugural speaker at the popular Ahiajoku Lecture series: "We have a language which is so efficient in its structure that some say it was first spoken in Eden" (1979, 7). He entitles that lecture "Ahamefula" ("A Matter of Identity") to mark, like his diasporic forebears, the employment of the English language at the service of the Igbo. The 1998 publication of Echeruo's comprehensive *Igbo-English Dictionary*

11. The most revelatory aspect of Olufemi Taiwo's article "Prophets without Honor" is the discourse on the groundbreaking work of the diasporic Igbo, Dr. James Horton, and his science of racial redemption (11–15).

by Yale University Press marks a critical point in the globalization of the Igbo language and culture in modern discourse. In spite of the peculiar circumstances of his enslavement Equiano's book arguably launched that project of globalizing the Igbo over two hundred years earlier when, in repeatedly proclaiming his Igbo-African heritage, it became the most edited best-selling slave narrative in the world, going through nine English editions, one American printing, and Dutch, German, and Russian translations in the author's lifetime (Sollors 2001, xxvii–xxviii, 399). That globalization continued with the emergence of Achebe's *Things Fall Apart* as a great African and world classic, and the recognition of such Igbo female novelists as Buchi Emecheta and Chimamanda Ngozi Adichie among leading names in contemporary literature and writing.

Igbo-English Dictionary is a milestone in Echeruo's long research in Igbo studies, beginning with his first meeting in 1960 with F. C. Ogbalu, the acclaimed "father" of Igbo linguistics. Echeruo and such notable Igbo linguists as E. N. Emenanjo, P. A. Ezikeojiaku, Omen Maduka-Durunze, and Ebo Ubahakwe have no doubt about the immediate need for the reinvention of the Igbo language in light of the invasive colonial intervention in the social life of Africa. The comprehensive scholarship of Echeruo's dictionary validates Kay Williamson's postulation about the difference it would make when the Igbo themselves are involved in the development of their language. Such a commendable vision shows up the limitation of Inno Uzoma Nwadike's puritanical prescription, which circumscribes itself by legislating on the borders, entries, dos, and don'ts of postcolonial language study, as seen in his separate attacks on Achebe and Echeruo ("Achebe Missed It" (2000), "Echeruo's *Igbo-English Dictionary*" (2001)).

Echeruo's contributions to the development of Igbo studies began tentatively with the publication of such work as "The Dramatic Limits of Igbo Ritual," "Igbo Thought through Igbo Proverbs: A Comment," *Igbo Traditional Life, Culture, and Literature* (coedited), and *A Matter of Identity*. It blossomed into what may be considered the third phase of his writing career (from 1998 to the present), which includes the *Igbo-English Dictionary, Nwogure* (edited, an Igbo novel by Phillip N. Edomobi), "Igbo Gbaa Verb," "Igbo Verb and the Lexicon," "Holiness in Igbo," and "Usoro Ohuru Ibiputa Mkpuru Edemede Igbo" (New Guidelines for Igbo Orthography).

Echeruo completed an English translation of the best-seller Igbo pioneer novella by Peter Nwana, *Omenuko* (1933), in 1998, and he published the first Christopher Okigbo poetry *Concordance* in 2008. One of the most significant innovations that Echeruo has made in contemporary Igbo linguistics is not so much in relation to his introduction of the New Standard Orthography, which proffers the controversial umlaut (super-dot) as replacement for the sub-dotted vowels, but more so in relation to his creation of the I. K. Imprints prefigured program disk for easier application in writing Igbo characters using both Word Perfect/Corel WordPerfect and Microsoft Word. He has continued to collect both African and diasporic materials, organize workshops and interviews, and employ the services of field assistants in Nigerian schools, colleges, urban cities, and remote villages in preparing a new edition of the dictionary.

Echeruo has proven to be ahead of his peers and many an African language and literary scholar in computer technology and web support. More will be said in the future about his leadership in tech-savvy innovations in Igbo linguistics, a dictionary, and an African literary concordance. Yet this is hardly surprising since interest in science and technology runs deep in his family. His father, Eze Echeruo, was the first African chairman of Shell Petroleum in Nigeria, a position that enabled him to offer college scholarships to many distinguished students, including such notables as the late Adiele Afigbo and Ken Saro-Wiwa. His brother, Senator Emeka Echeruo, was a petrochemical and explosives engineer. His son, Chinedu Echeruo, was the founder of HopStop.com, Inc. (branded as "HopStop"), an online transit guide for over 140 metropolitan cities worldwide. In 2001, HopStop was named one of the fastest growing software companies in the United States. Apple Inc. dropped support for Windows Phone after it acquired HopStop for, reportedly, a billion dollars in July 2013 (Bajaj 2005; Gundan 2014).

Echeruo's emergence in African scholarship was announced with the publication of such sustained book-length critical studies in the early phase of his writing as *Joyce Cary and the Novel of Africa* (1973), *Victorian Lagos: Aspects of Nineteenth-Century Lagos Life* (1977), *The Conditioned Imagination from Shakespeare to Conrad: Studies in the Exo-Cultural Stereotype* (1978), and *Joyce Cary and the Dimensions of Order* (1979). Contrary to the proclamation of the earlier French traveler, but in tandem with the thesis of the latter French analyst, what Echeruo and others before him have done is to demystify the imperial order by insisting on inscribing Africa on the monument of history. That is what Echeruo means by the phrase "Fate is a fully determined thing," in reference to the closing line of an Old English poem at the end of his 1966 Nsukka lecture on Nigerian poetry. This is the foundation of the revelation of the word to which he is a witness through his circuitous pursuits in the transatlantic Western academy. This is the unique vision and the staying power and philosophic humility of the Echeruoan scholarship that the very best of Echeruo's generation have graciously hailed as unorthodoxly ubiquitous.

Michael J. C. Echeruo: Selected Publications

1962 "Concert and Theater in Late Nineteenth-Century Lagos." In *Drama and Theater in Nigeria: A Critical Source Book*, edited by Yemi Ogunbiyi, 357–69. Foreword by Stanley Macebuh. Lagos: Nigeria Magazine, 1981.

1966 "James Wait and *The Nigger of the 'Narcissus'*." *English Studies in Africa* 8, no. 2: 166–80. Rpt. in Echeruo, *Conditioned Imagination from Shakespeare to Conrad*, 93–112.

"Traditonal and Borrowed Elements in Nigerian Poetry." *Nigerian Magazine* 89: 142–55.

1968 *Mortality: Poems*. London: Longmans.

1971 *Igbo Traditional Life, Culture, and Literature*. Edited by Michael J. C. Echeruo and Emmanuel N. Obiechina. Lagos: Conch Magazine.

"Igbo Thought through Igbo Proverbs: A Comment." In Echeruo and Obiechina, *Igbo Traditional Life, Culture, and Literature*, 63–66.

"The Dramatic Limits of Igbo Ritual." Presented at the Seminar on Igbo Language and Literature organized by the Institute of African Studies, University of Nigeria, Nsukka (November 24–27). Rpt. in Ogunbiyi, *Drama and Theater in Nigeria*, 136–48.

1973 *Joyce Cary and the Novel of Africa*. London: Longman.

1975 *Distanced: Poems*. Enugu, Nigeria: I. K. Imprints.

"Literature, Religion, and Cultural Renewal." *West African Religion* 16: 13–21.

1977 *Victorian Lagos: Aspects of Nineteenth-Century Lagos Life*. London: Macmillan; New York: Holmes & Meier.

"Language and Currency." Presented at the Conference on the Second Black and African Festival of Arts and Culture (FESTAC '77), January 15–February 12, Lagos, Nigeria.

1978 *The Conditioned Imagination from Shakespeare to Conrad: Studies in the Exo-Cultural Stereotype.* New York: Holmes & Meier.

"Chinua Achebe." In *A Celebration of Black and African Writing,* edited by Bruce King and Kolawole Ogungbesan, 151. Zaria, Nigeria: Ahmadu Bello University Press.

1979 *Joyce Cary and the Dimensions of Order.* New York: Barnes & Noble.

A Matter of Identity: Ahiajoku Lecture. Owerri, Nigeria: Ministry of Information.

1980 *The Tempest.* Edited by Michael J. C. Echeruo. New Swan Shakespeare. London: Longman.

"The Future of Igbo Studies: A Very Modest Proposal." In *Igbo Language and Culture,* vol. 2, edited by F. C. Ogbalu and E. N. Emenanjo, 228–37. Ibadan: University Press.

1989 "After Derrida." Review of Rand Bishop's *African Literature, African Critics: The Formation of Critical Standards, 1947–1966. Yearbook of Comparative and General Literature* 38: 186–88.

1991 "From Transition to Transition." *Research in African Literatures* 22, no. 4: 135–45.

1992 "Theologizing 'Underneath the Tree': An African Topos in Ukawsaw Gronniosaw, William Blake, and William Cole." *Research in African Literatures* 23, no. 4: 51–58.

"Edward W. Blyden, W. E. B. Du Bois, and the 'Color Complex.'" *The Journal of Modern African Studies* 30, no. 4: 669–84.

"Gabriel Okara: A Poet and His Seasons." *World Literature Today* (Summer): 454–56.

"Culture as a Base for Science and Technology." In *Culture and Nation Building,* edited by Ebun Clark and Dele Jegede, 85–89. Lagos: National Council for Arts and Culture.

1993 "Tennyson and 'Victorian' West Africa." *English Studies in Africa* 36, no. 1: 29–45.

"Negritude and History: Senghor's Argument with Frobenius." *Research in African Literatures* 24, no. 4: 1–14.

"Post-Negritude: The Odor of Grandfathers." *The Journal of Modern African Studies* 31, no. 4: 719–24.

1995 "Derrida, Language Games, and Theory." *Theoria*, no. 86 (October): 99–116.

1996 "Modernism, Blackface, and the Postcolonial Condition: Review of *The Dialect of Modernism: Race, Language, and Twentieth-Century Literature* (1994), *Vicious Modernism: Black Harlem and the Literary Imagination* (1990), and *The Subaltern Ulysses* (1994)." *Research in African Literatures* 27, no. 1: 172–87.

"Joyce's 'Epical Equidistance.'" *English Studies* 39, no. 1: 1–12.

1998 *Igbo-English Dictionary: A Comprehensive Dictionary of the Igbo Language with an English-Igbo Index*. New Haven, CT: Yale University Press.

Nwogure (Novel in Igbo), by Phillip N. Edomobi. Edited and preface by Michael J. C. Echeruo. Dewitt, NY: I. K. Imprints.

1999 "An African Diaspora: The Ontological Project." In *The African Diaspora: African Origins and New World Identities*, edited by Isidore Okpewho, Carole Boyce Davies, and Ali A. Mazrui, 3–18. Bloomington: Indiana University Press.

Omenuko (Novel in Igbo), by Pita Nwana (unpublished translation, 1963). Transliterated by J. O. Iroaganachi. Reillustrated by Tony Kamen. Ibadan: Longman Nigeria.

2000 "Igbo Gbaa Verbs." Presented at the 31st Annual Conference on African Linguistics, March 2–5, Boston University, Boston, MA.

"Holiness in Igbo." Presented at the African Studies Association Conference, November 16–19, Nashville, Tennessee.

"Usoro Ohuru Ibiputa Mkpuru Edemede Igbo." Presented at the African Studies Association Conference, November 16–19, Nashville, Tennessee.

2003 "*Te Deum Laudamus*: The Legacy of Chinua Achebe." Citation at the award of the Langston Hughes Prize to Chinua Achebe, Lincoln University, Lincoln, PA.

2004 "Whiteness, African-ness, and Post-Apartheid South African Literature and Culture." Keynote Address to the Conference on Africa and Its Challenges in the 21st Century," March 22, Kutztown University, Kutztown, PA.

"Christopher Okigbo, *Poetry Magazine*, and 'Lament of the Silent Sisters.'" *Research in African Literatures* 35, no. 3: 8–25.

2006 "Figures in a Dance: The Theatre of W. B. Yeats and Wole Soyinka (review)." *Research in African Literatures* 37, no. 1: 165–66.

2008 *A Concordance to the Poems of Christopher Okigbo (with the Complete Text of the Poems, 1957–1967)*. Edited and introduction by Michael J. C. Echeruo. Foreword by Isidore Okpewho. Lewiston, NY: The Edwin Mellen Press.

2014 "Foreword." *Uka Wu Ilu: A Compendium of Igbo Idioms and Proverbs*, by Florence Chinyere Duru, 4–5. Lagos: Oyster St. Ike.

"Character, Leadership, and Community Development: The Role of Town Unions." A Keynote Address to the 2014 Mbano National Assembly Convention, May 24, Washington, DC.

Part One

African Literature and Global Imaginaries

2

The Figuration of the *Un*

Between African and World Literature

MAIK NWOSU

It needs to be noted right from the outset that the term "world literature" is not an alternative nomenclature for Western or non-Western literature. World literature privileges a relational perspective (not a list of preferred or nonpreferred texts) that highlights the transnational and the intertextual in the grand human narrative constituted by literatures from all over the world—without deemphasizing or denying the different cultural-ideological contexts of these constituent literatures. But clarifications or instantiations of what constitutes "world literature" often tend to gloss over African literature. To truly appreciate the transnational or global applicability of "world literature," however, is to (further) examine the figuration of the *un* that luminously explains both *African* and *world* literature. To examine the multidimensionality of African literature is to (further) appreciate the essence of the term "world literature." It is African *and* world literature because of its rooting in African experiences or memory (including contemporary memory) and its figuration of the *un*—the generative transformation or presential application of the *un*said, the *un*seen, the *un*done, and other pertinent *un*s. The *un* is perhaps the most important principle in the appreciation of literary transnationalism. Understanding the progression and contexts of a regional literature, especially one like African literature that is often referenced as a singularity, can further illuminate the idea and basis for world literature.

One of the most touching incidents in African literature occurs at the end of *Palace Walk*, the first book of Naguib Mahfouz's *The Cairo Trilogy*. Al-Sayyid Ahmad Abd-al-Jawad has just been informed of the death of his favorite son, Fahmy. He ponders: "How can I have a home without him? How can I be a father if he's gone? What has become of all the hopes attached to him?" (Mahfouz 1989, 495). He goes home, troubled by conjectures and questions: "He remembered Amina [his wife] for the first time and his feet almost failed him. What could he say to her? How would she take the news? She was weak and delicate. She wept at the death of a sparrow" (497). When he arrives home, his heart an inferno of pain, he hears his younger son, Kamal, singing with melodious abandonment: "Visit me once each year/For it's wrong to abandon people forever" (498). Fahmy's death, al-Jawad's humanizing pain, Amina's troubling shadow, Kamal's exultation in the supposed absence of his dictatorial father—all these weave, in one short chapter, an evocative tapestry of ironic forces and the gravity of a tragic movement of history. This terminal chapter affectively opens the second book, *Palace of Desire*. In *Sugar Street*, the concluding book of the trilogy, the overtones of Fahmy's death still register in the cumulative questions and resolutions of Kamal the philosopher: "Anyone slain for a cause greater than himself dies a martyr. The relative worth of causes may vary, but a man's relationship to a cause is a value that does not"; "Perhaps patriotism, like love . . . is a force to which we surrender, whether or not we believe in it" (Mahfouz 1992, 26, 31). Fahmy's death becomes, therefore, a focal event that ripples throughout *The Cairo Trilogy*. Both the root cause and the consequent waves point to aspects of modern African history, on which the literature of the continent is mostly grounded.

There are many other similar instances in literature, regardless of temporal and spatial distinctions. In *Oedipus Rex*, we feel for Oedipus, who in trying to run away from his prophesied destiny only fulfills it by killing his father and marrying his mother. Insofar as we interpret Okonkwo's suicide in Chinua Achebe's *Things Fall Apart* as the epilogue to the life of a man overtaken by a negating force, it also engenders a similar response. The Magistrate in J. M. Coetzee's *Waiting for the Barbarians* suffers a similar reduction, although without the same tragic response. When he settles down, however, to try and write "the annals of an imperial outpost or an account of how the people of that outpost spent their last year, composing their souls as they waited for the barbarians" (Coetzee 1999, 151), he cannot help a plaintive nostalgia worsened by his banishment to the marginalia of an imperial textualization of power:

> "No one who paid a visit to this oasis," I write, "failed to be struck by the charm of life here. We lived in the time of the seasons, of the harvests, of the migrations of the waterbirds. We lived with nothing between us and the stars. We would have made any concessions, had we only known what, to go on living here. This was paradise on earth." (151)

In *Texaco,* Patrick Chamoiseau's novel about the founding of a Creole town, even the vibrant Marie-Sophie Laborieux is eventually limited by age in a manner that signifies beyond her own personal history:

> My shack remained the same, with its share of asbestos, tin, and its crate wood leprosy, as if my time had stopped. Adieu, I told myself, adieu, I'm leaving, I'm leaving, as if to put out the life still rising in me. When you oppose it, you realize that life is both in us and well outside of us. Like an inaccessible light scattered in our flesh, everywhere and nowhere, a law unto itself, outside of the spirit. I would say Adieu, adieu, I'm leaving. But she wouldn't move, still as an old cat that a broom does not scare any more. So more and more I took refuge in my notebooks and my nightly rum. I no longer participated in Texaco's progress, intervening only to settle some squabbles, give out advice, and complete such or such a file still dragging in the courts. (1998, 365)

Laborieux's battle with time is as universal, or even more universal, as it is Creole—even though Laborieux is an important embodiment of Creoleness in Chamoiseau's novel.

In all these instances, the writers—Naguib Mahfouz (Egypt), Sophocles (Greece), Chinua Achebe (Nigeria), J. M. Coetzee (South Africa), and Patrick Chamoiseau (Martinique)—simultaneously draw from their immediate environment as well as imbue their works with a universalizing latitude that makes them able to "please all people at all times"—Longinus's index of the "truly beautiful and sublime" (Longinus 1962,

394). In this wise, transnationalism registers as a basic condition of universalism. In her essay "On Literary Realism," Alice Kaminsky writes: "Aquinas, following Aristotle, believed that the objects we observe are indeed real, but that buried in them is another aspect of what is real, namely, the form or universal" (1974, 25). This interior essence or form "makes the body what it is" and "makes us grow and mature from childhood to manhood" (215). Kaminsky attributes to novelists like Dostoyevsky and Tolstoy "this same view of reality as consisting of individuals in whom the universal is reflected" (215). Although the last attribution somewhat raises the question of whether the universal—if it is indeed so—is not reflected in all individuals, this inquiry does not invalidate the underwriting philosophy about an essential core in all individuals that defines our common humanity.

Literature often focuses on significant experiences that illustrate human relationships, thus highlighting as well as ranging beyond cultural and temporal boundaries. Interestingly, the Nobel Prize for Literature citations often stress this point. In 1986, the prize went to Wole Soyinka for fashioning "with poetic overtones the drama of existence" (Nobelprize.org 1986). Two years later, Mahfouz was honored for forming "through works rich in nuance—now clear-sightedly realistic, now evocatively ambiguous— . . . an Arabian narrative art that applies to all mankind" (Nobelprize.org 1988). In 1991, Nadine Gordimer became the third African to win the prize; she was described as a writer "who through her magnificent writing has—in the words of Alfred Nobel—been of very great benefit to humanity" (Nobelprize.org 1991). When J. M. Coetzee won the prize in 2003, the press release noted: "It is in exploring weakness and defeat that Coetzee captures the divine spark in man" (Nobelprize.org 2003). The citations only build on the fact that the core lessons of literature are fundamentally not national ones but universal or adaptable "truths" often perceived through national or personal lenses. Being "a creative interpretation of history," as Shatto Gakwandi specifically described the African novel (1977, 10), literature attempts to explore in the human consciousness the essence of human actions. And because members of the human species (in a taxonomic sense) are basically not national types, even if they are obviously affected or shaped by their environment, literature can be borderless in its appeal. J. V. Landy argues this point in "Is There Anything as a National Literature?":

> The most memorable characters in fiction are not types at all; they are individuals. Take Jane Austen's *Emma*. What makes this young English lady come to life and keeps her lodged in our memory is, not her nationality, but her incommunicable individuality, her improbable mixture of snobbery and patronizing bossiness with unaffected kindness and good disposition. To my mind she is the most miraculous of Jane Austen's heroines. And the least important thing about her is that she is English.
>
> Furthermore, and this is even more to the point, the great characters of literature, in so far as they are types, are not national types, but human types. In Oedipus we see, not just a Greek, but ourselves. (1975, 50)

Despite the relative modernity of the term "the global village," the literature of diverse peoples at different periods has always been a literature of the global village—a literature of humanity. Even when literature reflects or probes the world of nonhumans, as is also the case in African and other literatures, the underwriting logic is often animated by human concerns and imagination.

This literature of humanity accords with Goethe's vision of *Weltliteratur* or a world literature that transcends particular national borders and time frames. David Damrosch identifies three main characteristics of this "world literature": it is "an elliptical refraction of national literatures," it is "writing that gains in translation," and it is "a mode of reading: a form of detached engagement with worlds beyond our own place and time" (2003, 281). Damrosch's schema reminds us of Hans-Georg Gadamer's proposition of a transformative "fusion of worlds" as a way of relating to other cultures (quoted in Taylor 1994, 67) or of Kwame Appiah's note in *Cosmopolitanism*: "[A] world in which communities are neatly hived off from one another seems no longer a serious option, if it ever was" (2006, xx). In his own theory of world literature, Pascale Casanova speaks of a "world literary space" constituted "by writers, who make and actually embody literary history" and whose works—along with the writers themselves—should be situated in "a sort of spatialized history" (2004, 4–5). Neither Damrosch nor Casanova denies the importance of culture and history in interpreting world literature, although they seem rather inclined to understate or deemphasize attention to historical and cultural particularities. But literature is often rooted in those particularities and world literature involves relationality or comparativity at several levels. While he argues against what he calls "simplified binaries," Timothy Reiss makes the point that a novel "may not only make us aware of differences of life, custom, culture, and language, but provide—require, it may be—access to them" (2004, 112, 136).

Notably, the term "African literature," as in the instance of "world literature," is itself a transnational description of a geopolitical assumption or relationship between several national literatures. In this sense, "African literature" is a regional exemplification of "world literature." Rarely do "African" novels, for instance, traverse or speak about "Africa." Instead, many African novels focus on national issues or examples—Nigerian or South African or Egyptian or Kenyan particularities that register as "African" only in a transnational sense or because of a common continental grouping. Reading "African"—to read a Nigerian novel in light of or in relation to Kenyan history, for example—is one instantiation of the figuration of the *un* (the generative transformation or presential application of the *un*said, the *un*seen, and the *un*done). In the case of "world literature" across regions or continents, this figuration is aided by the fact of a common humanity (which in this case suggests a similarity of instincts and experiences, not a uniformity of consciousness). In the example of "African literature," the figuration of the *un* is facilitated by the perception of Africa as an interlinked continental space and, in some cases, by a shared history or experience across Africa's rather haphazard borders. Whether as a result of geopolitical proximity or because of a universal humanity, it is this figuration of the *un* that truly explains the idea of "world literature." And it is an idea that explores as well as transcends cultural and national specificities.

When, in Moses Isegawa's *Abyssinian Chronicles*, for example, Serenity discovers in the history of Rome an ironic resemblance to his own childhood in Uganda, he is also comparing cultural particularities about parenting norms and deviations from the norm. And he is able to make this comparison because he understands each historical and cultural context:

> Serenity bought souvenirs, but his heart was stolen by a bronze plaque depicting the legend of Romulus and Remus. This was what he had subconsciously come to get; this was what the blackbirds carried unseen in their beaks. In the middle was the wolf, big, dominant, her snout pointed menacingly at unseen intruders. Her large puffy teats were hanging down like strange fruits. Her eyes looked glazed with what could only be the joy and sensuousness of breastfeeding. The twins, nude and silky like hairless piglets, were sucking the diabolical milk as the wolf protected them with the arch of her body.
>
> This was overwhelming for a boy abandoned by his mother to the wolfish quirks of his dad's wives. He held the plaque as if somebody were about to snatch it from him. The vendor, an old man with a thick mustache and little gray eyes, was intrigued. Serenity was his first customer that day, and how strangely he acted! (2001, 235–36)

Besides Serenity's engagement with history—at the public and the personal levels, within the literal and the figurative dimensions—his experience exemplifies world literature *as a mode of reading* because of Isegawa's figuration of the *un*. The *un* in this case refers to the *un*seen, the *un*said, and the *un*done elements in a particular situation or text that signify (or are capable of signifying) their presence nevertheless. It is in this manner that the same text is able to speak personally to different readers—subliminally, according to and yet beyond their particular history and culture—and allow them to insert or reference their personal experiences and perspectives. In Serenity's case, the plaque signifies to him both by what he sees in it and by what he does not see in himself. The experience is dialogic not just at the cultural level but also as an interface between presence and absence.

The *un* also refers to the seen, the said, and the done that speak to or invoke our unseen and unexpressed (within the context of the narrative) histories and cultures. It is this aspect of the *un* that enables us to appropriate a text that does not otherwise directly address or narrate us.

In a *Paris Review* interview, Chinua Achebe speaks of the appreciation of *Things Fall Apart*—the character of Okonkwo in this case—in countries outside Africa (by non-Africans):

> INTERVIEWER. Are you ever surprised, when you travel around the world, by what readers make of your writings, or how they bond to them?
>
> ACHEBE. Yes. Yes, yes, yes. I am. People make surprising comments to me. I think particularly of a shy-looking, white American boy who came into my office once—in the seventies, I think—at the University of Massachusetts and said to me, That man, Okonkwo, is my father!
>
> INTERVIEWER. You were surprised!
>
> ACHEBE. Yes! I was surprised. I looked at him and I said, All right! As I've said elsewhere, another person said the same thing: in a public discussion—a debate the two of us had in Florida—James Baldwin said, That man is my father. (Achebe 1994)

And Okonkwo, regardless of his race or ethnicity, *is* their father in a profound sense. In another interview, Achebe notes: "I suspect, from some of the things readers from abroad say to me, that they find something in this book which resonates with their own history, people in different places. An example is a school, a class in a women's college in Korea. This whole class wrote to me many years back, because they just read *Things Fall Apart*, and what they said was, 'It's our history'" (Achebe 2008). It *is* their history because they see in Achebe's story about British colonialism in Nigeria the untold story (in *Things Fall Apart*) about Japanese colonialism in Korea. Naguib Mahfouz's allegorical *Children of the Alley* presents us with another example of the figuration of the *un*. The tales that constitute the novel highlight the communal construction of reality based on (or around) a significant absence. The stories that are told gesture toward other stories that are not expressly narrated; the literal points to—or points up—the literary. Toward the end of the novel, even the death of Gabalawi, the novel's principal but mostly unseen character, assumes the status of an indeterminate truth. "Gabalawi is fiction," explains Mahfouz. "Like all art, it can be the vehicle of meanings that are the construction of the reader" (2001, 81). As a fable or myth, the story of Gabalawi embeds an elemental tale that travels beyond its Cairenne setting. As a figuration of the *un*, Gabalawi belongs to a Mahfouzian mythology that transcends national literature or cultural specificity.

But the idea of world literature does not negate the existence or perception of such a category as a national literature. The former, however, raises the question of how to define the latter. If literature is fundamentally the narrative of humanity, what then is national or regional (African) literature? It seems easy to determine the nationality of a literary work by reference to its setting and local color. In this respect, *Things Fall Apart* belongs to Nigerian literature, Sophocles's *Oedipus Rex* to Greek literature, *The Cairo Trilogy* to Egyptian literature. In these works, the internal geography appears to suffice as a be-all argument for nationality determinations. However, this criterion can also raise difficult questions—as is evident in Eurocentric novels on Africa or what Michael J. C. Echeruo has described as "the European novel of Africa" (1973, 26). Joseph Conrad's *Heart of Darkness* and Joyce Cary's *Mister Johnson* are both set in Africa, but their setting does not make them African. In Cary's case, he wrote a number of novels set in Africa (Nigeria specifically)—*An American Visitor, Mister Johnson, The African Witch,* and *Aissa Saved*. Unlike Conrad, who only visited the Congo briefly, Cary served as an officer in most of the areas he wrote about. Yet he was clearly one of Philip Curtin's "European travellers" who "wrote to please their [European] audience . . . Thus the reporting often stressed precisely . . . aspects of African life that were repellant to the West and tended to submerge the indications of a common humanity" (1964, 23). Some African novels—such as Yambo Ouologuem's *Bound to Violence*, Hampate Ba's *The Fortunes of Wangrin*, and Elechi Amadi's *The Great Ponds*—also appear to stress the spectacular and the repellent in traditional African life. But there is an important distinction. In his criticism of *Heart of Darkness*, Achebe observes: "One of the best images in *Heart of Darkness* is of a boat going upstream and the forest stepping across to bar its return. Note, however, that it is the African forest that takes the action: the Africans themselves are absent" ("The Song of Ourselves"). One difference between the Afrocentric and the Eurocentric novels on Africa, therefore, is that whereas the former are novels of presence, the latter are of absence, the defining criterion being the extent to which the humanity of the African is recognizable in the identifiable locales of these novels.

Perspective or point of view appears to be a superior indicator of the nationality or regionality of a literary work. Remarking that the African novel should be about Africa, Achebe has described Africa as "not only a geographical expression; it is also a metaphysical landscape—it is in fact a view of the world and of the whole cosmos from a particular position" (1982, 50). That position does not necessarily have to be physical; it can also be cultural-ideological. But African history has not been a never-ending glory parade. So the African writer has also closely—and critically—examined African society. Although Ouologuem portrays the exploitation of Africa by Arab slavers and European colonizers in *Bound to Violence,* he also paints a picture of internal exploitation by native lords, a tale that incorporates cannibalism. In *The Fortunes of Wangrin,* Hampate Ba's colonial-era African clerk is an incarnation of mischief and evil, yet Ba's novel is an outstanding instance of an interface between African oral narrative art and the European novel form. Ba widens Wangrin's targets to include whites and tries to turn his story into a morality tale, but Wangrin mainly highlights the extent of corruption among some Africans of that milieu. Finally, his nemesis comes—in the form of a white colonial officer. Amadi's *The Great Ponds* is a story of an unrelenting war between two villages over a small pond. The focus of the conflict itself is less important than the villages' vaulting ideas of themselves and their ancestry. "Who has ever grown rich from the proceeds of the cursed Pond of Wagaba?" wonders Eze Okehi's senior wife in the novel (1969, 72). Still, the battle rages. Amadi's aim is the figuration of the *un* or the particularization of the general. He situates the conflict in 1918 and therefore invites a parallel reading between the Aliakoro-Chiolu conflict and World War I ("the Great War" in the novel). In *Ethics in Nigerian Culture,* Amadi points out: "For some obscure reason, man has never learned from history . . . It becomes very difficult to dismiss the suggestion that man's pugnacity originates in instincts planted in him not merely to ensure survival but also to check his population" (1982, 41). Unlike Conrad and Cary, Amadi does not paint a picture of Africa as the locus of darkness or unusual buffoonery but as a human setting with human failings and tragedies. Africa is not characterized by the absence of evil, but it is also not bereft of dignity.

In the Eurocentric African novels, the African characters, when they have any distinguishable life at all, are more or less marionettes foredoomed by their historical circumstances. But in the Afrocentric African novels, evil can often be interpreted as a human condition. Both novel types sometimes tend toward propaganda—without the occurrence of an aesthetic transubstantiation to (further) problematize the issue of literary nationality. In *A Connecticut Yankee in King Arthur's Court*, for instance, Mark Twain sets down a nineteenth-century technician in the fifth century court of King Arthur and his Knights of the Round Table. This "new" world is depicted with a measure of realism, but Twain's novel ultimately registers as a portrait of a triumphant American able to overcome Merlin the magician and the best of the knights in combat. If Twain arguably achieved only a qualified success, Kazuo Ishiguro in *The Remains of the Day* and Robert Graves in *I, Claudius* achieve the sort of aesthetic transubstantiation that makes it tempting or compelling to conclude that the novels belong to English and ancient Roman literature, respectively—regardless of the authors' native nationalities. Ishiguro's central character, setting, and point of view are "authentically" English. "It is sometimes said that butlers only truly exist in England," the butler in *The Remains of the Day* muses. "Other countries, whatever title is actually used, have only manservants. I tend to believe this is true. Continentals are unable to be butlers because they are as a breed incapable of the emotional restraint which only the English race are capable of" (Ishiguro 1988, 43). The narration is duly restrained and is a fitting illustration of a perspective-style synthesis. If Ishiguro, a Japanese, could write an *English* novel, Graves demonstrates that a twentieth-century Englishman could produce an "authentic" work on ancient Rome. He especially achieves verisimilitude by his use of carefully selected historical and cultural markers. The passage on Claudius's forced ascension as emperor is illustrative:

> I made no more protests. What was the use of struggling against Fate? They hurried me out into the Great Court, singing the foolish hymn of hope composed at Caligula's accession. *"Germanicus is come Again, to*

> *Free the City from her Pain.*" For I had the surname Germanicus too. They forced me to put on Caligula's golden oak-leaf chaplet, recovered from one of the looters. To steady myself I had to cling tightly to the corporals' shoulders. The chaplet kept slipping over one ear. How foolish I felt. They say that I looked like a criminal being hauled away to execution. Massed trumpeters blew the Imperial Salute. (Graves 1934, 493)

Whereas Ishiguro strategically uses a butler as his central character, Graves adroitly adopts a historian as narrator. Graves's account accords with Suetonius's remark in *The Twelve Caesars*—notably translated by Graves—that "Claudius became Emperor, at the age of fifty, by an extraordinary accident" (1989, 191). Twain and Graves, in particular, transcend not just national boundaries but temporal ones as well. What is especially remarkable in *A Connecticut Yankee in King Arthur's Court* and *I, Claudius* is the time travel that the authors invite the reader to undertake without a loss of comprehension or applicability. The thrust of both narratives, Twain's especially, tends to be relational—to connect the past to the present, even though Twain's point of view privileges the American and the modern. To what nations do these works—exemplars of literary transnationalism—belong? Ishiguro, though Japanese, has lived in England since he was six years old—that is, since 1960. Graves has authored (with Joshua Podro) a study of early Christianity, *The Nazarene Gospel Restored*; compiled a dictionary of Greek mythology, *The Greek Myths*; and translated Apuleius, Lucan, and Suetonius. *The Remains of the Day* and *I, Claudius* signpost a contemporary modernity marked by physical and intellectual migrations—a world that provokes many hard questions but not as many easy answers. "Am I an American writer because I have lived in America?" asks Vikram Seth. "Or am I an Indian writer? Or am I a Commonwealth writer, that strange beast? Or am I a rootless cosmopolitan?" (Iyer 1993, 51).

Contemporary African literature also provides us with interesting examples. It is not incidental that some modern Nigerian poets, for instance, are particularly fond of the journey motif. Esiaba Irobi aptly describes his *Cotyledons* (1988) as a poet's "attempt to capture the beauty of his landscape and the larger world with a critical, sensitive, psychic camera" (no page). In Uche Nduka's poetry, experimentation and the globalization of the poetic form are pronounced. Artistic freedom is obviously important to Nduka, and this involves a journey without boundaries. In his first poetry collection, *Flower Child,* Nduka aligns himself with the phenomenon of social power in the American decade of the flower children. In *Bremen Poems,* his "songs" are set against the psychic background of his "hometown" in Germany. His *Chiaroscuro* is a personal gallery of national and transnational icons. In Irobi, Nduka, and some other modern Nigerian poets, the definition of poetry as an artistic form is rather spectral and incorporates a creative dialogue with a wide range of writers across different cultures. The artistic temperaments point to the convergence of the local and the global. In the novel form, Chris Abani's *The Virgin of Flames* is remarkable for the way it examines the issue of diasporic identity. Abani tells the story of Black, the son of an Igbo father and a Salvadorian mother, who tries to re-create himself within the context of a city, Los Angeles, that is also a transnational crucible. *The Virgin of Flames* is as much about the mystique of Los Angeles as it is about Black's quest for a larger self and seems as American as it is African.

Comparing the opening pages of two novels highlights the long journey that modern African literature has made in the past six decades. Amos Tutuola's *The Palm-wine Drinkard* (1952):

> I was a palm-wine drinkard since I was a boy of ten years of age. I had no other work more than to drink palm-wine in my life. In those days we did not know other money, except COWRIES, so that everything was very cheap, and my father was the richest man in our town.
>
> My father got eight children and I was the eldest among them, all of the rest were hard workers, but I myself was an expert palm-wine drinkard. I was drinking palm-wine from morning till night and from night till morning. By that time I could not drink ordinary water except palm-wine.
>
> But when my father noticed that I could not do any work more than to drink, he engaged an expert palm-wine tapster for me; he had no other work more than to tap palm-wine every day. (1994, 191)

Chris Abani's *The Virgin of Flames* (2007):

> This is the religion of cities.
>
> The sacraments: iridescent in its concrete sleeve, the Los Angeles River losing faith with every inch traveled. A child riding a bicycle against the backdrop of desolate lots and leaning chain-link fences, while in the distance, a cluster of high-rises, like the spires of Old Cathedrals, trace a jagged line against the sky, ever the uneven heart of prayer. The inevitable broken fire hydrant surrounded by an explosion of half-naked squealing children bearing witness to the blessed coolness of water. World-weary tenements and houses contemplating a more decadent past, looking undecided, as if they would up and leave for a better part of the city at any moment. A human silhouette on a park bench reading a book. Junkies hustling the afternoon. And out of sight, yet present nonetheless, the tired bounce of heat-deflated basketballs against soft tar. And a dog. Old, ancient even. And curious. (3)

"To what nation, or region, does this work belong?" is a question that hardly applies to Tutuola's *The Palm-wine Drinkard*. Not only do references in Tutuola's novel ("palm-wine" and "cowries") suggest an African setting but its folkloric texture also believably indicates an oral African character to the narrative. Abani's novel exemplifies the unraveling of a new chapter in modern African literature, one relatable to the virtual relocation of African literary production to Euro-American spheres.

But it is not simply the consequence of physical location—the fact that many African writers currently reside abroad (mostly in Europe and America). Many of the foundational modern African writers went to school in Europe and America. Wole Soyinka's "Telephone Conversation" is set in England. Tayeb Salih's *Season of Migration to the North* travels from Sudan to England and back. Tutuola's *The Palm-wine Drinkard* was first published and acclaimed abroad. The Heinemann African Writers Series that has played a role in the shaping of modern African literature since 1962 has its main operational office in London. So too the British Broadcasting Corporation that "played a significant role in the development of contemporary African theater of English expression" (Amankulor 1993, 148). The Négritude movement—founded by Aimé Césaire, Léon Damas, and Leopold Senghor—took shape not in Africa but in France. Senghor's poetry follows the poet's trajectory from Senegal to France to the United States of America. Modern African literature has always been in some sort of relationship with external factors or outside forces. Today, more African writers still write about Africa than anywhere else regardless of their various locations in the world, but the relationship of modern African literature with the world outside Africa has intensified with the relative amplification of the rhetoric and the reality of global diversity.

In determining what other works, apart from those done for African audiences by Africans and in African languages, belong to African literature, Chinweizu, Onwuchekwa Jemie, and Ihechukwu Madubuike set out four criteria: the primary audience for which the work is done, the cultural and national consciousness expressed in the work, the nationality of the writer whether by birth or by naturalization, and the language in which the work is done (*Toward the Decolonization of African Literature* 1980, 13–14). But while it sometimes seems easy to tell for which audience certain books were intended, this sort of certainty can be misleading. Was Tutuola's *The Palm-wine Drinkard*, for instance, intended exclusively for a European or an African audience? Are literary audiences effectively conceived in such singular (or binary) terms? In any case, many literary works, even if written for a particular audience, truly endure because of their figuration of the *un* so that different people around the world find in them appealing elements or can relate to them in their own way. A work of art that cannot transcend a specific audience might arrive, perhaps, but probably never travel. Many non-African readers will find in Soyinka's *The Road* or Coetzee's *Waiting for the Barbarians* rich metaphors of the ghost road in consonance with their different experiences. When the Professor conducts his benediction in Soyinka's *The Road*, his immediate audience barely understands him. But his message speaks about rites of passage that resonate beyond the characters'—and the writer's—location in place and in time:

> Be even like the road itself. Flatten your bellies with the hunger of an unpropitious day, power your hands with the knowledge of death. In the heat of the afternoon when the sheen raises false forests and a watered haven, let the event first unravel before your eyes. Or in the dust when

> ghost lorries pass you by and your shouts your tears fall on deaf panels and the dust swallows them. Dip in the same basin as the man that makes his last journey and stir with one finger, wobbling reflections of two hands, two hands, but one face only. Breathe like the road. Be the road. Coil yourself in dreams . . . (Soyinka 1982, 228)

It is also not impossible to read literature outside physical geography as a journey from one state of consciousness to another.

Language is the other consideration promoted by Chinweizu, Jemie, and Madubuike. But this criterion is also problematic. While it seems easy to situate works written in a national language, where it exists as such, as constituting the core of a national literature, modern African literature has been written more in European than in African languages. Should we then insist or recommend that African literature in non-African languages evidence transliterations or transpositions of the speech patterns and semantic codes of the writer's vernacular—such as in Achebe's *Things Fall Apart* or Okot p' Bitek's *Song of Lawino*? This inquiry highlights the language question (raised by Cheikh Anta Diop in 1948 and Obi Wali in 1962) that has been one of the central debates in modern African literature. Should African writers write in foreign languages (which creates a problem of identity, according to Diop, or leads to a dead end, according to Wali) or only in African languages? Is the answer simply a matter of choice, as it has sometimes been presented? Every language (including English or French in Africa) embeds in some form the history of its speakers and is expanded by their experiences. Although the language worlds of *Things Fall Apart* and Ben Okri's *The Famished Road*, for instance, are different, both mirror what it means to be a Nigerian or an African in a postcolonial or contemporary sense. So, too, the difference between the language worlds of Wole Soyinka's *Death and the King's Horseman* and J. Ene Henshaw's *Second Chance*. Language is at the heart of literature, and the hearts of different writers—according to their different personalities and circumstances, regardless of national identity (or identities)—beat differently.

It seems convenient, therefore, to define literary nationality in relation to a writer's (native or assumed or hyphenated) nationality and sensibility—with the understanding that the national and the global or the local and the universal do not necessarily cancel out each other. To be local is (or can) also (be) to be global. To be African is also to be universal. Whereas a writer's "complete break with all traditional forms is rare in literature," as Landy argues, traditions connect and expand as the world relationally contracts through international linkages. According to Landy, when such a break occurs, "as it did in varying degrees with such writers as Whitman, Joyce, the Imagists, and Gertrude Stein, the result is often stillborn. Most good writers borrow shamelessly. What distinguishes them from third rate writers is that they never borrow slavishly, mechanically. Their very imitation is creative" (1975, 49). Thus, writers and books connect—knowingly and unknowingly—across national boundaries in terms of similitude in thematic concerns and stylistic patterns. Camara Laye's *The Radiance of the King* connects with Franz Kafka's *The Castle*, V. S. Naipaul's *Miguel Street* with Naguib Mahfouz's *Midaq Alley*, Alice Walker's *The Color Purple* with Mariama Ba's *So Long a Letter*. Mahfouz instructively explains his "first concept of the novel" as having been "formed by the Qu'ran" (2001, 66) but also acknowledges that he was influenced by French literature: "As for myself, I was deeply influenced by Flaubert, particularly *Madame Bovary*. I read most of Balzac in translation. But I read Zola's *Nana* in French" (90). To define or delineate contemporary African literature—African *literatures* in reality—entails looking beyond fixed notions of "authenticity." Such a description should take into account the contemporary phase of transnationalism that goes back to several important moments in international history (including Bartolomeo Diaz's circumnavigation of the Cape of Good Hope in 1487 and the maturing of the Internet in the late twentieth century).

If we emphasize the role of the writer as the individual synthesizer of different inspirations, literature can arguably be divided simply into the literature of presence and the literature of absence. In one, we see our world vividly presented (or in a particularistic manner). In the other, we behold a nowhere or anywhere world in which the narrative is more or less a psychological poem. Jose Ortega y Gasset makes a comparable distinction in "The Dehumanization of Art" between "realistic art" and "artistic art" (1968, 3–54). These distinctions are primarily stylistic. Writers employ what Morse Peckham calls "mediate signs" (Kaminsky 1974, 220)—words for which referents may not actually exist in the physical environment, such as Okonkwo and Marlow or Miguel Street and Midaq Alley. The living stage on which literary characters act out their lives are the theaters of the writer's imagination. In this sense, is the writer as a writer really bound to any particular place or nation? In creating the fictive world of his/her works, the experiences of the writer as a person intersects with the mythopoetics of the writer as an artist to yield a world that if it has any consistent nationality at all is a nationality of the mind—the writer's. Kaminsky specifies: "A novelist works with a special kind of hypothetical question, the subjunctive conditional, 'What would happen if such and such were to happen?' Note that he does not use the material conditional form of the hypothetical question: 'What does happen if such and such does happen?'" (1974, 229). These are private creative decisions, as writing is a private activity. Should Okonkwo commit suicide and thus deny himself a proper burial in his social circumstances? Should the Magistrate, the representative of empire, suffer imprisonment at the hands of imperial agents? All writers are mythmakers insofar as their fictive worlds are their own individual creations or simulations. And it is this mythmaking or ideational order (fashioned from the chaos of the nation or the world) that defines the writer.

Still, the national (or regional)—whether as an objective reality or a strategic imaginary—is (or can be) important because the writer does not exist in a void, and meaning systems are usually culturally-ideologically grounded. "Every nation, every race, has not only its own creative, but its own critical turn of mind," T. S. Eliot argues in "Tradition and the Individual Talent" (Eliot 2001, 1092). But the same Eliot also notes that "the historical sense involves a perception, not only of the pastness of the past, but of its presence; the historical sense compels a man to write not merely with his own generation in his bones, but with a feeling that the whole of the literature of Europe from Homer and within it the whole of the literature of his own country has a simultaneous existence and composes a simultaneous order" (1093). Expanded beyond its Euro-American focus, Eliot's essay gestures toward the challenge that the modern or contemporary era poses to the writer—to be creatively national and international at the same time, to be international (or global) without necessarily ceasing to be national (or local). For African literature, the challenge is no different, as it reflects not only what has happened to the continent but also what is happening to its peoples. In its modern phase, African literature is both the literature of creative translation (as in Chinua Achebe's *Things Fall Apart*) and of experiential diffusion (as in Abani's *The Virgin of Flames*). It is African and world literature because of its rooting in (or relation to) African experiences or memory (including contemporary memory) and its figuration of the *un*, perhaps the most important principle in the appreciation of literary transnationalism.

3

In "the Vortex of the Expulsion"

The Search for an Asian African Imaginary

RASHNA B. SINGH

On August 4, 1972, General Idi Amin issued an order for the expulsion of all Asians in Uganda who did not hold Ugandan citizenship and ultimately of all Asians, with very few exceptions, as many found their citizenship revoked. Amin allowed three months for the Asians to clear out. Although there were similar exoduses of Asians from other East African nations, such as Kenya, where there was a much larger community, or Tanzania, where there was a smaller community, they were far more gradual and not expedited by an actual expulsion order. Pressures on the Indian Ugandan community began during the presidency of Milton Obote but came to a head after Idi Amin took the reins of power in a coup. Even in Kenya, President Jomo Kenyatta had held off signing the independence agreement in 1953 until he had received an assurance that the British government would remove all Asians from Kenya, although over a period of years.

What Peter Nazareth has termed "the vortex of the expulsion" (1981, 60) has exerted a pull on Ugandan writers of Indian descent since then and has become the dominant theme of their literary works. Amin's putative dream brought things to a head, not only because Asian Africans had to hurriedly plot their futures but also because they had to hurriedly figure out who they were. On a socioaffective level, Amin's expulsion order disrupted thousands of lives. On a political level it compelled new configurations of power and modalities of agency in our understanding of the neocolonial nation-state. On a more metaphysical level it forced Asian Africans, as they have come to be called, to confront their own constructions of identity. This essay will consider the expulsion as a historical moment that precipitated a search for an Asian African identity and an Asian African imaginary. I will explore how Asian African writers saw the expulsion as a situation that forced a showdown, as it were, with the structures of their being, with their very selves, and with the constitutive elements of their social, cultural, and national identities. For Asian Africans identity is intricate and always in flux. It is constituted not only by citizenship but also by historical and cultural memory. It is contingent on changing contexts and discourses of authenticity, which, this essay will theorize, create an imaginary that is not bound by the claims of citizenship or the strictures of the nation-state. Instead, it is a constructed identity that is not tethered to passports but enacted through everyday experiences. Peter Nazareth's novel *The General Is Up*, Jameela Siddiqi's *The Feast of the Nine Virgins*, Shenaaz Nanji's *Child of Dandelions*, Yusuf K. Dawood's *Return to Paradise*, and Mira Nair's film *Mississippi Masala* all focus on the expulsion as a defining experience, and this essay will examine how these texts explore the crises of identity and existence compelled by the expulsion order and the consequent exile.

The critical response to the literature compelled by the expulsion has been sparse and sporadic, so this essay constitutes a significant intervention in our understanding of the expulsion as an impetus for an imaginary. Most scholars have concerned themselves with the historical, political, economic, social, and experiential fallout of the expulsion. A few focus on single writers, for example, John Schecter's piece on Peter Nazareth, "Peter Nazareth and the Ugandan Expulsion: Pain, Distance, Narration," in *Research in African Literatures* (Summer 1996). Abasi Kiyimba's article "The Ghost of Idi Amin in Ugandan Literature," published in *Research in African Literatures* (Spring 1998), is one of the few that addresses the literature in general. It is a useful survey of prose fiction that features Idi Amin, whether directly or in disguise. However, whereas Kiyimba mostly deals with Ugandan writers of African descent, as well as some white writers such as Donald Westlake, I focus on Asian African writers who had to wrestle with the actual experience of expulsion. The novels that emerged from the expulsion often lack literary merit in terms of style and technique; they are not particularly nuanced, nor are they innovative or inventive. The writing is often pedestrian, and the characters are often clichéd or underdeveloped. But these novels do offer personal narratives to set against the mostly collective histories that have been written about Asians in Uganda or in East Africa as a whole. They also allow us to look at the expulsion not simply as a historical or political event, but as a larger phenomenon that prompts a new consideration of terms such as "diaspora" and "transnational" as literal, cultural, metaphorical, and bureaucratic all at the same time.

Ten years prior to the expulsion, at the first African Writers Conference in 1962 at Makerere University in Kampala, Uganda, the most fundamental questions about African literature were hotly debated. Some of these questions were later addressed by the noted Nigerian author Chinua Achebe in an essay entitled "Thoughts on the African Novel." As to what constitutes the African novel, Achebe answers simply that "the African novel has to be about Africa," but then immediately complicates the issue by going on to qualify Africa as more than "a geographical expression." It is also, Achebe insists, "a metaphysical landscape" and "a view of the world and of the whole cosmos perceived from a particular position" (Achebe 1975, 50), a position, one might postulate, that derives from being part of a physical as well as a metaphysical African landscape. Achebe then asks whether the African novelist is defined by passports, individual volition, or perspective, the most elusive item of all (50). Amin allowed three months for the Asians to clear out. Suddenly the definition of an African (in this case, of course, specifically a Ugandan) became entirely a matter of passports, and in the end even passports did not matter. Individual volition meant little, and something as frangible as perspective, which Achebe "touched with the timidity of a snail's horn" (50), meant nothing.

Cultural critics such as Stuart Hall and Homi Bhabha have since encouraged us to regard identity as complex, unstable, transitional, and negotiable. But thousands of Indian Ugandans discovered that identity is also legislated and thus nonnegotiable. Those who already had Ugandan passports found that their citizenship was just a piece of paper that could be torn up. Those who had British passports discovered that there was a difference between being a British citizen and a British subject: for the latter there was no "right of abode." Most Indian Ugandans had no desire to settle in India, the land of their ancestors but a land where they had never even set foot. "It took an expulsion to make Uganda feel like home," affirms Jameela Siddiqi (Hawley 2008b, 3), who was a student at Makerere University in 1972 when her Ugandan citizenship was revoked, and she was expelled along with other Ugandans of Indian descent.

The concept of "hybridity" that emerges from literary and cultural theory interrogates the construction of culture and identity within the historical context of colonialism and racial conflict. For Homi Bhabha, hybridity destabilizes the singular identity of any particular culture and disrupts notions of purity or essentiality. Additionally, it disrupts binary constructions of racial or national character, postulating instead a continual process of negotiation between the colonial paradigm and the postcolonial experience. Hybridity becomes an interstitial or liminal space where negotiation occurs, a space Bhabha terms a "Third Space" (Bhabha 1994, 36). The "Third Space" of enunciation "quite properly challenges our sense of the historical identity of culture as a homogenizing, unifying force, authenticated by the originary Past, kept alive in the national tradition of the People" (37). For Ugandans of Indian descent, however, a national or historical identity and an originary past was ruptured by multiple ethnic identities. This is evident in *The General Is Up*, as Nazareth's characters postulate their primary identity as Goan rather than Indian, Goan arbitrated by their domicile in Damibia, the fictitious country clearly based on Uganda, where the novel is set.

Nazareth's characters, as well as those of Jameela Siddiqi, Shenaaz Nanji, Yusuf Dawood, and the characters in Mira Nair's film, are more than a "masala" or spicy mix. For them identity, as Stuart Hall would have it, is always in the process of becoming as well as of being. More than perhaps any other group, Indian Ugandans especially and Asian Africans in general bear out Hall's contention that identity is a production that is always in process and always constituted within, not outside, representation. However, the enunciation of Indian Ugandans was also mediated by political and practical expediencies. As Hall indicates, "We all write and speak from a particular place and time, from a history and a culture which is specific" (Braziel and Mannur 2003, 234). Forced to "enunciate" themselves in a historical moment, their narratives of displacement are nevertheless multifaceted and sometimes self-contradictory. Yet the characters in all these novels, and Jay in Nair's film, are unequivocal about their national identity: it is Ugandan. What the expulsion order forced was a confrontation with their ethnic and cultural identities. In Mira Nair's 1991 film *Mississippi Masala,* Uganda is not fictionalized but becomes almost fantastical as it is processed through the filters of memory when an Ugandan Indian family settles in a small town in Mississippi after the expulsion. The father refuses to give up his material claim to his property in Uganda and cannot free himself from the imaginative and emotional hold the country has on him. His wife has reconciled herself to the reality of the present, while their daughter, whose memories of early childhood in Uganda are now hazy, embraces the various influences that have configured her: Ugandan, Indian, and the American South (and the resulting hybridity or "masala"). Here too different worlds are mapped on each other, but Uganda before the expulsion becomes a trope of exilic nostalgia as the film explores various expressions of racism and cultural hybridity.

Remembering Uganda becomes in these works an act of imaginative rediscovery, a recovery of a purloined identity. Hall discusses identity as a production grounded in the retelling of the past, not in its archaeology. As an example he uses the work of Armet Francis, a Jamaican-born photographer whose photographs of the peoples of the Black Triangle is "an act of imaginary reunification" (Braziel and Mannur 2003, 235). Similarly, Mira Nair attempts an imaginary reunification in *Mississippi Masala* where Ugandans, Ugandans of Indian origin, and African Americans of the American South find, to use Hall's words, "an imaginary coherence on the experience of dispersal and fragmentation" (235). Nazareth, Nanji, Dawood and Siddiqi, on the other hand, do not strain after an imaginary coherence but allow their characters to break apart in all the constitutive elements of their identity before arriving at an uneasy but functional truce, a simple strategy of survival. It is possible to think of the expulsion of people of Indian descent from Uganda as a clear case of economic determinism. But it is also possible to think of it as identity by decree. In the end Ugandan passports did not save Indian Ugandans from expulsion.

Within the community itself the politics of identity collided with the politics of passports.

We can use Hall's diagram of black Caribbean identities as framed by two axes or vectors, simultaneously operative, to understand Asian African identities. The vector of similarity and continuity for the Asian community was obviously India, whereas the vector of difference and rupture was first Africa and then Western nations. Most Asians found their way to the United Kingdom, but many went to Canada, some to Australia, some to the United States, and some to other lands. Only a few went to India. The dialogic relationship between these two axes, however, is somewhat different for the contemporary Asian African. Identity is always relational, and for Asian Africans in the diaspora the grounding axis is now Africa, not Asia, or Uganda, not India. Asian African migrants see their identity as distinct from Indian migrants in the lands where they have settled and distinct from Indians themselves in the case of those who settled in India. The articulation of cultural relations between Africans and Asians, in Hall's sense of the term, was mediated by the inherited racialized perceptions each group had of the other, inherited from their common colonial rulers, and thus one must acknowledge that they are overdetermined. In an essay on black attitudes to the brown and white colonizers of East Africa, Dent Ocaya-Lakidi stresses the role of the colonial context: "It is at once clear that black African attitudes and views of the Asians arose largely out of the social, political, and economic dynamics generated within such a context" (1975, 82). The expulsion unwittingly afforded coherence to the experiences of Indian Ugandans, a coherence or suture that ironically resulted from a splitting apart of identities, an enunciation of a collective experience that was particular, if not unique, and powered by memory and reconstruction of personal histories into a collective whole.

Although the first interactions between Asians and Africans far predate the British Empire, in modern times they met in a colonial contact zone, which produced the very ambivalence of meaning articulated in Homi Bhabha's intervention of the "Third Space of enunciation" (1994,36). Many in the Asian community, as well as many outside the community, perceived the historical identity of their culture as homogenous, unifying, and derived from an originary past. Nazareth, however, disrupts this notion by creating a narrator who embodies the disunities of his present: "The solution was to create a narrator who would have moved through the different worlds, including that of the erstwhile British rulers, which would unite in his consciousness. He would be Goan by race, British by education, and African by experience and commitment" (1981, 57). Just as "the disruptive temporality of enunciation displaces the narrative of the Western nation" (Bhabha 1994, 37), the disruptive temporality of the expulsion of Indians from East Africa displaces the narrative of an originary Indian presence. From the colonial construction of Uganda, from the multiplicity of the cultures from which it was constructed, and from the compounding of identities such as Asian and African, we can well understand why Bhabha states that "hierarchical claims to the inherent originality or 'purity' of cultures are untenable" (Bhabha 1994, 37). It is within the "Third Space," which is not representable in itself, that all cultural statements and systems are constructed. It is in its very nature contradictory and ambivalent, but it is there that the meaning and symbols of cultures are destabilized and "can be appropriated, translated, rehistoricized and read anew" (37). In this "split-space of enunciation" (38) we may find an *inter*national culture based not simply on multiculturalism or diversity but on hybridity. It is in the "inter," in Bhabha's sense of the *inter*national, the *in-between* space (38) where Asian Africans lived and still live, and where a rehistoricized story of the expulsion as loss of home, not merely loss of assets, can be told. It is perhaps this vision that lay behind *Transition* magazine, founded in Kampala in 1961 by a twenty-one-year-old Ugandan of Indian descent named Rajat Neogy, who proclaimed in an early editorial: "There will be no birth without miscegenation" (Tuttle 2007). The early issues of *Transition* make clear that the story of Uganda that was being told was of a hybrid identity in an *inter*national cultural space. But it was also a transitional space that could be traversed continually.

Stuart Hall's discussion of identity as a production, never complete and always in process, clarifies those who are enunciated from different positions, people who have multiple cultural, linguistic, and social identities, and people in the diaspora. Hall famously notes two ways of thinking about cultural identity. The first, as something shared, obviously will not encompass both Asians and Africans or, specifically, Indians and Ugandans. Such a conception lay at the center of Négritude, and certainly Asians in Africa did not partake in Négritude. However, as Gupta indicates, many did partake in a vision shared by Nehru and other Indian nationalists "of a resurgent Asia working hand-in-hand with a resurgent Africa; the two strands of resurgence being anti-imperialism and anti-racialism" (Twaddle 1975, 127). They also shared in the experience of being colonized and of becoming postcolonial societies, in the need to restructure not only societies but also perceptions, as Frantz Fanon so memorably described it (Fanon 1967, 196). Hall's other configuration of identity is situated not in imaginary and textual coherence but in difference: "This second position recognizes that, as well as the many points of similarity, there are also critical points of deep and significant *difference* which constitute 'what we really are'; or rather—since history has intervened—'what we have become.'" So, in speaking of commonalities, we must also speak of discontinuities (Braziel and Mannur 2003, 236). And, indeed, Amin's expulsion order disrupted emerging transnational alliances. Cultural identity in Hall's second sense is about becoming as well as being and belongs to the future as much as the past. It is clearly here that we must locate the cultural identities of Asian Africans, not fixed in some essentialized past but subject to the continuous "play" of history, culture, and power (Braziel and Mannur 2003, 236).

Hall's contention that cultural identity is contained within history is the starting point for an examination of the identity of Indians in Uganda and, more generally, for Asians in Africa. India, as well as all the African nations where there was and is significant Indian settlement, were once part of the mighty British Empire, and this is where the imbricated identities of Asians and Africans must be positioned. Although the presence of India in Africa is usually attributed to the coolies brought in to build the railways, in his essay "Was the Expulsion Inevitable?" Michael Twaddle indicates that this sort of essentialization is inaccurate. Nor is it accurate to think of Indians by what Twaddle calls "the new myth," that they were all *dukawallahs* or small traders (Twaddle 1975, 2). Many Asian immigrants were clerks brought in to run the Zanzibar Sultanate and the nascent administrations of the British protectorates on the East African mainland,

Twaddle points out, while others were artisans. The Indian community in Uganda comprised large-scale industrialists as well as petty traders and shopkeepers. Among them were doctors and lawyers as well as clerks and mechanics. Considered economic middlemen, a buffer or intermediary class, the material identity of the community is enunciated by that very positionality. However, these novels reflect a positionality in constant negotiation. As Ocaya-Lakidi points out, there were three rather than two colonial layers; the Asians were "colonizing" immigrants above the indigenous people and the British were above everyone else (Twaddle 1975, 82). "Life was segregated, courtesy of official British policy," notes the narrator in Moses Isegawa's epic novel *Abyssinian Chronicles* (2000, 114). These are the points of identification to which Hall refers.

It is exactly the law of origin, however, that was applied to people of Indian descent in Uganda. For Amin, and for many black Ugandans, as the film and the novels expose, the law of origin *was* unproblematic. Nationality was configured not by virtue of birth or domicile but by origin. How does an identity of becoming mediate a state of being? The expulsion forced Asian Africans in Uganda to choose a nationality, but often that label did not correspond to their own sense of who they were, which was as much a facet of the past as of the future. In effect, the exiles have created a separate diasporic space that transgresses the borders of the various nations in which they have settled, just as the expulsion order itself forced a suturing of originary and discrete religious and cultural identities. Cultural identities, as Hall points out, come from somewhere and have histories; they undergo constant transformation (Braziel and Mannur 2003, 236). How are those transformations and negotiations occasioned by a political act and necessitated not only by more abstruse explorations of self but also by the very need for survival?

Shenaaz Nanji's novel *Child of Dandelions* is a coming-of-age story about Sabine, an Indian Ugandan girl, and her friendship with Zena, a black Ugandan girl; the friendship is strained as radio stations count down the days for all Asians to leave the country. For Sabine, self-identification is straightforward. When the radio announces the expulsion order, her mother says to her husband in fear: "Sadru, we are Indians." Sabine immediately corrects her, saying "Ugandans," and looks for affirmation to her father, who nods (Nanji 2008, 11). With all the idealism and nationalism of youth, Sabine underscores the point that her family chose to be Ugandan citizens where most other Indians in Uganda remained British subjects (11). Sabine and her friend Zena rehearse the politics of identity playing out in the country as they get into a heated discussion: "But we are Ugandans," Sabine keeps insisting. However, Zena, the indigenous daughter of the country, replies: "You are Indian, I'm African." Her ethnic, political, and social positionality all enable the legitimacy and authority with which she defines and represents Sabine. Sabine has a comeback: "I'm African too. Indo-African." But so does Zena: "You are brown. I'm black," she explains (92), summoning the imperial cartography of race, the subjective sovereignties of self-definition, and the geo-spatial categories of the postimperial nation-state. Zena's response recalls Nadine Gordimer's question in *Writing and Being*: "Could one, in fact, make the claim, 'my country' if one could not also say 'my people'?" (Gordimer 1995, 128). Sabine would like to be able to say "my people," but Zena precludes the possibility by reminding her that she is a weed, an undesirable encroachment, the child of dandelions.

Although outwardly they were seen as a homologous community, internally Asian Africans identified by ethnicity and religion. It is perhaps not wholly accurate, therefore, to refer to Indian Ugandans as a discrete community but to reference the politics of religion and ethnicity as well as that of national origin. Each religious group of East Indians maintained an individual identity, and often that was further mediated by linguistic subgroups. "We are all children of Divide-and-Rule," thought Ronald, one of the characters in *The General Is Up* (Nazareth 1991, 19). Throughout these novels, and in Mira Nair's film, Asian African characters struggle to organize their identities, as ethnic enclaves give way to national and finally transnational collectivities. Siddiqi notes in *The Feast of the Nine Virgins* that Asians loved the old popular movie song "Mera juta hai Japani . . ." for its crucial message that one's attire could be from anywhere, but one's heart was essentially Hindustani or Indian (2001, 145). Interestingly, in *Mississippi Masala,* this is the very song that plays on Kinnu's tape recorder when the soldiers take it out of her suitcase at a checkpoint, and they dance to it in a derisive manner. It is this hybrid "masala" identity that Sabine in *Child of Dandelions* embodies as she clutches her mother's *tasbhi* or rosary and prays in English, Gujarati, Swahili, and Arabic. And it is this identity that Mina in *Mississippi Masala* insinuates when she is mistaken for Mexican or introduced as Indian in Mississippi but confuses everyone by explaining that she has never been to India.

Jamilla Siddiqi's *The Feast of the Nine Virgins* also describes a fictional East African country, this one called Pearl. That the African country where Siddiqi's novel is set is Uganda is clearly indicated when it is referred to as "the Pearl of Africa's Crown. Just Pearl, for short." (2001, 3). It uses a layered technique to map disparate worlds onto each other: East Africa in the 1960s, nineteenth-century Lahore (now in Pakistan) and London in the 1990s. After the expulsion order has been issued, Siddiqi reveals the general attitude of Asians toward Africans as one of resentment and anger. She ascribes to Asians the notion that the blacks are simply ungrateful, throwing them out after they have sacrificed their lives to the place. "All our hard work, our sweat," Indian Ugandans grumble, "What have we not done for Pearl? And now just look at them! Rounding us up like cattle and wanting to brand us with a special mark if they think we are good enough to carry on running our noble businesses in their blessed country" (275–76). The expulsion order provoked a sense of confusion about nationality: "It's our country too! Well, it's not our real country—we're Indian and proud to be Indian. Our soul belongs in India, but we live here. Our livelihoods are here" (276). Uganda is described as Mohanji's "beloved homeland" but then immediately qualified as "never home, but . . . the homeland. Real home was always India, Bharat" (51). Mohanji asserted that he would return to India when he had enough money, but he had been saying this for forty years, and in his way of thinking he would never have enough money. So the intention to return was specious. Had he not been forced out of there he would never have left small town "Pearl." That Uganda is the natal home is reiterated insistently in these novels, and in *Mississippi Masala* Jay tells his friend: "Okelo, this is my home." But Okelo replies, "Not any more, Jay. Africa is for Africans. Black Africans." And it is an answer Jay can never forget nor forgive until much later when he returns to Uganda and finds that Okelo had been killed in the Amin era. In *Return to Paradise*, Azra, whose last memory of Uganda was her brutal rape on the way to the airport, still thinks of it as "her cherished country . . . now bleeding to death" (Dawood 2000, 197) when she returns with her English husband after the fall of Amin.

Hall points out that Martiniquans and Jamaicans are positioned as both the same and different, and that the boundaries of difference are continually repositioned in relation to different points of reference (Braziel and Mannur 2003, 238). And so with black Ugandans and Indian Ugandans. We see just such a repositioning when a family friend asks Sabine's mother if they too are leaving town like the rest of the Indian community. Sabine's mother's first response to the expulsion order was to say with trepidation, "We are Indians," but now she reconfigures their identity with a shrug: "We are Ugandan citizens" (Nanji 2008, 44). The myriad ways in which Indians in Uganda represent their identity (and are represented) illustrate Hall's claim that diasporic identities are those that constantly produce and reproduce themselves anew through transformation and difference (Braziel and Mannur 2003, 244). It also illustrates Hall's point that we do not stand in the same relation to metropolitan centers. What was the metropole for Indians in Uganda? Was it Kampala, Bombay, or London, or even Lisbon for the Goans? Or was it all of the above? In *Child of Dandelions* Lalita applies an old adage that describes tangential thinking to Ugandan Indians as "'Looking London, Talking Tokyo,'" but "we are talking Bombay," she giggles (Nanji 2008, 45). Hall's contention that identity is not "once-and-for-all. It is not a fixed origin to which we can make some final and absolute return" (Braziel and Mannur 2003, 237) is metaphorically borne out in Nazareth's *The General Is Up* when George attends a farewell gathering for David at the club and presents him with traditional beaded sticks made by his wife. Each has a motif in black, green, and brown to remind David and his family of their three parents: Goa, the father, India the stepfather, and Damibia the mother (1991, 98). In *Child of Dandelions,* Sabine's father shows her a sculpture made by Makonde tribesman of the Tree of Life, which depicts past and present generations supporting each other. He takes Sabine's hand and places it on top of the sculpture, explaining that she is standing on the shoulders of her father and grandfather (2008, 52).

Peter Nazareth's novel *The General Is Up* records the frenzied days between the issuance of the expulsion order and the exodus. His characters had until then configured their identity as African-Goan but suddenly found themselves in long queues to obtain passports with "East Indians," a group with whom they had not previously identified. The Goan characters in the fictitious country of Damibia, clearly based on Uganda, must determine not only where their allegiances lie but also where their hearts and souls belong. It is no accident that the first Indian to whom we are introduced in Nazareth's *The General Is Up* is a humble mechanic. Nazareth intentionally chooses someone humble in occupation and vulgar in manner to crack open the stereotype that all Indians were rich and exploitative. That Nazareth opens his novel with the General himself, a character clearly based on General Idi Amin, is no accident either. Nazareth builds up an image of a man who is ingenuous as well as dangerous. Despite its title, Nazareth's book is more about the expulsion than it is about Amin. But Amin is a deliberate starting point because Nazareth wants the reader to be clear where responsibility for the expulsion lies and he wants to foreclose any blaming of the victims.

One of the main characters in *The General Is Up* is George Kapa, a Damibian of the Karamoli tribe from the West of Damibia who feels something of an outsider himself in Lubele because it is a stronghold of the Gembe and thus "slightly foreign territory" (Nazareth 1991, 23). Political leaders would occasionally accuse East Indians of refusing their offer of citizenship and "sitting on the fence." George himself wondered why more of them had not become Damibian citizens, thinking that this option was open to all who sought it unless there was something specific against the individual (25). George likes the Goans and cannot believe the rumors that such useful and inoffensive people will be deported until he turns on the news and "Thomas Kisirwa came on, with his horn-rimmed glasses and his horn-rimmed Damibian-BBC accent," announcing the expulsion order: "His Excellency the General has announced that, in accordance with a dream from God, East Indians have to leave Damibia by the next moon" (27). In George, Nazareth deliberately presents us with the figure of a reasonable and temperate Damibian without tribalist instincts as a foil to Amin. That an outrageous order can be modulated by a Damibian-BBC accent is an instance of internal focalization, which draws out the tension between the credible heirs to British governance and Amin's abrogation of power.

Anirudha Gupta indicates that the Government of India expressly instructed its missions in East Africa to persuade Asians to surrender their British passports and accept local citizenship, but since many applications were denied, Asians argued that citizenship was not entirely a choice. East African governments were not interested in giving citizenship to a large number of Asians (Twaddle 1975, 130). Official policy in postindependence India sought to champion the cause of people oppressed under colonial and racial domination. India's first prime minister, Jawaharlal Nehru, was prophetic in admonishing Asians as early as 1953 that the Indian government could not protect them if they went against the people of Africa "because you are their guests; and if they do not want you, out you will have to go, bag and baggage" (Twaddle 1975, 129). The experience of Nazareth's protagonist, David D'Costa, is offered as a rejoinder to those who wonder, as George does, why more Goans (or Indian Ugandans in general) had not taken Damibian citizenship. Further, it responds to those who automatically assume that Indians in Uganda were not interested in citizenship because of their lack of identification with the country or a perceived sense of superiority. Of course, David is a fictional character, but Nazareth's characters tend to be barely fictionalized constructions of various types, and David is clearly intended as a prototype of the kind of Asian African who did indeed identify as both Asian and African and did desire to remain. Soon after independence he had "in a burst of patriotism" applied for Damibian citizenship (Nazareth 1991, 28), and this was well before the accusations that East Indians were simply sitting on the fence. Nazareth then goes on to record the daunting and labyrinthine bureaucracy that David must hack his way through to get that citizenship ratified. David comes up against the Kafkaesque bureaucracies of both the new state and the old one as he shuttles between the British High Commission and the Damibian Passport Office. Nazareth shows that there is more than one sense in which people of Indian descent were middlemen. Whereas the office workers in the Ugandan Passport Office treat him like a criminal, the British immigration official at the airport in

London treats him with suspicion and condescension. David's anger is directed against her and the government she represents more than anyone else. Sabine's father similarly accuses Britain of stabbing the backs of forty thousand British Indians in claiming that England is a crowded little island that cannot take in more than the quota of three thousand a year (Nanji 2008, 50).

Nazareth loses no opportunity to expose the empire as a rapacious and corrupt organ of oppression. Their distinction between "British citizens" and "British passport holders" might make them seem magnanimous, David reflects, but "Britain could pick and choose the ones she needed to prop up her tottering, empire-less economy" (Nazareth 1991, 35), and she could do this surreptitiously while hiding behind a mask of humanity. In somewhat didactic asides, Nazareth uses his narrative authority to squarely place the bulk of the blame on the British: "Wherever they went, they brought in a buffer, scapegoat middle-class, usually from another part of the empire" (55). The idea is to make East Indians feel that Damibians envied and hated them and that both before and after independence protection was provided by European arms: "Voila! Divide-and-Rule!" (55). The General is too simpleminded and stubborn to understand this Orwellian game, which all other leaders know how to play: "Blame the alien middle-class but throw out only a few hundreds and keep the rest for continual use" (55–56). In locating responsibility within the British Empire itself, Nazareth is backed by Ocaya-Lakidi, who states unequivocally that "the real and proper colonizers of East Africa after all were white Britons, not brown Asians" (Twaddle 1975, 81). Ocaya-Lakidi indicates that "the Asians were 'colonizing' immigrants to East Africa, even if under direct British supervision, in that they came to be above and to dominate the indigenous people of East Africa in many sectors of life" (82). But he goes on to make the qualification that they themselves were a colonized people, both in East Africa and in their original homeland, notwithstanding their talk of being British citizens (82).

Thus the Indian community became foreign scapegoats who were blamed for everything from the cost of clothing to the lack of housing. While African anger was directed at Asians because they put colonial exploitative policies into effect, "the real authors of the system, the British, were largely spared because they operated, often invisibly, from behind the buffer" (Twaddle 1975, 82). This is illustrated in Moses Isegawa's *Abyssinian Chronicles,* where whites are portrayed as "locked in their privilege and elitist corporate power" and enjoying the protection of nuclear arms in silos back home and warships in the Indian Ocean over here." Whites "were the goldfish in mobile aquariums, gawked at as they rolled through the city on the way to their schools, their clubs, their power jobs" (Isegawa 2000, 120). Mugezi echoes prevailing attitudes when he talks about how the local elite had entered the political arena, but Indians stayed out of it, "content with their 90 percent control of trade and their royal role as the geese that lay the golden eggs" (116). In *Child of Dandelions* Lalita reminds Sabine's mother that they are called Jews and are too successful for their own safety (Nanji 2008, 45). So what was often presented as a bilateral problem misses a very important third dimension, as Ocaya-Lakidi points out. He distinguishes between two levels of anti-Asian resentment: the practice of investing abroad money earned in East Africa was an issue for the African elite, while the alleged Asian habit of cheating his buyers was an issue for the ordinary African (Twaddle 1975, 93).

The reputation of Asians as crafty bamboozlers emerges in Siddiqi's novel, which focuses on the Mohanji family. Mohanji sees his community as a hardworking people who get up at five in the morning to fetch goods from wholesalers and who stay up long after darkness has fallen to count the day's takings and stock up for the following day. It is a self-image very different from the stereotype of the *dukawallas,* but Siddiqi deconstructs that self-image by exposing the racism inherent in it: "What does the government know about running a business? What did the natives know about running a shop? No work ethic, these Blacks. Only Indians could do this sort of thing. It was in their blood" (2001, 12). Throughout the novel Siddiqi makes it a point to reiterate stereotypes of the *dukawallas* as crafty, small-minded and miserly people who made obscene profits off the backs of black people. Siddiqi focuses on the derogatory view of Africans held by the *dukawallas,* who refer to them as "savages, junglees, kaalias" (290) and "live with the constant dread that some day, these not-to-be-trusted Black chaps would be in charge of everything (123). Siddiqi is not inaccurate with regard to social facts, as when she notes that the *dukawallas* kept their property circulating among themselves through endogamous marriages, and the racist traits she describes are not wholly inaccurate either. But the over-the-top language she imputes to them risks the production of caricatures rather than credible portrayals, simplifying where Nazareth at least tries to complicate.

Siddiqi's most effective uncovering of the de facto apartheid in play in Pearl is not only in her reference to the separate residential areas that Asians inherited from Europeans but also in her description of the distribution of drinking water in the Mohanji store. Mohanji sets up a clandestine business of selling ice-cold tap water to black Africans for ten cents out of a cooler that was designated by a soft drink manufacturer for its own products only. Africans were sold their drinking water in empty jam tins, with jagged edges, while Indians got their water for free in stainless steel cups. Europeans, being at the top of the pecking order, received real glass tumblers for their sodas and beers with candy striped straws from which to sip (Siddiqi 2001, 17). The drinking vessels become allegorical for race and class divisions and disparities, and selling the natives their own tap water becomes a trope of the Asian exploitation of Africans that recurs throughout Siddiqi's novel. In *Child of Dandelions* drinking vessels also serve as social commentary. When events have reached a crisis point, Sabine decides that it is time to make some changes and insists that Katana, their domestic help, drink his tea from the china cups the family uses, not his usual plastic mug on the top shelf (Nanji 2008, 134). However, one must note that there is a similar separateness maintained for servants in India, not just the "untouchables" Nanji mentions (134), but all servants, and that it is as much a class issue as a racial one. But it becomes even more complicated in Uganda, where "race was class, and class was still determined by race," as Mugezi notes in *Abyssinian Chronicles* (Isegawa 2000, 121).

In Nanji's novel as well, Asians refer to the untrustworthy nature of the *golas* or blacks (2008, 44). Nanji, however, introduces a range of Asian characters, from the shopkeeper who acts in a disdainful manner toward Zena to the respect and kindness with which her own family treats fellow Ugandans. Similarly, she offers a range of Ugandan characters, from the violent Colonel Butabika and the gratuitously cruel army men who search Sabine's home to the tender Katana (himself in danger during Amin's regime as a Langi[1]) and the humorous "Bodyfinders." Nanji cannot always resist a patronizing superiority in her authorial voice, a superiority that reflects what Africans resented in Asians, even as she simultaneously endeavors to expose such attitudes. When Lalita pronounces Katana "a good African," (180), it is clear that Nanji is not exposing Lalita's sense of superiority so much as betraying her own. While it is clear that many of the viewpoints and descriptions of Africans ascribed to Indians were inherited from the British, Ocaya-Lakidi points out that the same is true of the viewpoints and descriptions of Indians as the local Jews, crafty, cunning, and avaricious, held by black Africans (Twaddle 1975, 85). Both groups were victims of a mental colonization. As Ocaya-Lakidi indicates, Africans had their own assumptions about Asians, seeing them as lazy because they did not engage in sweaty, dirty work, and weak because of their spicy diet. Asian habits such as constant hawking and spitting in the street and living in congested urban quarters afforded a reputation of ill hygiene, but they were also considered rich, showy people who sported an arrogant attitude and maintained a social exclusiveness (Twaddle 1975, 95).

Factual accounts of the expulsion by black Ugandans such as Dent Ocaya-Lakidi's essay and Henry Kyemba's memoir *A State of Blood* tend to be scrupulously fair toward the nature of the Asian presence in Uganda, but fictional accounts such as Isegawa's or Ngugi wa Thiong'o's often depict Asians as economically and sexually exploitative and segregationist profiteers. Ngugi's novels *Weep Not, Child* and *Petals of Blood* both put forth negative portraits of Indian shopkeepers, but *Wizard of the Crow* takes a more epic and transnational approach. In Isegawa's *Abbysinian Chronicles,* Mugezi describes the Indians in "Mini Bombay" as "sealed off in their mansions, their schools, their hospitals, ever a mystery to the Africans" (2000, 120). Mugezi's father, Serenity, describes the departing Indians with complete emotional detachment and in almost bestial terms: "He knew

1. Members of the Langi tribe were targeted because it was the tribe to which Amin's predecessor, Milton Obote, belonged.

that the Indians would not leave without a fight: the geese that lay golden eggs would claw, and flutter, and bite, and break the eggs if possible" (122). Mugezi explains the stranglehold on trade and the perceived role of Indians as agents of the British who had left the political arena but still ran the economic show by remote control. Mugezi's grandfather is euphoric about Amin's expulsion order: "He could see the mighty padlocks on Indian businesses falling away like rusty trinkets, opening the way for Africans to storm the bastions of economic power" (118). However, to describe the Asian African presence in East Africa as essentially or entirely an exploitative one is simplistic and reductionist.

In *Quest for Equality: Asian Politics in East Africa, 1900–1967,* Robert Gregory notes that storied industrialist families such as the Madhvanis, the Mehtas, the Chandarias, and, of course, the Aga Khans donated large sums of money to libraries, hospitals, schools, temples, civic buildings, and recreational facilities in Africa as well as in India (Gregory 1993, 54). The Madhvani contribution is also referenced in *Return to Paradise* by Yusuf Dawood (2000, 7), where the pseudonym Manghnani is used, but the attribution is clear. Madhvani was one of the first Asians to apply for Ugandan citizenship; he continued his father's program of providing educational, health, housing, and recreational facilities for his African employees, and he employed handicapped Africans wherever feasible. Unlike most other Asian industrialists Madhvani also employed Africans in top management (Gregory 1993, 55). The stereotype of overseas Indians as economically exploitative is difficult to come to terms with; as Michael Twaddle points out, it is "at best simplistic, at worst immoral" (1975, 3). But it finds frequent countenance in many of these novels, even though they are by Asian African authors, whether through an internalization of this stereotype or a somewhat guilty struggle to confront it.

Unlike most of the other writers, however, Nazareth makes an effort to debunk the notion that Indian *dukawallas* were universally hated. David D'Costa's housegirl, Rosa, tells his wife, Josephine, that she misses the Indian *dukawallas* because tribalism does not enter into their treatment of African customers, whereas a Gembe would say: "'You are a Muroto, you won't buy anything.' And he refuses to show me anything" (Nazareth 1991, 44). Nazareth does not deny that the *dukawalla's* main function was to make a profit, but he points out that Africans were equally capable of exploiting each other, and tribal differences factored into it. For instance, he exposes the hypocrisy of the Minister of Citizenship and Internal Affairs, who was known to be exceedingly corrupt himself, but rants that they cannot let these "bloody *Muinidis* keep on sucking our blood!" (42). However, because they handled money, Asians were suspect, as David Gwyn indicates in his book on Idi Amin (1977, 115). Nazareth also responds reflexively to the perception that all Damibians had a fanatical hatred of East Indians or rejoiced at Amin's order. In this he is backed by Gwyn, who records "the widespread sympathy that Asians reportedly received from the majority of Uganda's Africans" and notes that "the country is clearly bigger than Amin and his entourage" (1977, 122). In *The General Is Up*, David D'Costa recounts that many Damibians of all classes came to apologize to him, to weep, and to bring gifts after the expulsion order, feeling as though the General had abused their deep sense of hospitality.

The anguish felt by Indian Ugandans is recorded by both Nazareth and Isegawa, who recount stories, apocryphal perhaps, about Indians taking their own lives when the expulsion order was issued. It was rumored that the only Ugandans who regretted the order were domestic workers who would lose their source of employment, but when the buses start rolling toward the airport, George notices that Damibians by the roadside stop to watch them silently, not dance with joy as shown in the photos printed in the foreign press. In *Mississippi Masala* as well there are sorrowful scenes of farewell as families part tearfully from friends and from their domestics. While it is certainly true that such sentimental scenes belie the iniquitous treatment of domestics in many instances, as well as unequal race relations, they also remind us that the story is many-sided and multifarious.

Integration, or the lack thereof, remained one of the great sticking points in Asian fears and African resentment. The term "integration" was "thundered" by Amin, says Gwyn, and mentioned in the official Ugandan government report on Amin's case for expelling the Asians (1977, 118–19). Gupta notes that neither African nor Asian leaders cared to define the term, but the report spells it out. The term "integration," Gupta indicates, has a legal as well as a sociocultural connotation (Twaddle 1975, 130).

Asian settlers argued that integration would involve surrendering their traditions and customs but also, and worst of all in their view, giving their daughters in marriage to Africans. Integration in terms of accepting African leadership was not controversial. Integration in business terms was complicated on a number of levels. But the biggest bogey was the threat of miscegenation. Whereas Gwyn rejects as probable nonsense the rumor that Amin's hatred of Asians resulted from his rejection by an Asian widow who refused his offer of marriage (1977, 118), Nanji gestures toward a version of it in her novel when Sabine's mother claims that Amin arrested the multimillionaire Indian businessman Madhvani because his actress daughter-in-law turned down the President's invitation for an evening of pleasure (2008, 103). Gwyn acknowledges that "much of the racial tension in Uganda and elsewhere certainly seems to be concerned with sex" (1977, 118), and this is borne out in these texts. In *Child of Dandelions* the official who issues Sabine's identity card makes a move on her. The policeman who opens Kinnu's suitcase in *Mississippi Masala* thrusts the phallic barrel of a rifle into her face and uses it to rip her necklace off in an act of simulated rape just before he tells her that she can go. Azra, the female protagonist in Dawood's *Return to Paradise*, experiences an actual rape, graphically described in unequivocal detail and unmistakably racial terms.

In *Feast of the Nine Virgins*, forced miscegenation was undeniably the greatest fear of the Asian community, prompting Mohanji to ask indignantly, "Is this what integration is all about? Should our Indian girls become pregnant with Black babies and then be allowed to marry innocent, unsuspecting Asian boys . . . ?" (Siddiqi 2001, 250). Mohanji points out that exogamy is proscribed even in India, so to contemplate marrying someone of a different race and religion would be unthinkable. Mohanji's idea of integration would instead be mutual tolerance and respect for each other's traditions, a sort of separate-but-equal philosophy, and he expresses his admiration for "real" African traditions such as respect for elders, especially the father, and holding the family unit sacrosanct, values held before the "shameless Whites came and wiped out what little culture these people had" (250). Mohanji has a simple and straightforward solution to the internecine tensions in Pearl: "Africans and Asians could live in such harmony if only all this inter-marriage nonsense goes away. We own the shops, we sell them stuff. They buy, we sell. They're happy, we're happy" (250). As if legitimizing the community's fears of miscegenation, fifteen-year-old Sabine in *Child of Dandelions* has a crush on Ssekore, the brother of her best friend, Zena. But it was the very real fear of rape by Amin's henchmen at the time of the expulsion that gave physical form to the old specter. Bodies rather than borders was the site where difference was most sharply marked. Despite the fear of miscegenation, however, many of these writers take pains to offer a counternarrative. The friendship of Jay and Okelo as young boys in *Mississippi Masala*, the mixed-race children in *Day After Tomorrow* and *The Feast of the Nine Virgins*, Sabine and Zena's friendship in *Child of Dandelions*, George and David's friendship in *The General Is Up*, and Imran and Princess Malika's romance in *Return to Paradise* are all instances of racial contravention.

When David D'Costa finally reaches the head of the slow-moving queue in Nazareth's *The General Is Up* and enters the Immigration Department building, he is faced by a harassed black man who veers between anger at his discomfort in the stifling heat and musty air of the building and his "civil service politeness" (1991, 65). David is asked to surrender his Certificate of Citizenship and his passport, which he does. For David, identity is suddenly no longer a choice. Nor is it a social or cultural matter. It is, quite simply, a bureaucratic decision: "What did it mean to be a Stateless person? What would it be like going to a concentration camp? What did it mean not to have a country?" (65). When he returns home, he repeats over and over again to his wife, "They took away my citizenship," while she struggles, yet again, to convince him of the necessity of leaving (71). Nanji also writes extensively about the *kipande* or identity card for Indians: the long lines in the hot sun and bureaucratic hassles, the corruption and exploitation of the soldiers and some of the officials. Sabine is the only member of her family awarded a *kipande*, but when the immigration officer tries to sexually exploit her she seeks asylum through the auspices of the United Nations. When she hears that her entire family has found refuge in Canada, she rips the identity card to pieces, for she is as determined to leave as she had once been to stay. Her treasured Ugandan citizenship had been no more than a piece of paper after all.

For the Asians of Uganda, even passports were no guarantee of nationality, as they were revoked in so many instances. But identity cannot be revoked, and for David D'Costa and other Asian Africans, identity was constituted by many factors: historical, geographical, cultural, metaphorical, and perhaps most of all a sense of place. It is a sense of place that is rendered most powerfully in these novels; it is expressed in descriptions of the land and the connectedness of the characters with the land. This is the geographical expression and metaphysical landscape of which Achebe speaks. The characters must determine not only where their allegiances lie but also where their hearts and souls belong. For Ronald D'Mello, walking home in the darkness with a Damibian woman he picks up, it is the land of his nativity: the land is like a "black womb" (Nazareth 1991, 21). In *The Feast of the Nine Virgins* the child narrator wonders how family friends leaving for England for a whole month could bear to stay away for so long: "All kinds of things will be happening in Pearl and they'll miss them all. The crickets will be singing. The fireflies have special dances this time of the year . . . I would be inconsolable if I ever had to leave Pearl even for a day . . ." (Siddiqi 2001, 198). Pearl is a musical place where "everything and everyone made music" (245). In one of her more resonant passages, Siddiqi brings together the natural sounds of this sonorous land: the symphonies of crickets, mosquitoes, snakes, and geckos, and the flashing of fireflies along with the hymns of the various religious communities: Hindu bhajjans, Muslim congregations, church choirs, and the indigenous songs of the land.

The connection with the land is embodied in dramatically visual terms in *Mississippi Masala*. Nair, like these authors, takes pains to show that the Asian attachment to Africa was not all about money and profiteering; they were in love not only with the landscape but with the very land itself. As they leave their home Jay plucks and holds a red hibiscus flower, while his small daughter, Mina, carries their pet African grey parrot on her shoulder. Before embarking on the plane a man kneels to kiss the land, while a woman prays her rosary over it. There are idyllic scenes of Jay as a child splashing in the stream with Okelo, both boys in loincloths, one brown, the other black, jostling each other, embodying Bahadur Tejani's words from *Day After Tomorrow*, his novel of preexpulsion Uganda: "they felt a call in the blood: of the black African to the brown Indian" (1971, 7–8). Nair's camera lingers lovingly over sloping green hills, rapids, cattle, villagers carrying water pitchers, and other pictographs of the lush landscape for which Uganda is known.[2] When, at the time of their departure, Mina asks, "Why do we have to go, Papa?" and "When are we coming back home?" he is too choked up to answer. Tears pour down Okelo's face as he says goodbye and Kinnu hands him the keys to their car. Boys selling the *Uganda Argus* newspaper yell out the headline: "Last day!" A Sikh boy and an African boy share a laugh over the Mercedes Benz insignia, a symbol of Asian wealth. At the airport, Ugandan schoolchildren in uniform sing a song of farewell. A soldier throws into the mud a portrait of Jay in his legal robes, abrogating his authority, neutralizing his claim to the country, and yet symbolically burying him in the soil of Uganda.

Sabine has posters of Indian movies stars and Russian nesting dolls in her room, but Uganda is represented by skipping stones from Kasenda farm and cowrie shells from Bamburi Beach, as though to suggest that her bond to Uganda is with the land itself. On her grandfather's skin Sabine "could smell the red earth of Kasenda and the aroma of coffee beans" (Nanji 2008, 139). Later he tells her that he cannot leave Uganda no matter the danger. Scooping a fist of red soil from a flowerpot he opens his palm to show Sabine the earth, saying, "Beta, the Kasenda earth is soaked with my blood, my sweat, and my tears. My farms, the coffee beans, they're part of who I am. This is home" (183). Sabine's father, Sadru, insists, "But we are—body, soul, and by law—one hundred percent Ugandan," thus summing up the totality of their identity (48). Most Asians, unlike other minority groups, owned businesses rather than land. Land tenure constitutes a physical belonging, a stake in the very soil of a nation. In *Weep Not, Child,* dispossession is the dispossession of land: the appropriation by white settlers of Gikuyu land, not the dispossession of property, as in the

2. Mira Nair, who is married to a man of Indian Ugandan extraction but was born and raised in India, has said in an interview with Carrie Rickey of the *Philadelphia Inquirer*: "My clothes hang in three places, but I have a garden only in Kampala . . . Where you plant your garden is your true home."

case of Asians. The lament for their lost land by the Gikuyu is poignant. We see Ngotho fondling the soil (Ngugi 1964, 30), but the only presence of Asians in the novel is at its very end, as exploitative shopkeepers. Jay thinks about Uganda all the time and has an ongoing battle with the government to reclaim his property. He wants to call Kampala to tell the person who is living in his house to get out, but when he eventually returns he finds his property in a state of decay and disrepair.

R. Radhakrishnan, a literary and cultural scholar, asks: "Is the 'Indian' in Indian and the 'Indian' in Indian-American the same and therefore interchangeable? Which of the two is authentic, and which merely strategic or reactive?" (Braziel and Mannur 2003, 123). Indian identity, for Asian Africans, was both strategic and reactive. It allowed them to preserve a distinct if sometimes detached presence in their land of domicile while permitting a sense of superiority over the native population. Hugh Tinker, in his chapter on Indians abroad, points out that Indians tried to go in three different directions, first trying to become the equals of the whites, then trying to establish a claim to be British citizens in Africa, and finally falling back on their Indian resources and attempting to mobilize the support of the Indian government and of Indian nationalism (Twaddle 1975, 17). Gupta goes so far as to call it a "'dependency-complex' towards India," seeking advice from Indian officials and visitors on such relatively minor matters as licenses, the higher education of their wards, or the settlement of their in-group rivalries (Twaddle 1975, 126). Radhakrishnan also asks: "To what extent does the 'old country' function as a framework and regulate our transplanted identities within the diaspora? Should the old country be revered as a pregiven absolute, or is it all right to invent the old country itself in response to our contemporary location?" (Braziel and Mannur 2003, 123). From the extensive participation of Jawaharlal Nehru and the Indian government and its representatives in East Africa we can see that the "old country" functioned as an active framework and attempted to regulate the transplanted identities of Indians in East Africa. In 1953 the All-India Congress Committee issued a directive in the form of a resolution that supported the just struggle of Africans against the domination of one race over others and noted with gratification the growing cooperation between Africans and Indians. It also cautioned Indians abroad to demand no official privileges at the expense of the country in which they lived (Twaddle 1975, 128). The old country functioned as a framework not only in an official sense but also in a cultural sense. Notwithstanding their long stay in Africa, and whether or not they were citizens, Asians, as Gupta suggests, preserved their native traditions and culture (Twaddle 1975, 125). The enthusiastic participation of Asian Africans in all things Indian "have tended to accentuate their 'Indianness' to a point which is most irritating to the Africans," who then question their bona fides, says Gupta (125). Apparent apathy toward African causes and problems, traditions and symbols, compounded the perception.

By following their characters into their postexpulsion phase in England and by going back to their antecedents in India, Siddiqi and Dawood extend their narrative space and recontextualize their characters' identities. The use of transnational and transcultural narrative space becomes a site for the contesting identities of the characters. National identity always intersects and affiliates with transnational correlations, but these writers claim in Uganda the singularity of "home" in order to reclaim the multiplicity of the identity that was stripped from them. In the final analysis, the idea of Uganda as home prevails. What Amin exploited was the politics of origins, and no one clarifies this more succinctly than Henry Kyemba. Kyemba does not mince words, describing Amin's actions as "brutally racist" (1977, 241) and exposing Amin's talent for taking a partial truth and twisting it to his own advantage. Kyemba is referring to Amin's argument that the Asians had been brought to Uganda by the forces of imperialism to build the railway that was then used to take away the country's wealth. Asians, Amin claimed, were non-Ugandans who were "milking the cow without feeding her" (Kyemba 1977, 241). In that manner he presented himself as a black leader protecting the rights of other blacks against foreign exploitation and as "Ugandanizing" the country and getting rid of the last traces of white imperialism (241). It was a beguiling message that beckoned black peoples in a number of African nations and even resonated with many black Americans who were ready to regard Amin as a great African nationalist leader, according to Kyemba (242). When Kyemba describes Amin's move to expel Asians it is interesting to note that he describes it not only as "an act dictated by his extraordinary greed" but also as "an act of piracy whereby he handed over the property of one minority to another minority—his own" (241). In so doing, Kyemba is saying something very significant, and he is saying it intentionally and mindfully. He is saying that the Asians were one minority among many in Uganda. Besides minority tribes, Gwyn observes that the 1969 census indicated the presence in Uganda of substantial communities of people born in Kenya, Tanzania, Rwanda, Burundi, Zaire, and the Sudan (123). Their numbers equaled or exceeded the numbers of Asians in most instances, but of course they were black Africans and thus did not trouble those with nativist inclinations.

The Asian African imaginary clearly constructs Africa as home. Africa is the land, the soil, the scenery, but it is also the people, not simply a stage prop of scenery without people: Marlow's "*blank spaces*" in *Heart of Darkness* (emphasis added). In these novels the focus is naturally on Asians, but Africans people their pages prominently as well, unlike so much of the literature of empire where Africans are nonexistent or only shadowy figures in the background. For Asian Africans India was an illusory place; East Africa was their domicile, and physical and political boundaries were both fungible and negotiable. Through memory, boundaries are crossed continually. Asian Africans struggle to describe a journey that has often taken place across four continents: Asia, Africa, Europe, and the Americas. Shailja Patel uses the term "Migritude" in order to describe her 90-minute spoken-word theater show. Patel uses saris inherited from her mother to tell the story of her ancestors' migration from India to East Africa, the expulsion and emigration of East African Indians to the global North from the 1970s onward, and her own emigration from Africa to Europe to the United States. Today, blogs and social media sites have become repositories for memory and sites for the ongoing production and negotiation of Asian African identity. Such sites are self-reflexive spaces that allow for constant positioning and repositioning.

It is no surprise then that the metaphors these writers use to describe the experience of the exodus are drawn from relations of kinship. Peter Nazareth sees himself as the bastard son of Africa: "'Goodbye, Mother Africa,' I said, as the plane lifted off. 'Your bastard son loved you'" (Nazareth 1972, 150). Siddiqi uses the metaphor of "Bidaai," the sadness of the ritual departure of the bride for her new home: "The scene at the Market Square bus station resembled a typical Indian wedding. All the men in their best western suits, and all the women in shiny gold and red saris and heavy jewellery" (Siddiqi 2001, 280, 282). Siddiqi sees the bridal colors of red and gold reflected in the spectacular sunsets of the region, once more connecting Asians with the geography of the land itself. Dawood describes the scene graphically, with the emphasis yet again on kinship: "The sight of men, women and children, standing in unending queues at banks, embassies and airline offices, millionaires becoming paupers overnight, men savagely beaten, women raped, children crying, families relieved of their life savings and personal belongings, and third and fourth generation residents of Uganda arriving in the UK as destitute refugees begging for handouts . . ." (Dawood 2000, 153). The life of exile is the life of memory. Returning to the land of his childhood and birth, Imran finds that "The Pearl of Africa had been reduced to a festering wound, weeping and bleeding" (156). But Imran, like most Asian Africans, knows that the lands they once called home must remain a construct of memory and home a moveable place. When Jay returns from Uganda to Mississippi, after his failed attempt to reclaim his property, he tells Kinnu: "Home is where the heart is and my heart is with you." Sabine, in *Child of Dandelions*, resolves: "*I will carry my home with me*," since "Turtles carry their homes with them so they are always at home (Nanji 2008, 174). "Everyone lives in a space inside their head," insists the narrator in *The Feast of the Nine Virgins* (Siddiqi 2001, 1). Such sentiments may sound like clichés, but this is not simply the trivialization of history or of histories that R. Radhakrishnan disparages with regard to *Mississippi Masala* (Braziel and Mannur 2003, 124). It is an acknowledgment that for Asian Africans home must forevermore be transportable and constantly re-created, a virgin space, not the erroneous "empty space" that European colonizers saw for the taking but a space of imaginary reunification and coherence, a space of the mind and of the heart. For Asian Africans Uganda remains the country that could have been. When Gordimer talks about "the discovery of what could be my own country," something she "could begin to lay claim to," she is looking toward the future of South Africa; Asian Africans must relinquish that possibility to the past. "We did not know how to go about putting our country, ourselves, together," Gordimer says (1995, 127–28). While there have been more recent and less significant arrivals of migrants from India, as well as a few returnees, for the original Indian Ugandan communities that prospect was made moot by the expulsion order. An imaginary must be grounded in a physical and perceptual reality, and for the children of exiles that reality is no longer Uganda but rather the mostly Western countries where their parents settled. Uganda, however, has replaced India as the land of mythic origin.

Part Two

African Literature and Consciousness

4

Jacques Lacan in Africa

Travel, Moroccan Cemetery, Egyptian Hieroglyphics, and Other Passions of Theory

OBIWU

Jacques Lacan's essays, seminars, interviews, and correspondences are invaluable in their relation to the analyst's African travels and his discourses on the subject of reading, writing, the book, the father, and racism. Lacan toured Morocco in 1928 and toured Egypt in 1947; that is, twenty-five and six years (respectively) before the inception of his seminars in 1953. Three remote and four immediate scenarios present themselves as sources of inspiration for Lacan's quest in Africa. On one level, the respective trio of Charles de Gaulle, Sigmund Freud, and André Gide would provide the remote albeit sociopolitical and intellectual influence that could have overdetermined Lacan's African journey. On another level, Lacan's immediate motivation for embarking on his African journey may have everything to do with his respective critical encounters with the French master psychiatrist Gäetan Gatian de Clérambault and the Swiss psychologist Carl Gustav Jung, his relationship with Marie-Thérèse Bergerot, and his later engagement to Sylvia Maklès Bataille.

Lacan did not have any physical contact with Freud and I could not ascertain that he ever met with either de Gaulle or Gide. Charles de Gaulle (class of 1909) was one of the alumni heroes of the College Stanislas and its Saint-Cyr military academy, and he was celebrated by the school's younger generations for his military and political exploits in colonial Africa. The College Stanislas was an upper-middle-class school for the most promising of French Catholic youth. Lacan, who graduated from College Stanislas in 1919, according to the psychoanalytic historian Elisabeth Roudinesco, was discharged from military service for supposedly being "thin" (1990, 104). Lacan's younger brother, Marc-Francois (who would later become a Benedictine monk), had his military service as a reserve officer at the same Saint-Cyr in 1927. Could Lacan have had de Gaulle at the recesses of his mind as he planned his African trips?

Given their antecedents and the adventurous paths that each took to Africa and global recognition, it is not surprising that Jean-Paul Sartre would compare Lacan with his old school great alumnus, de Gaulle. "Trapped between the id and the super-ego," avers Sartre, "the psychoanalyst's subject is a bit like de Gaulle between the Soviet Union and the United States" (Roudinesco 1990, 417). Following Sartre's grand historical gesture, Roudinesco likewise compares Lacan with the war strategists de Gaulle and Hannibal:

> The founding act pronounced by Lacan at the summer solstice of 1964 was not without recalling de Gaulle's celebrated speech of June 18, 1940: majestic in tone, splendid in style, impeccable in its legislation. Lacan spoke in the first person, denounced "deviations" and "compromises" and presented himself as the absolute head of a great movement of reconquest. Rediscovering all at once his baroque inflections, he mobilized the signifiers of his culture and was intent on being the savior of a Freudian France gone decadent . . . As opposed to Freud, Lacan agreed to be a master who politically and juridically occupied the position of the master. Sovereign, emperor, or pope? I would suggest, rather, legislator or founding father. Against the empire, he raised his head anew to avenge his ancestor and reestablish the might of the Carthaginian cause, the symbol of that Hannibalian situation which Freud had dreamed for psychoanalysis. (1990, 417–18)

The comparisons are apt because the perennial military histrionics of both Hannibal and de Gaulle exemplify the characteristic restlessness of the unconscious that is central to Lacan's analytics. Similarly, when paired with Lacan's own professional battles and realignments with the International Psychoanalytic Association and the French Psychoanalytic Society, the resurgences of the two warriors speak to the resistances of the subject and its compulsion to repeat. Moreover, the highs and lows of Hannibal and de Gaulle's respective war engagements in Africa and Europe would prove revelatory to the expanding geopolitical associations and complications of Lacan's own illustrious career.

Lacan learned about Freud's theories for the first time in 1923 (Roudinesco 1997, 13). That was five years before his first travel to Africa and nine years before he defended his doctoral thesis in psychiatry. Though Freud never visited Africa, Lacan makes copious references to the trove of African ethnographic materials in Freud's *The Interpretation of Dreams* (1900), *Totem and Taboo* (1913), and *Moses and Monotheism* (1933). Leaning on *The Interpretation of Dreams*, Lacan references what he describes as "the dreams of the botanical monograph" in his 1953 seminar, and speaks of the book's "mythological, anthropological and cultural topics" (1991a, 269, 9). *The Interpretation of Dreams*, according to Lacan, is the book in which Freud reintroduces the subject of meaning, a theme that is at the core of dream reading and the problematic of repression. On the one hand, Lacan connotes the complexity of dream interpretation when he says (in "The Agency of the Letter in the Unconscious or Reason since Freud") that "taking the tour is simply continuing in the *Traumdeutung*" (1977, 160). On the other, he speaks to the pure satisfaction of a physical pilgrimage to the land of the dreams that would supersede all secondary ethnographic accounts of his greatest intellectual hero, Freud. Freud's description of the scarcely trodden but "adventurous" road of interior Africa in Rider Haggard's novel *She: A History of Adventure* (1886) would prove irresistible to an ambitious votary who hankered after the hidden treasures of a master discourse from the beginning of his career.[1] After defending his thesis (entitled "Paranoid Psychosis and Its Relation to Personality") in November 1932, Lacan sent a copy to Freud, who responded with a postcard that read: "Thank you for sending your thesis" (Roudinesco 1997,

1. The British analyst Helton Godwin "Peter" Baynes reports that *She* was one of Jung's favorite novels and that Jung led a seminar on the novel in the spring of 1925 just before his Bugishu expedition to East and Northern Africa (Burleson 2005, 30).

58). That was apparently the closest personal contact on record that Lacan ever had with Freud.

André Gide was a pioneer of surrealism, an artistic movement that heavily impacted Lacanian psychoanalytic discourse. In his youth, notes Roudinesco, Lacan and his friends attended public readings at "Shakespeare & Co," a Parisian bookstore that hosted such famous writers of the day as Paul Claudel, Gide, James Joyce, and Jules Romain (Roudinesco 1997, 12–13, 371). It is not certain if Lacan met with Gide during any of those readings, but the surrealists would later become a great source for Lacan the way they could never be for any other psychoanalyst. He became close friends with many of them, including André Breton, René Crevel, Salvador Dali, Joyce, and Marcel Proust. Lacan's second wife Sylvia's oldest sister, Bianca Maklès, was also married to Theodore Fraenkel, who was reputed as "the 'fourth musketeer' of French surrealism" (Roudinesco 1997, 122). Gide and Breton made the acquaintance of Freud, though Freud, by his own words, was not as enthusiastic about surrealism as the surrealists were of psychoanalysis (Roudinesco 1990, 31). Gide's friend and translator, Dorothy Bussy, was the sister of Freud's friend and translator, James Strachey. When Gide broke off his analysis under Eugenie Sokolnicka, the first-generation French analyst and one of the twelve founders of the Paris Psychoanalytic Society in 1926, he turned her into a tragic character, "Sophroniska," in his only novel *The Counterfeiters* (1925).

Gide traveled to North Africa in 1893, 1894, and 1895, and toured extensively in Algeria, Morocco, and Tunisia. He traveled to Equatorial Africa from 1926 to 1927, during which he visited the Francophone countries of Cameroun, Central African Republic, Chad, Republic of Congo, Guinea, and Senegal. He lived in Tunisia from 1942 to the end of the Second World War. His accounts of these travels are the focus of *Travels in the Congo* (1929) and *If It Die . . . : An Autobiography* (1935). His comparison of French colonialism and the exploitation of the rubber plantations to a new slavery aided the cause of the decolonization movement in Africa. Gide would hold more significance for Lacan, as much for his language and structure as for his politics and travels (see note 7 below). The allegation of linguistic obscurantism that dogged much of Lacan's career echoes

Clément Vautel's position—as Gide himself excitedly cites in *Travels*—that because of their "abstruse" writing, "France has no wish 'at any price'" for the company of Gide, "Rimbaud, Proust, Apollinaire, Suarès, Valèry, and Cocteau" (Gide 1986, 116). Lacan invokes Gide's experience of indecisiveness to illustrate what he calls the "empire of confusion" in *Écrits* (1977, 173). He also invokes Gide's *The Counterfeiters* in the seminar on *The Ego in Freud's Theory* (1954–55) to emphasize the superficiality of Erik Erikson's analysis (1991b, 153).

In his 1958 review essay of Jean Delay and Jean Schlumberger's "psychobiographies" of Gide, "The Youth of Gide, or the Letter and Desire," Lacan specifically notes Gide's interest "in psychoanalysis" and his failed attempt "to undergo analysis with Mrs. Sokolnicka." He describes *The Counterfeiters* as an "elaboration of Gide's own drama" (Lacan 2006, 630). The "botanical monograph" that Lacan references in Freud's *The Interpretation of Dream* could have equally applied to Gide's *Travels in the Congo*, in which Gide describes an actual "visit to the Botanical Gardens" of Dakar, the largest city of Senegal (1986, 5). Gide's observations on imperialism, racism, and slavery are especially remarkable in their foreshadowing of Lacan's later readings on slave labor and the frustrations of *jouissance* in the three books, *Écrits*, *Ethics*, and *Television*. According to Gide:

> The black races are described as being indolent, lazy, without needs, and without desires. But I am inclined to believe that the state of slavery and wretched poverty in which they are sunk, only too often explains the apathy. What desires can a person have who never sees anything desirable? Every time that a well-stocked factory offers the native blankets, stuffs, household utensils, tools, etc., people are ingenuously surprised to see his desires aroused—if, that is to say, a fair remuneration of his work gives him the means of satisfying them. (1986, 44)

Gide shows us, Lacan posits in "The Youth of Gide," "how the tree of the bourgeoisie that arose under Louis XIV grew from a farmer, Nicolas Rondeaux, who acquired wealth by trading staples from the colonies" (2006, 628). Gide could have been one of the earliest influences on Lacan's acerbic condemnation of colonial imperialism and its Christian missionary instrument in Africa. I will come back to this.

Besides Freud, Lacan professes his career indebtedness to none other than his teacher de Clérambault. De Clérambault was a decorated veteran of the Moroccan Army during World War I (1914–18). He also achieved acclaim with his essays on local Moroccan textiles and his photographs of native people. On his return from Morocco, he was appointed psychiatrist-in-charge at the Special Infirmary for the Insane of the Paris Prefecture of Police from 1920 to his death by suicide in 1934. De Clérambault was notable for his devotion to "Roman togas and drapings" and his expertise on the "art and manner" of Arab fabrics and costumes (Roudinesco 1990, 105). One could see how his flamboyance would have rubbed off on Lacan's constant dapper dressing, presentational swagger, and theoretical flourish.

Lacan came under the mentorship of de Clérambault at the Special Infirmary in the academic year 1928–29. He effusively declares the power of de Clérambault's influence on his own professional development at the beginning of his seminar on *The Psychoses* in 1955:

> I was certainly still a young psychiatrist then, and I had been introduced to psychiatry largely through the works, the direct teaching, and, I would even be so bold as to say, the intimacy of someone who played a very important role in French psychiatry at that period, M. de Clérambault, whose personality, action, and influence I call to mind in this introductory discussion. (1997a, 5)

Such adulation from the eminent Lacan himself explains why de Clérambault is especially celebrated in the field of psychiatry. His incisive description of the condition of erotomania in 1921 led to the founding of the term "de Clérambault's syndrome." In his presentation on "The Meaning of Delusion," Lacan notes that it is "precisely at the level of psychological distinctions that [de Clérambault's] work is the most significant" (1997a, 18). It was in the same year of their meeting that Lacan went on his grant-funded study tour of Morocco. Roudinesco thoughtfully notes that the Moroccan trip was "the first sign of a strong hankering for the East that would later take him to Egypt and Japan" (1997, 56). Lacan dedicated his definitive collection of essays, *Écrits* (1966), to Gäetan Gatian de Clérambault: "Sole master in psychiatry." In the essay "On My Antecedents"

(1966), Lacan is even more possessive in describing de Clérambault as "my only master in psychiatry" and declaring that it was through de Clérambault and de Clérambault's own teacher, Emil Kraepelin, that he "was led to Freud" (2006, 51–52).

Carl Gustav Jung traveled to Africa, specifically to Algeria and Tunisia in North Africa, for the first time on the invitation of the oil magnet Hermann Sigg in March 1920 (Bair 2003, 339). On October 15, 1925, Jung embarked on a six-month second tour of Africa, but this time to East and North Africa (ending in April 1926). The journey was widely advertised as the "Bugishu Psychological Expedition" or "Expedition to Interior Africa" (339–55). He traveled to Mombasa, Nairobi, and Mt. Elgon in Kenya; to Jinja in Uganda; to Khartoum in Sudan; and to Port Said, Abu Simbel, and Cairo in Egypt. Jung's "expedition" was marked by its unnecessary cruelty, with descriptions of his wielding whips on natives in Uganda and Sudan (351). It was also marked by inordinate sacrilege, when Jung violated a taboo by deliberately going through an Egyptian Coptic monastery with a woman. He made his female companion, Ruth Bailey, "dress like a boy" and falsely introduced the "boy" to the monks as his "disciple" (353). The expedition was so scandalous that it would be better left in the disturbing visual imagery of Blake W. Burleson's characterization in *Jung in Africa* as "the lunatic express" (2005, 55–56). The biographer Deirdre Bair also reports on the strained "tensions" between Jung's "short-tempered" co-travelers, the wealthy American expedition sponsor George Beckwith and the British analyst Helton Godwin "Peter" Baynes (2003, 22). Though Jung had placed Beckwith under the analysis of Baynes, he had to make both men sleep in tents far apart from each other, with his own tent in the middle, during the expedition (Burleson 2005, 22; Bair 2003, 347).

One of Lacan's earliest institutional contacts with Jung was from August to September 30, 1930, during his study under Hans Maier at the Burgholzi clinic of the University of Zurich, a place made famous by the works of Eugen Bleuler (Freud's rival), Jung (Freud's dissident former apostle), and Otto Binswanger (Marini 1992, 98). Roudinesco also reports that Lacan attended a meeting of the Swiss Psychiatric Society at Prangins on October 1933, where Jung presented a talk "about his experiences among African tribes" (1997, 76). In a discussion with the Jungian disciple

Roland Cahen in 1954, Lacan disavows any connection between the Lacanian "signifieds" and the Jungian "archetypes." Lacan subsequently met with Jung at his home in Zurich in an attempt to "reinforce the hypothesis about the subversiveness of Freudianism" (Roudinesco 1997, 264). Stuart Schneiderman, Lacan's first American "analysand," would support this suggestion with his assertion that Lacan adjudged psychoanalysis "to be a subversive and revolutionary occupation," for which he had to adopt a defensive, if obfuscating, language style (1983, 11).[2] In the course of his November 7, 1955 Viennese lecture on "The Freudian Thing, or the Meaning of the Return to Freud in Psychoanalysis," Lacan revealed a confidence from his interview with Jung. Said he:

> Thus Freud's words to Jung—I have it from Jung's own mouth—when, on an invitation from Clark University, they arrived in New York harbor and caught their first glimpse of the famous statue illuminating the universe, "They don't realize we're bringing them the plague," are attributed to him as confirmation of a hubris whose antiphrasis and gloom do not extinguish their troubled brightness. To catch their author in its trap, Nemesis had only to take him at his word. We would be justified in fearing that Nemesis had added a first-class return ticket. (1977, 116)

Lacan speculates that if the threatened "plague" or "subversiveness" of psychoanalysis failed to take hold in the United States, as Freud had expected during his 1909 first American visit with Jung and Sandor Ferenczi, it would be because of the repressed "bad memories" of the Europeans who left for the New World. In other words, America would subvert psychoanalysis, and not the other way round. Freud and Europe would be paid back in kind with a first-class return ticket. Many, including Marcelle Marini and Elisabeth Roudinesco, have joined the ensuing controversy as to whether Freud used specific words (like "plague") or whether Jung supposedly said what Lacan reported (Marini 1992, 29; Roudinesco 1997, 265). Though Jung lived and wrote his memoirs for six years from the date of Lacan's lecture, and Lacan himself lived for twenty

2. An "analysand" is a student who is in analysis under an analyst.

years more after Jung, no one has disproved the veracity of Lacan's narrative. Contemporary Jungian scholars and biographers, in particular, have not helped the cause of elucidating the circumstances or exactitude of Lacan's report on his final meeting with Jung. It is perplexing that in spite of the half-century old furor that links Freud's and Lacan's names to their subjects', neither Bair (2003) nor Burleson (2005) mentions either Lacan or the controversy once in their extensive biohistorical texts on Jung.

I pointed out earlier that Lacan was an intellectual tourist in Morocco. The same is certainly true of his visit to Egypt, during which Roudinesco notes that "he demonstrated all his old interest in seeing and understanding everything" (1997, 56, 184). It seems equally true that a new love affair was usually an occasion for Lacan to embark on international passion trips. His travel to Morocco at age twenty-seven in 1928 coincided with his blossoming relationship with Marie-Thérèse Bergerot, a widow who was fifteen years older than him. He took her to the Saadian Tombs in Marrakech, which were rediscovered in 1917, where his daughter Judith Miller reports that he "scrupulously noted down the complicated genealogies" of the Saadi dynasty (Miller 1991, 46–47, 66–67).[3] In 1929, while he was still dating Bergerot, Lacan found a new love interest in Olesia Sienkiewicz, whom he took on romantic trips to Madrid, Corsica, and the coast of Normandy. Though Sienkiewicz helped to type his medical thesis in 1932, Lacan dedicated the thesis to "M.T.B." (Bergerot's initials), with a note in Greek: "Without whose help I would not have become what I am." Lacan also toured Egypt in 1947 with his Jewish actress fiancée Sylvia Maklès Bataille, who had officially divorced her first husband, Lacan's friend and renegade surrealist writer Georges Bataille, on July 9, 1946. The couple married on July 17, 1953, the same month and year that heralded the epoch-making Lacanian seminar series. It is noteworthy that the 1955 lecture on "The Freudian Thing" was dedicated "To Sylvia" (Lacan 1977, 114). In the Freudian-Lacanian doctrinaire, therefore, the pursuits of the

3. Judith Miller, married to the Lacanian scholar and editor Jacques-Alain Miller, was Lacan's daughter with his second wife, Sylvia, who was formerly married to the writer, playwright, and Lacan's friend Georges Bataille.

intellect, the conquests of cupid, and the excavations of the unconscious all evidently fly on the same wavelength.

Lacan presented his first lecture on "The Symbolic, the Imaginary, and the Real" at the inaugural meeting of the Société Française de Psychanalyse (SFP) in Paris in July 1953, and presented his lecture on "The Function and Field of Speech and Language in Psychoanalysis" to the Rome Congress of Psychoanalysts at the Institute of Psychology, University of Rome, on September 26–27, 1953 (Lacan 1977, 30–113). These presentations would enable Lacan not only to go back to Freud's *The Interpretation of Dreams* and *Totem and Taboo*, both of which had been published before his Moroccan journey, but also to revisit Freud's *Moses and Monotheism*, which was published before his tour of Egypt. In light of Freud's guidance, therefore, Lacan already knew what he was looking for in the two trips. In Morocco, he was drawn to the curious royal cemetery and the genealogical historiography of the 150-year-old bloody expansionism that saw the Saadi dynasty leap from its Principality of Tagmadert in the south of Morocco (1509–54) to the Sultanate of Morocco (1554–1659) after decimating the old Wattasids Sultanate at the Battle of Tadla. In Egypt, Lacan was after the textual profundity of the hieroglyphics.

Like Shakespeare, Marx, Freud, and even the younger Derrida, all of whom he invoked in his essays and seminars, Lacan always had a fascination for the dead, ghosts, and tombs. These afterlife, transitory, and often mythologized states and symbols usually came in handy as the objects of his allusions and illustrations.[4] They would become the leitmotif of his lecture on "The Subversion of the Subject and the Dialectic of Desire in the Freudian Unconscious," which he presented to the conference on The Dialectic at Royaumont, September 19–30, 1960. Says Lacan, "No doubt the corpse is a signifier, but Moses's tomb is as empty for Freud as that of Christ was for Hegel. Abraham revealed his mystery to neither of them"

4. Some photographs of Lacan in various books show masks, possibly African and Asian, hanging on his office walls. Roudinesco observes that "Lacan was a great collector of master paintings. Picasso, Masson, Balthus, Zao-Wou-ki were his favorites. He also collected books and primitive art" (1997, 139).

(1977, 316).[5] If the audience strains too long on the rhetorical flair of the signifying corpse and the disemboweled tombs of Moses and Christ, it misses the *point de capiton* of the analyst's location of the dead father in the Freudian myth. In the "Function and Field of Speech" lecture, Lacan speaks of the censorships of the unconscious and the recovery of truth from the storage of monuments as "the hysterical nucleus of the neurosis" that is "deciphered like an inscription," archival documents as "childhood memories" that defy penetration without knowledge of their provenance, and traditions and legends as "heroicized" bearers of history (1997b,Ethics 50). This burden of history and writing is even more categorically stated in his 1957 declaration that the symptom is "already inscribed in the process of writing" (Grigg 1999, 69).

In the 1959 seminar on *The Ethics of Psychoanalysis*, Freud's *Totem and Taboo* and *Moses and Monotheism* would aid Lacan's discourse on the taboo of the "Symptom-God" or "Totem-God" and the myth that is the vehicle of the God of truth.

> It is by means of the [myth] that truth about God could come to light, namely, that God was really killed by men, and that once the thing was reenacted, the primitive murder was redeemed. Truth found its way via him who the Scriptures no doubt call the Word, but also the Son of Man, thereby admitting the human nature of the Father. (1997b, 181)

For Lacan, as for Freud, the killing of the father of the horde (in *Totem and Taboo*) and the eminent personality of Moses the Egyptian (in *Moses and Monotheism*) would aid a recognition of the function of the father in human experience as an essential sublimation toward the apprehension of reality. "The sole function of the father is to be a myth," Lacan says in the 1960 seminar on "The Moral Goals of Psychoanalysis," "to be always only the Name-of-the-Father, or in other words nothing more than the

5. During their meeting in New York in 1975, the artist Salvador Dali had sought to show Lacan the proper way to make Lacan's famous "Borromean knots." "I learned all about it in Italy," Dali said to Lacan. "If you go to Charles Borromeo's tomb you'll see what I mean" (Roudinesco 1997 377).

dead father" (1997b, 309). Here then is the basis for Marcelle Marini's assertion that Lacan replaced the Freudian genetic system with his own structuralist system in 1953 (1992, 43). Lacan's framework of the symbolic, the imaginary, and the real father (later revised to real, symbolic, imaginary) would henceforth privilege "the three registers of human reality" over the Freudian birth-to-adulthood development of the individual with its reliance on biology, neurology, and physics.

But for the Lacanese obliquity that occludes the source or allusions of his presentation, it is not surprising that Lacan uses the occasion of his discourse on "The Highway and the Signifier 'Being a Father'" to draw a comparison between the Parisian highway and the elephant track of an equatorial forest.[6] In the context of the colonial period of Lacan's 1955–56 seminars on *The Psychoses*, "equatorial" was an amorphous term that identified the geopolitical space including tropical and sub-Saharan Africa on the equator. Solange Faladé, Lacan's disciple, was from the Benin Republic.[7] Abdoulaye Yerodia, Lacan's personal driver and the husband of

6. In his essay, "Construing Lacan," Jean-Michel Rabaté argues that Lacan's language is difficult by choice, as evident in the psychoanalyst's use of "constant and deliberate paradox" and "post-Joycean tongue-twisters" (2000, xvii–xix). The portrayal of popular remarks, notes Rabaté, is that "Lacan is perversely obscure, impenetrable, all the more so with an English-speaking audience facing translation problems and increased cultural distance" (xvii). In his lecture on "The Agency of the Letter," Lacan stresses the kind of convoluted ambiguity that inhabits his idea of writing: "Writing is distinguished by a prevalence of the text in the sense that this factor of discourse will assume in this essay a factor that makes possible the kind of tightening up that I like in order to leave the reader no other way out than the way in, which I prefer to be difficult. In that sense, then, this will not be writing" (1977, 146). Schneiderman's account of Lacan's defense of his "impenetrable prose style" suggests a Christ-against-the-Philistines form of politico-linguistic subterfuge. "If they knew what I was saying," Lacan had said during a seminar, "they would never have let me say it" (Schneiderman 1983, 11). This would, of course, recall the reported Freudian quip about a psychoanalytic plague invasion of America.

7. The Beninois Solange Adelola Faladé (1925–2004) was the first black woman to study under Lacan, having entered into analysis with the master in 1952. Brigitte Nölleke reports that the subject of Faladé's medical thesis was on "the psychomotor development of African children from Senegal." Faladé's writing includes studies on the sociocultural experiences of women in Dakar and Senegal, as seen in her essay "Women of Dakar." The

Lacan's personal secretary and will executor, Gloria Gonzalez, was from the Congo. Benin and Congo were former Francophone colonial states and both are representative of Lacan's "equatorial forest." Lacan posits that whereas humans stop along the Parisian highway, thereby forming agglomerations that lead to impassable viscosity, elephants do not languish on their pathways, tracks that invariably lead to some mythical cemeteries or "bone depots" (1997a, 291). The highway polarizes meaning since it is a site of contestations, of departures and returns (qua *fort da*), houses and dwellings, interpersonal contracts, vast communications, diffusion of statues, and modes of written transmissions. The highway marks a stage in the history of human experience because it is the "undeniable signifier" that gives a full sense to paternity and death, to procreation, and to sexual relations with a woman. Lacan's reading of the Parisian highway and the equatorial pathway is metonymic of the postcolonial superhighway that redefines global channels of communication and the traditional relationship between the signifier and the signified.

Lacan's early discourse on reading is owed directly to his travels on the mountain chain of northern Africa where he encountered a curious "case of someone pretending to read." The bird's-eye precision and narrative detail of the passage both acquitted the experienced clinical analyst who had seen through the restless whims of psychoneurotic conditions and also paid tribute to the professional listener whose keen imaginative leaps pointed to the hours and years spent under the oracular gaze of Edgar Allan Poe and James Joyce:

> Long ago, when I was traveling in countries that had just gained their independence, I saw a gentleman, the attendant to a lord of the Atlas, take a small document that was intended for him, and I noticed immediately that he didn't understand one word of it, for he was holding it

---

Egyptian Moustapha Safouan, Lacan's first African male "analysand," began analysis with Lacan in 1945 and remained in his supervision for fifteen years. To demonstrate the friendship between master and student, Lacan recommended Safouan to the "Jews of Strasbourg" and suggested him as an analyst to his son-in-law Jacques-Alain Miller over Charles Melman, though Miller decided to go with Melman (Miller 2002, 38).

> upside down. But, with great seriousness, he uttered something—a story about not losing face before the respectful circle. (1997a, 207)

Coming in the middle of his seminars on *The Psychoses* the theme was signifying since it marks the opening of his presentation on "Secretaries to the Insane," during which he advanced his thesis on the three functions of the father. When the said North African government official held his travel document "upside down," Lacan was intrigued that the man's inability to read had not vitiated his judgment—that Lacan's "credentials were sound." To Lacan, therefore, the man was reading the essential part since one supposedly reads what one already knows by heart. From his point of view, a discourse is fundamentally directed by a mechanism that orientates every participant to keep within a specified limit. "It seems that the ultimate point of the discourse is to give a sign to its readers and to prove that the signatory is . . . a non-nobody, that he is capable of writing what everybody else writes" (Lacan 1997a, 207–8). In a sense, reading—as much as writing—is a group act, organized by structures laid out by a visible or invisible collegial standard and assessment committee. Each reader or each writer comes to the act with established expectations and protocols.

Six years before Lacan's seminar, George Orwell had launched a theory of reading in the ninth chapter of his widely controversial novel *1984* (1949), in which he claims that part of the attraction of a good book is that it reassures since it tells nothing that is new. "The best books . . . are those that tell you what you know already." By its global reception Lacan could have been aware of Orwell's novel, though it is not clear that he knew of his shared vision of reading with Orwell. In reference to the same novel, the psychoanalytic historian Paul Roazen uses his essay "What Is Wrong with French Psychoanalysis?" to draw a critical analogy between Orwell's *1984* and Lacan's postulation on writing history in his first seminar: "When Lacan refers to 're-writing history' (p. 14), one has to be careful that Orwell's *1984,* in which truth-holes suck up the past, does not get fulfilled" (2000, 47). Paul Wendkos acquiesces with the Orwellian-Lacanian view of reading in his television drama *Blood Vows: The Story of a Mafia Wife* (1987), when mafia boss Frank's blindsided wife exasperatingly avers,

"I read in a book once that people see what they want to see." In *Culture and Imperialism*, however, Edward Said suggests that the vision of Lacan, Orwell, and Wendkos is part of a cultural flux that has been sweeping through the world since the beginning of the Western imperial project: "Texts create not only their own precedence, as Borges said of Kafka, but their successors. The great imperial experience of the past two hundred years is global and universal; it has implicated every corner of the globe, the colonizer and the colonized together" (Said 1994, 259). In effect, the praxis of reading and writing is beyond the transference of interpersonal, intergroup, or interracial activity, but is part of a vast globalizing culture of human experience.

By his 1959–60 seminars on *The Ethics of Psychoanalysis*, Lacan's thesis on reading and writing has developed into a theory of the book that begins his discourse on desire and the second death in "The Demand for Happiness and the Promise of Analysis." The apocalyptic image of eating the book becomes for Lacan a metonym for the consumerist's incorporation of the signifier, representing God as "the object of the incorporation itself" (1997b, 294). But Lacan is simply rereading the biblical Book of John that places the Word at the beginning where the book becomes flesh through sublimation, as he shows in the discourse on "The Paradoxes of Ethics."

> The hunger in question, sublimated hunger, falls in the space between the two, because it isn't the book that fills our stomach. When I ate the book, I didn't thereby become book anymore than the book became flesh. The book became *me* so to speak. But in order for this operation to take place . . . I definitely have to pay a price. Freud weighs this difference in a corner of *Civilization and Its Discontents*. Sublimate as much as you like; you have to pay for it with something. And this something is called *jouissance*. I have to pay for that mystical operation with a pound of flesh. (1997b, 322)

The eaten book, however, neither displaces nor substitutes the hunger and, therefore, comes at the cost of *jouissance* (see below). Unfortunately, *jouissance* is the object or good that one pays for the satisfaction of desire. Those who have "eaten the book" are those who wrote with their labors and their blood (325). The question ultimately is what happens to one after one has eaten the book.

The foregoing leads back, on the one hand, to the continuing need for a reconsideration of Africa's experiences of slavery and colonialism, apartheid and civil wars, genocides and HIV/AIDS epidemic, hunger and kwashiorkor, migration and perennial political instability, as seen in the twenty-first-century Arab Spring that engulfed all of North Africa and parts of the Middle East. On the other hand, it harps on the question of the status of the writer and the problematic of literary representation. Africa is obviously important to Lacan's analytic especially as it relates to the phenomenology of writing, history, and what the analyst describes as the "complex of cultural encirclement."

As in the instance of Morocco, the subject of documentary tradition and the signifying highway was another occasion for invoking his Egyptian visitation. In the Roman lecture of 1953, "The Function and Field of Speech," Lacan compares Freud (especially in *The Interpretation of Dreams*) with the French Jean-Francois Champollion, who reputedly deciphered the Egyptian hieroglyphics. Freud, according to Lacan, deciphered the "primary language" of dreams as the subject's language of desire, "in which, beyond what he tells us of himself, he is already talking to us unknown to himself" (1977, 81). In other words, the primary language is that which the subject negates or elides in his discourse with the analyst, but which is always already present—in spite of the subject—in the slips, ellipses, and hide-and-seek games of the unconscious. The primary language, therefore, represents the symbols of the subject's symptom that the analyst decodes in analysis. Lacan draws a pointed comparison between dreams and hieroglyphics in the 1954 seminar on "The Creative Function of Speech." As a transmission of desire the subject's speech can be recognized in any organized symbolic system, the absence of which marked—at least before Freud—the "undecipherable character of dreams."

> It is for the same reason that for a long time no one knew how to understand hieroglyphics—they were not set up in their own symbolic system, all anyone could see was a little human silhouette, which might mean *a man*, but might also represent the sound man, and, as such, might be a

> part of a word by virtue of its being a syllable. The dream is constructed like hieroglyphics. (1991a, 244–45)

The "dream is constructed like hieroglyphics," says Lacan, who in another context also posits that the "unconscious is structured like a language." In effect, since the dream is an immanence of the unconscious, and the subject's speech is a repressed desire, it does not allow for a direct translation. It is in this connection that, in his May 14–26, 1957 lecture on "The Agency of the Letter," Lacan equates what he calls the "alphabet," "phonematics," or "day-residue," to such signifiers as the "dream-image," "rebus," "proverb," "figuration," "ideogram," "cryptogram," and "pictograph" (1977, 159–61). These are all elaborate abstract-to-concrete forms that would equally characterize the Egyptian hieroglyphics, or even the cultic sign writing of the Igbo *Nsibidi*. When Lacan returns to the discourse again in his November 20, 1963 lecture on "Introduction to the Names-of-the-Father," he underscores the fact that the dream is to the subject what the hieroglyphics are to the people, an inscription of history and a testimony of the unconscious. He references "a few hieroglyphics bearing witness to the customs of the Egyptian people" (Lacan 1990, 94).

Lacan goes further to confront the provocative subject of racism and imperial exploitation of Africa. In a letter to the analyst D. W. Winnicott on August 5, 1960, Lacan was vehement in his support of his stepdaughter Laurence Bataille and his nephew-in-law Diego Masson, both of whom were arrested in 1958 and subsequently jailed for their "resistance to the Algerian war" (1990, 77).[8] Laurence Bataille had earlier toured Algeria with a theater company in 1954 and had subsequently joined the French Communist Party. In 1958 Bataille and Diego Masson became fund-raisers for the Algerian Freedom Fighters. Bataille also enlisted her half sister, Judith Lacan (later Judith Miller), in the anticolonial movement. It is noteworthy that Algeria was also the birth country of three of Lacan's acquaintances and seminar attendees, namely, the 1957 Nobel literature

8. The analyst Laurence Bataille was the daughter of Sylvia and her ex-husband Georges Bataille. Diego Masson was the son of the painter and Lacan's friend André Masson.

laureate Albert Camus, the feminist scholar Helen Cixous, and the deconstructionist philosopher Jacques Derrida.[9] Lacan brought the typescript of the seminar on *The Ethics of Psychoanalysis* to read to Laurence Bataille during her six-month incarceration at the Prison de la Roquette in 1960.

Lacan's 1973 television interview with Jacques-Alain Miller gives him the opportunity to tackle an aspect of the Algerian crisis, his prophecy on the rise of racism in Europe and Africa. In the 1959–60 seminars and the 1973 interview, Lacan speaks out against European stigmatization of Africa as "underdeveloped." In the seminar he derides the salvation "fantasm," which drives Christian missions and their denegation of desire in man through the centuries. "Those gods who are dead in Christian hearts are pursued throughout the world by Christian missionaries" (Lacan 1977, 262). In the interview he lashes out against the "fantasies" that drive "the empty forms of humanhysterianism [*humanitairerie*] disguising our extortions" (Lacan 1990, 32–33). He insists that the "precariousness" of the European mode of *jouissance* should not be imposed on the *jouissance* of the other. All this would give credence to the exceptional tribute of Roudinesco in her praise of Lacan as "the great theorist of persecution" (Lacan 1997, 320).

A highpoint of the seminars is Lacan's introduction of the schema of *jouissance* into psychoanalytic praxis. But for the work of the Haitian Willy Apollon, it is surprising that the basic principle of *jouissance* in racial dialectic is elided in much of black analytics. Jacques-Alain Miller translates *jouissance* variously as "enjoyment" (*joie*), "bliss," "pleasure," or "orgasm," and notes that Lacan counterposes the term with "joy" (Lacan 1991a,

9. In his interview "Unsealing ('the Old New Language')," Derrida spoke of the anti-Semitic attacks against the Algerian Jews that drove him from El Bair to France at the age of nineteen. "Then, in 1940, the singular experience of the Algerian Jews. The persecutions, which were unlike anything in Europe . . . Jewish children expulsed from school . . . Friends who no longer knew you, insults, the Jewish high school with its expulsed teachers and never a whisper of protest from their colleagues. I was enrolled there but I cut school for a year . . ." (1995, 120–21). Roudinesco describes the discipleship of the French Jewish Serge Leclaire, the black Beninois Solange Falade, and the Arab Egyptian Moustapha Safouan as the universalist signifier of Lacanianism (1990, 418).

204–5). In Lacan's postulation, *jouissance* is at the core of the ego of frustration and the alienation of desire. It negates narcissistic embrace since the image in the mirror—by which the subject makes an object of himself or herself—is the image of misapprehension, and therefore of contempt. It is the schema of *jouissance* that enables Lacan to arrive at the *meconnaissance* of the notorious discontent and "aggressivity of the slave whose response to the frustration of his labor is a desire for death" (Lacan 1977, 42). Lacan echoes Gide in this perspective of desire and dissatisfaction, hope and humiliation.

The symbolic nature of the law establishes the relation between *jouissance* (pleasure) and work (labor). This in turn imposes on the slave—dual embodiment of subject and object (chattel)—to satisfy the desire and *jouissance* of the other (signifier/master). The imaginary of human action betrays a "fatal intersubjectivity" dialectic, the automaton of master-slave Hegelian myth, which "implicitly implicates a rule of the game" (Lacan 1991a, 223–24). In this light Apollon avers that the political discourse that legitimates the monopoly of violence always already deals with the "basic truths that confront the subject to its difference," identity, *jouissance*, and death (1996, 34). The recurrent harsh lights of slavery, colonialism, and genocide denote *jouissance* as a place of anguish and defect in the "purity of Non-Being." As Lacan notes, the Oedipal castration complex means that "*jouissance* must be refused, so that it can be reached on the inverted ladder . . . of the Law of desire" (Lacan 1977, 317, 324).

Apollon's work is a good example of the time-honored interventions of black and Africanist scholars to the advent of Jacques Lacan and psychoanalytic theory in the discourse of the continent and its diaspora.[10] This phenomenon now calls for immediate exploration.

10. Two of the major book-length literary interventions on Lacanian analytics in Africa are the South African Teresa Dovey's *The Novels of J. M Coetzee* and the Nigerian American Obiwu Iwuanyanwu's *In the Name of the Father.*

5

(Re)Defining the Self through Trauma in West African Postcolonial Short Fiction

BOJANA COULIBALY

The argument developed by Tanure Ojaide and Joseph Obi among many other critics of African literature who collectively insist on the interrelation between African texts and the African context is no longer contested. Ojaide and Obi argue indeed that African writers evolve in a "historical vortex to which they respond" (2002, viii). Our purpose in this study is to show how West African postcolonial and Anglophone short fiction carries signs of traumatic daily experiences in relation to the individual and collective urge for a creation of a new cultural and national identity in a changing world. Through these narratives, West African short story writers offer healing strategies to trauma faced by the characters, strategies that help the represented individuals regain their sense of agency often lost under and after the occurrence of the traumatic event. We will illustrate this study with texts by major Nigerian authors including Chinua Achebe and Flora Nwapa as well as two prominent contemporary authors, Chris Abani and Chimamanda Ngozi Adichie. We will also include short fiction by the famous Ghanaian writer Ama Ata Aidoo.

Throughout the second half of the twentieth century, a great number of African short narratives emerged as an expression of traumatic events that allow protagonists—through means of resistance and counterdiscourse—to build new negotiated identities. Stylistic particularities emphasize traces of trauma in texts that represent a daily context of decolonization, war, nation building, expatriation, and globalization. On the one hand, postindependence experiences of the dehumanization of war, family dismemberment, and the incongruities of nation building and political activism are extensively portrayed, as well as the conflict between European values brought by colonization and traditional customs. On the other hand, in a period that could be considered as *post* postcolonial and dwelling at the threshold of the twenty-first century, traumatized individuals face new challenges in relation to questions of identity formation, cultural clashes, and alterity. In both of these contexts, the self emerges within a new set of norms that are experienced as traumatic, and it is through personal resistance strategies that these characters adapt and re-create a sense of agency. As Judith Butler explains, "when the 'I' seeks to give an account of itself, an account that must include the conditions of its emergence, it must, as a matter of necessity, become a social theorist" (2005, 8). It is indeed remarkable that the characters represented in these texts come to occupy the function of commentators of their social and traumatizing conditions that further illustrate the conditions of their global society. As it has been widely understood, storytelling helps us make sense of our existence and our identity.[1] It allows victims of trauma to build narrative strategies of healing. As expressed by Van der Merwe and Gobodo-Madikizela and referencing the notion of Aristotle's "catharsis," the narrative through which trauma is reenacted heals the writer as much as the reader and therefore the whole of society from the traumatic pain (2007, ix). Similarly, Gay Wilentz (2000) bases her reflection on "alternative healing," which to her is the capacity of members of suffering and oppressed communities to cure cultural "dis-ease" and reclaim through novel writing their sense of cultural dignity. She exemplifies her study with texts by women novelists from different ethnic and cultural backgrounds and shows how protagonists move from a state of mental or

1. The notion known as "narrative identity" is understood, for instance, in Descartes's "I think, therefore I am," or Walter Fisher's "homo narrans," also identified by Niles in *Homo Narrans* (2010). Freud's "talking cure," developed in his theory of psychoanalysis, and which identifies narrative as a healing process, specifically relates to the issue of trauma. In a similar way, Gay Wilentz in *Healing Narratives* refers to the "curative power of the word" (2000, 6).

physical disease toward wellness through a reconnection with their cultural traditions and the healing practices of their culture. Hence, the narrative as it is widely understood takes a prescriptive role, which teaches members of society to deal with traumatic experiences of colonization, war, and sociopolitical and economic tyranny. In the same way, West African postcolonial short fiction offers modes of resistance to trauma that guide readers to a better understanding of their traumatic situation and helps them heal through the trauma.

The short story form has been and is still widely produced by well-known and less famous African writers. It is a genre that was commonly defined as a line of continuity between oral transmission of narratives and the written form.[2] Short fiction has also been described as mainly depicting slices of everyday life.[3] Michel de Certeau, in his well-known book *The Practice of Everyday Life* (1988),[4] explains that through everyday creative practices individuals reestablish a space of agency previously denied to them. Throughout the societies depicted in West African short narratives we discover that these quotidian creative experiences allow the protagonists to reemerge as active subjects either individually or as part of a collective endeavor. For instance, the everyday political activism during the Biafra War is evident in the short stories by Achebe and Nwapa. And in the recent Abani novella *Song for Night* (2009), the everyday traumatic life of a boy soldier in the process of daily survival is narrated. Similarly, the collective nation-building efforts taking place in a context of political and cultural decolonization are broadly described in the short fiction by the first generation of writers enumerated above. Frank O'Connor

2. The link between the short story genre and orature is emphasized by Andres in *La nouvelle* (1998, 89); Godenne in *La nouvelle* (1995, 143); and Eileen in "Of Traditional Tales" (1983, 147). Eileen argues that the narrative structure and the characterization of the short story are similar to the ones in the traditional tale. See Azodo's "(Re)defining Africa's Limits" (1999, 297). Azodo stresses the intrinsic link between the short-story genre and the African traditional tale as compared with the novel.

3. See Obiechina's preface to *African Creations* (1985, vii–viii); Chukwuma's "Two Decades of the Short Story" (1989, 2); and Shaw's *The Short Story: A Critical Introduction* (1983, 47).

4. Originally published as *L'invention du quotidien: Arts de faire* (1980).

suggests that the short story genre portrays the ordinary man and woman in their everyday quest for existence. "The short story has never had a hero," O'Connor explains, "what it has instead is a submerged population group" (1962, 18). He also argues that the main feature of the short story is "an intense awareness of human loneliness" (11). Chris Abani's short fiction, for instance, is pervaded by a general atmosphere of loneliness in which individuals face daily dilemmas of survival. Furthermore, as Helen Chukwuma identifies in her article "Two Decades of the Short Story in West Africa," West African short stories present individuals whose daily experiences reflect a broader cultural and socially collective phenomena:

> The short story by its very form reflects the sense of urgency shown by its writers to record an event, a feeling, a phenomenon, a slice of life. Thus the themes of the West African Short Story present this aspect of the individualism of the writers while at the same time reflecting their socio-cultural background. (1989, 2)

Literature of a Collective Cultural Restoration

Facing an environment of political collective consciousness, African authors—after the restoration of independence—aimed at reestablishing a new space of cultural action. African writers sought to create a literature away from the established belief that African culture was a product of European invention.[5] They regenerated a collective purpose to produce fiction based on an inside narrative of the African experience. Flora Nwapa, for instance, founded her own publishing company, Tana Press Limited, in 1977 with the aim of distributing literary texts produced by African writers. Other African writers have followed the trend, including Ayi Kwei Armah with the creation of Per Ankh Publishing based in Popenguine, Senegal, and Boubacar Boris Diop and Felwine Sarr with Jimsaan in Saint Louis, Senegal. Echoing Fanonist principles of decolonization,[6] this collective intention for a cultural restoration was emphasized by many African authors including Achebe, Chinweizu, Ihechukwu Madubuike,

5. See Appiah's *In My Father's House* (1992).

6. See Fanon's *The Wretched of the Earth* (1967).

and Kwame Anthony Appiah, among many others.[7] They further insisted on the major importance of restoring self-esteem after centuries of cultural denigration during the colonial period, as well as to decolonize African literature more specifically by re-creating a collective belief that, as Appiah expressed it, "the literature of one's own is that of one's own nation" (1992, 56). Or as Chimamanda Ngozi Adichie exclaimed in her speech "The Danger of a Single Story" (2009): "Stories have been used to dispossess and to malign, but stories can also be used to empower and to humanize." In "The African Writer and the Biafran Cause," Chinua Achebe writes about the necessity of the Biafran writer to be involved in the Nigerian political cause; he writes that "the involvement of the Biafran writer today in the cause for which his people are fighting and dying is not different from the involvement of many African writers—past and present—in the big issues of Africa" (1975, 78).

Achebe's "Girls at War," excerpted from *Girls at War and Other Stories*, shows the author's involvement in the Biafran cause. In this short narrative he describes aspects of daily life during the Biafra War. The story unveils a common characteristic of the Nigerian societal evolution during and after the civil war in Biafra, summed up in this sentence: "this particular girl . . . who had once had such beautiful faith in the struggle . . . was betrayed (no doubt about that) by some man like him out for a good time" (Achebe 1972, 108). We learn how Gladys, who at first typified the revolutionary spirit of activist young women during the Biafran struggle, later became the girlfriend of a "big man," one of the powerful and wealthy men employed as government agents or businessmen and generally considered as corrupted, presented by Nwankwo the protagonist as "some well-placed gentleman, one of those piling up money out of the war" (106). A snapshot of daily life during the war is sustained by a lexical field of political activism and nation formation, as the following terms demonstrate: "nation," "war" (101); "revolution," "the militia,"

7. See Achebe's "The Novelist as Teacher" in *Morning Yet on Creation Day* (1982); Chinweizu, Jemie, and Madubuike, *Toward the Decolonization of African Literature* (1985); and Appiah, *In My Father's House* (1992).

"Civil Defence" (103); "Ministry of Justice," "marching," "demonstrating" (102); "militia girl" (106); "a beautiful faith in the struggle" (108); "the government," "society," "a whole generation," "the mothers of tomorrow" (116). The first paragraph of this story calls attention to the daily political revolutionary involvement of men and women who took part in a collective fight for the formation of the Nigerian national identity: "that was in the first heady days of warlike preparation when thousands of young men (and sometimes women too) were daily turned away from enlistment centres because far too many of them were coming forward burning with readiness to bear arms in defence of the exciting new nation" (101).

The protagonist's reactionary interjection—"what a terrible fate to befall a whole generation. The mothers of tomorrow!" (116)—suggests that in the context described in this short narrative a great number of young men and women were initially revolutionary in thought and action but their struggle for a national identity in a newly independent nation transformed itself into a desire for personal material success. In the form of an interior monologue, which sets the reader in the position of the protagonist's partial observation, Nwankwo projects a reflection on the common phenomenon of political disengagement: "Gladys, he thought, was just a mirror reflecting a society that had gone completely rotten and maggoty at the centre" (116). He then initiates as a consequence of his observation a "saving operation" so as to bring Gladys back to her initial personality and take away from her, as he declares, the "terrible influence" (116). Gladys dies as a result of an explosion when she decides to go and help a wounded soldier who was trapped in a car that was being bombed. Her real personality is therefore revealed through her act of being prepared to sacrifice her own life in order to save another. Ironically, Nwankwo himself decides not to go and help the wounded soldier, which further unveils the inconsistency between his words and actions.

As suggested above, African short fiction reveals the existence of a new role for the African writer highlighting the importance of political, social, and cultural development. Focusing on the new political role occupied by African authors in a context of political and cultural decolonization, Flora Nwapa in her short fiction engages issues of political reaffirmation, activism, and economic and social development in the aftermath of Nigerian independence. She specifically focuses on women's collective activism and solidarity. Her civil-war stories mostly reflect the absurdity and irony of war, as illustrated in "Wives at War," excerpted from her second collection of stories *Wives at War and Other Stories* (1980). The narrative deals with Ebo, an employee of the Department of Military Intelligence during the war in Biafra. Ebo is willing to be politically involved, which is revealed in this sentence: "Ebo then traveled to Enugu to see what job he could do to help 'win the war' for Biafra." (Nwapa 1992, 1), but his actions progressively seem to unveil his lack of integrity. He indeed uses his position as an army officer for personal means and shows no compassion for a childhood friend who needs to be helped to survive. Ebo's inconsistent personality is unveiled through several devices. For instance, he was first an employee of the Ministry of Information at the department of "propaganda" (1). This first ironic element is expressed in the form of an antithesis, which appears as a political denunciation of the potential proliferation of misleading information during war (to which Ebo seems to participate). The term "information" in a political context generally implies a transmission of data that aims at being impartial concerning a particular situation. However, "information" in this narrative is closely followed by the term "propaganda," which on the contrary refers to an intention to influence people's opinions. This ironical device shows us that in a context of war information *is* propaganda, for it is designed to support the power structure.

Furthermore, in this short story Ebo's wife Bisi appears at first as a voice of reason, reminding her husband of the importance of being supportive with his friends in times of war. However, her own demands lack consistency, for she believes that her own survival should be protected "at all costs" (Nwapa 1992, 7). Ebo therefore decides that Bisi, his wife, "must be flown to Lisbon by any means" (8) to flee the war. Their departure by plane will be understood by the leaders of Biafran women's political organizations as a secret departure of representatives sent to discuss possible war relief with the Queen of England. The leaders will therefore protest against the fact that they have not been informed about the important discussion with the Queen involving, according to them, the nation's future. The short story, through devices of satire and irony, illustrates the existence of political organizations based on differences of opinion. But the positive actions of women are emphasized through their role in the civil war and national life with the use of anaphora that reveals a number of occurrences of the phrase "without the women . . . would . . .": "Without the women, the Nigerian vandals would have overrun Biafra; without the women, our gallant Biafran soldiers would have died of hunger in the war fronts. Without the women, the Biafran Red Cross would have collapsed" (13). However, as it seems to emerge in this short narrative, the use of anaphora as a rhetorical device in a context of war questions the truth of the statement uttered, for it seems to suggest that the women's declaration is a form of propaganda itself. The text also pinpoints clashes between leaders, which work against the collective political consciousness, creating many divergent groups who "were all bent on one objective—to make Biafra a great Nation" (11). The narrator's voice appears therefore as an outside critical speaker of the political contradictions found in the Nigerian civil war and nation-building contexts.

As previously hinted, experiences of cultural clashes in a daily postindependence context have been widely represented in African short fiction as a tool for cultural decolonization and a restoration of African identities. The portrayal of these experiences allows writers to highlight the presence of conflicting values, opposing on the one hand traditional cultures to the newly created urban way of life, and on the other hand African traditional and modern cultures are contrasted to the European colonial culture and more generally the European way of life. The questions of alterity, cultural self-definition, and identity negotiation have been raised through Ama Ata Aidoo's short fiction in a form of political discourse debating the cultural encounter between Europe and the African continent. "For Whom Things Did Not Change," excerpted from *No Sweetness Here and Other Stories* (1970), portrays elements of a sociocultural trauma that carries signs of painful memories of colonization and of a general cultural discomfort. The narrative deals with the need for a reaffirmation of Ghanaian culture as a means to distinguish itself from the European colonial influence. Colonization is presented as having initiated many changes in the collective behavior and traditional values and manners having been replaced by a new urban modern conduct highly shaped by European colonial standards. In the form of a dialogue the text is presented as a discussion about the evolution of Ghanaian society. The alteration from traditional to urban is announced in Setu's exclamation ("What times we live in!"), to which her husband Zirugu rhetorically responds: "Was it different in the old days, Setu my wife?" (Aidoo 1995, 10). Zirugu, a cook at a government rest house, discusses the evolution of values between the colonial and postindependence period with Setu, who further concedes that "times do change" (19). Kobina, a guest who is a young medical doctor, engages in a discussion with Zirugu through a second dialogue about the same clashes of values taking place ten years after independence.

The insistence on the change in times and behavior is expressed in the following sentence, highlighting the evolution between the past and the present, the native and the Western, the precolonial and the postcolonial, with the reiteration of temporal adverbs: "The big men we saw *yesterday* were bad. These we see *today* are worse. And be sure that those of *tomorrow* will be like those of *yesterday* and *today* put together" (Aidoo 1995, 12; emphases added). Kobina openly criticizes the newly born postindependent society, which has lost its original values. He complains about Zirugu, who offers him European dishes ("but that is not the food I eat"), to which Zirugu replies: "But 'e be white man chop." Kobina points out: "Zirugu, I no be white man" (16). Kobina insists on wanting to eat the "food of the land . . . the food of this land" (16). Zirugu is convinced that the new generation adopted the white men's values. Furthermore, language switches used as a stylistic device throughout the short narrative allow a reflection about language as a product of the same colonial encounter. In the dialogues, we notice the use of several different languages. Setu and Zirugu speak a Ghanaian language when addressing each other, while Zirugu speaks pidgin English when speaking to Kobina, who speaks standard English. We understand that Zirugu speaks pidgin English because it is directly transcribed in the dialogue. We also understand that Zirugu and Setu do not speak English: their dialogue is transcribed in standard English that appears to be a translation of their native language. The story told by Zirugu to Kobina is also transcribed in standard English because it is told from Kobina's point of view. We therefore come to understand that Kobina instantly translates in his mind Zirugu's story from pidgin English into standard English.

The multiple focalizations expressed through the use of language switches appear as a striking device to lead the reader to reflect on the clashes of values, cultural perceptions, and language use within the context of the encounter between colonial empires and African peoples. The question of language has been at the basis of the debate on African literature.[8] Other characteristics of the traumatic colonial encounter are denounced in the text, such as the master/slave dialectic as shown in Setu's brother's statement: "It all means that some fool who is big only because he is white or because he can read book will make me a dog . . ." (25). Zirugu concludes that his fellow men act toward him as the white men who colonized his country acted ten years before; he notes: "My own people who are big men do not think I should use these good things they use" (28). His final statement is left as an existential question hanging in the air and causing the reader once again to ponder over the collective human condition in a postcolonial context: "What does independence mean?" (29). Kobina's great esteem for Zirugu, his wife and their traditional way of life, brings hope and allows the reader to understand the kind of social and cultural behavior that would heal the society from the trauma of colonization.

Traumatic experiences of cultural clashes and expatriation pervade the lives of protagonists represented in West African short fiction. Through an attempt at cultural self-definition, characters face clashes between their native habits and a new hybrid space of daily activity, for as Kwame Anthony Appiah explains: "even those children who were extracted from the traditional culture of their parents and grandparents and thrust into the colonial school were nevertheless fully enmeshed in a primary experience of their own traditions" (1992, 7). Similarly, the contemporary societal phenomena of diaspora and expatriation projects individuals who are

8. See essays debating questions of language in African literature: Achebe in "The African Writer and the English Language" in *Morning Yet on Creation Day* (1982); Thiong'o in *Decolonizing the Mind* (1986).

impregnated by their original culture and who at the same time experience dilemmas of identity formation in a changing world.

The Exile as a Global Subject

The new generation of protagonists as represented in contemporary African short fiction illustrates a diasporic self still highly characterized by traditional experience and homeland culture. Characters, as depicted while traveling to major British and North American cities, deal with cultural encounters in a context in which experience of alterity seems to prevail. The new represented self becomes a global subject wandering between the homeland and the newly adopted country. In the context of an era of world economy, Kwame A. Appiah pinpoints the existence of a new feature of the African society widely dealt with in contemporary African short fiction. Appiah writes in *In My Father's House*:

> This novel self is more individualistic and atomic than the self of pre-capitalist societies; it is a creature of modern economic relations. I do not know that this new conception of the self was inevitable, but it is no longer something that we in Africa could escape even if we wanted to. And if we cannot escape it—let us celebrate it. (1992, 84)

National boundaries have disappeared and are being replaced by a global migrating engine of individuals who become world citizens. African literature was previously more about *us* than about *I*. The opposite phenomenon is taking place today. The individual experience prevails over collective experience. Characters, evolving no longer within a national sphere in which nation building and cultural decolonization take place, do on the contrary develop within a global geopolitical atmosphere in which diasporic experience is at stake. African contemporary short stories seek to represent new conflicts of values and the creation of new hybrid identities. Ama Ata Aidoo in her most recent collection of short fiction, *The Girl Who Can and Other Stories* (1997), shows characters that evolve and negotiate their new space of agency in the context of globalization. In "Comparisons," the narrator pinpoints elements of clashes between the African daily reality and the global media:

> I find him sitting in front of the TV watching CNN *Early Morning News* and trying to follow the stock market. On Wall Street, if you please. Sitting in Oguaa, Ghana, watching the New York Stock Exchange and commenting on the volatility or otherwise on NASDAQ. I mean, who has that kind of time in Africa and Ghana, before they go to work? (Aidoo 1997, 40).

Aku-Yaa, the narrator of "Nutty," also chooses to show her highly critical perception of globalization and cultural shock. In the context of an encounter with an American friend in the United States she describes American food habits in opposition to African food. She insists on the antagonistic values between two women from two parts of the world: she, a married teacher with two children; and her American friend, a married oil company worker who does not want kids, for she utters, "No kids please, not if I'll have to get pregnant first, and I shall never adopt. Can you imagine the hassle?" (Aidoo 1997, 48). They both "wonder at our changing world" (50). The opposition of values is further emphasized in the following utterances: "They are from different parts of the world? Different cultures? Silently judging one another?" (50). The narrator is also shocked by one of her friend's affirmations about an "exotic dish," for Aku-Yaa believes exotic means "strange, weird, dumb" (50). She questions the validity of neologisms and new practices coming from the West that perceive her traditional culture and food as "exotic," her traditional music as "world music" (53). Globalization according to her undermines many different cultures by considering them all as the same "exotic" culture, simply because they are different from the Western one. Her interior monologue reveals her painful thoughts about the situation: "thinking that in this global village where African music is only part of 'world music,' maybe African food becomes edible only when it is part of an exotic universal cuisine" (53). She therefore criticizes the new Western behavior that still relies on the basic relation of *us* and *them,* which further glorifies universalism, cultural essentialism, and stigmatism of customs from other parts of the world. She concludes with this agonizing statement left hanging in the air: "Such sad residents of the global village . . ." (54).

In "Some Global News," the use of satire and irony initiate discussion about the "global village" and NGOs (Aidoo 1997, 73). The narrator of the short story ponders over the value of terms such as "Third World" and states satirically: "So if Third World countries and First World countries are facing the same problems, then can we agree with those who think the world is now a global village?" (78). We are further reminded of the perpetual debate on language use in this global village in which distinctions and differences seem to persist: "in this global village, nothing is the same for everyone: and that includes language" (86).

Furthermore, in the context of self-restoration through quotidian acts, contemporary African short fiction presents characters depicted as lonely men and women. They face traumatic experiences of expatriation and cultural shock. Chimamanda Ngozi Adichie's "The Thing around Your Neck," excerpted from *The Thing around Your Neck and Other Stories* (2009), tells a common experience of a Nigerian young woman immigrating to the United States. In this short story the reader, who is directly addressed, deals with a very particular narrative voice, a second-person narrative, which suggests that the experience that the narrator faces could be faced by anyone. The young woman's narrative appears as an ordinary experience of an African woman coming to North America. Adichie in her particularly illustrative speech "The Danger of a Single Story" warns us about the potential misinterpretation of a culture when perceived from one single ethnocentric point of view. By way of a counterdiscourse to "the single story of Africa" this monologue, in an extensive use of irony, provides us with a possible narrative of the single story of the United States of America. In other words, Adichie illustrates the potential danger of assimilating American culture by referencing the possession of a big car, a big house, and a gun. For instance, in the following introductory sentence the repetition of "thought" may suggest an aggregation of partial ethnocentric perceptions: "You thought everybody in America had a car and a gun; your uncles and aunts and cousins thought so, too . . ." (Adichie 2009, 115). Given the extensive use of references in the text, Adichie seeks to caution us about cultural generalizations. As the narrative unfolds we quickly come to understand that there is no such thing as a single story of the United States of America. It is shown that each experience is unique in its own, however ordinary it might be. Life does not rely solely on owning a big house, a big car, and a gun; life is full of pressure, it is like a "thing around your neck that very nearly choke[s] you before you [fall] asleep" (119).

Indeed, like the protagonists in Aidoo's recent short fiction, Adichie's characters exemplify diasporic experience, global human and cultural exchange, and encounter between the African continent and the Western world. As Thomas L. Friedman argues in *The World Is Flat: A Brief History of the Twenty-first Century* (2005), the world has become flat in the sense that there is not one single pole of economic hegemony and cultural influence. This worldwide village has created a type of global hybrid culture, which is highly illustrated by contemporary African short fiction.

Trauma experienced in expatriation and exile in a process of identity self-restoration is particularly illustrated by Chris Abani in a recent short narrative, *Becoming Abigail* (2006). As the title of the novella suggests, Abigail—out of extremely traumatic mental and physical experiences—faces rebirth and the regeneration of her self. She is also an expatriate pushed out of her Nigerian homeland because her father, who is going to take his life away, believes he could not provide for her future. She is sent to London to stay with Peter, a relative highly regarded by the entire family, whose members believe he is a wealthy businessman. Contrary to this general belief, Peter earns his living as a procurer and he forces Abigail into prostitution when she is only fourteen. Because Abigail strongly resists being abused, Peter treats her like a dog, chaining her to a dog house, as described in her interior monologue: "Bent forward like a dog. Arms behind her back. Kneeling. Into the mud. And the food" (Abani 2006, 90). She is therefore, beside her previously experienced abuses, pushed into an animal condition.

Furthermore, as in Adichie's short story, we are dealing in this text with the issue of perceptions, cultural clashes, and alterity. One symbolic example referred to in the novella is the Needle sculpture on the Greenwich Meridian observed by Abigail (59). We understand that since throughout the world time is calculated on the Meridian Line's basis, this reference might emphasize the cultural centrality of Great Britain. In addition, Abigail's lover, Derek, a native of London, at times expresses himself on the basis of cultural prejudice. He believes, for instance, that Abigail comes from a "dark continent" (93), a concept that as we know was accompanied by far-reaching cultural misconceptions intensely criticized by Achebe in his essay on Conrad's *Heart of Darkness*.[9] From the outset and in an atmosphere of fatality, Abigail, dispossessed of her own human condition, seems as if she was never really born. For indeed in the eyes of her father—one of the "two men she loved" (Abani 2006, 34)—she remained until her expatriation the living reincarnation of Abigail, her mother who died when giving birth to her. This original experience of birth and childhood is going to be repressed by the protagonist because of its traumatic dimension. Expressed in the form of a fragmented syntactic and narrative interior monologue, Abigail allows the reader to face her daily experience of *becoming* a human being, and finally a woman. Trauma theory informs us that fragmentation—extensively present in the form and content of this short narrative—is caused by physical and mental trauma.[10] In the form of a written diary and putting pieces of a life story together, the protagonist who tells about her "desire to be noticed for herself" (45) allows this fragmented self to develop into a coherent identity, an experience referred to as "the burgeoning of a self, a self that was still Abigail" (26). By giving account of herself she recaptures her own being, for it is said that she was: "Wrapping herself each night in anecdotes about Abigail. Collected until she was suffused with all parts of her" (31). In this context, self-narration allows a self-reenactment.[11] Hence Abigail's narrative, which is told in a near-epistolary form and also through the markings that she engraves on her skin, becomes her major mode of catharsis. She indeed gives account of her trauma and re-creates a sense of agency through the narrative act. She further tells her story to Derek, who as a social worker and later as a lover allows her a total purgation of her traumatic experiences of abuse and exile.

As we have pointed out, West African postcolonial literature has been, in the aftermath of the restoration of independence, a literature of

9. See Achebe's "An Image of Africa" in *Hopes and Impediments* (1989).

10. See Horvitz's *Literary Trauma* (2000, 5); and Vickroy's *Trauma and Survival in Contemporary Fiction* (2002, 27).

11. See Vickroy, who writes that "storytelling is a personal and collective 'reconstructive' act" (2002, 34).

political and cultural collective counterdiscourses. Short fiction specifically described in this paper expresses—through the stylistic devices of irony, satire, rhetorical repetition, fragmented syntax and narrative, multiple focalizations, and language switch—the need for the restoration of a cultural identity through narratives of collective and individual trauma. We have suggested that signs of sociopolitical and cultural trauma are undoubtedly present throughout African postcolonial short fiction in its form and content. These traces of trauma allow the contemporary reader and citizen of the new global village to ponder questions of survival, political engagement, alterity, and the cultural encounter in a changing world. If we look at the current global situation of African literature, we must concede that cultural reaffirmation has taken place and African literature has found and reaffirmed its existence within a global atmosphere. African literary texts are indeed extensively published, valued, awarded, debated, and studied throughout the world. As Jean-Jacques Lecercle stipulates, postcolonial literature written in English is bound to the English literary canon because it mostly revises the British and American canon. There could be, according to him, no British literature of the nineteenth and the twentieth century without postcolonial literature, for it is through postcolonial literature that English literature continues to exist. Thus, with regard to the importance of African literature expressed throughout the world, we may presently consider the existence of African canons of literature in which trauma and the reestablishment of personal and collective agency are representative of a painful past, and which help readers, through prescriptive literary devices, reconsider the future of their transitioning societies.

6

African Postcolonial Imagination and the Moral Challenges of Our Times

CHIELOZONA EZE

In his acclaimed essay "How to Write about Africa: Instructions for Beginners," the Kenyan writer Binyavanga Wainaina satirized the Western media and its cultural representations of the image of Africa (Wainaina 2005). The essay plays into Africa's outrage at the West for not only the colonial encounter but also for the continued perpetuation of different forms of oppression and for the objectification of Africa. What is said of Wainaina's essay could also be said of Chimamanda Ngozi Adichie's 2009 TED talk "The Danger of a Single Story." It is laudable that these two authors, who are among the best known of the young and talented African writers, set out to confront the Western misrepresentation of the African image in their stories. These works by no means represent their entire writing, but they have come to define them and their worldviews: the authors are fiercely critical of the West, and Binyavanga Wainaina, at least, is very Afrocentric.

In their declared war on Western misrepresentation of the image of Africa in their discourses, Wainaina and Adichie bring to a full circle what Chinua Achebe began with *Things Fall Apart*. Simon Gikandi has argued that modern African culture was born at the moment *Things Fall Apart* was published. He defines modern African culture as that which is discoursed and "circulated within the institutions of interpretation" (Gikandi 2001, 4–8). In this understanding of African culture, literature adopts a preeminent role in the making of African subjects. Gikandi acknowledges the tremendous influence that Achebe's "works have had on the institutions of pedagogy and interpretation and the role his fictions have come to play in the making and unmaking of African worlds" (6). I identify Gikandi's short definition of modern African culture as the African postcolonial imagination. Gikandi and the other proponents of the idea of Achebe being the father of African culture do not ignore the influence of other works that preceded *Things Fall Apart* or the contributions of other writers of Achebe's generation.

It is true that modern African culture has been framed as a response to the colonial and imperial assault on Africa and is therefore born from the reaction to the gaze of the West. But it is also true that Africa's problems can no longer be simplistically reduced to the issues arising from the colonial encounter with the West. Although colonialism has had its own share of disrupting Africa's system, the truth is that most Africans can no longer realistically make the connections between their everyday experience of deprivation, injustice, and misery and the machinations of their erstwhile colonizing powers. It is important to explore how Africans produce or enhance the production of the images represented in the West even while they satirize and dismiss the Western misrepresentations of the African image. The serious challenge, therefore, is to confront African realities without losing sight of history. How can the African critical imagination be made to bear on African realities without the unproductive intervention of the gaze of the West? How can the African imagination adopt a radical introspection that would make it possible for Africans to relate fully and humanely to one another and to the world without adopting accusatory attitudes?

Chinua Achebe and Some Thoughts on African Literature

Since the publication of *Things Fall Apart* in 1958, African literature and cultural discourse have focused on the colonial encounter, its continued consequences, and the need to re-create the authenticity of African culture. This is certainly not Achebe's sole focus in *Things Fall Apart*, which is a complex and nuanced novel. But Achebe himself almost single-handedly drove the reception of the novel, and indeed all his works, in a decisively anti-imperial, write-back trajectory. Recently, Knopf published his collection of essays *The Education of a British Protected Child* (2009), a title that is as biting and far-reaching in the evocation of the pain of the inglorious colonial past as is *Things Fall Apart*.

Lending voice to the interpretation of his works, Achebe himself writes that he would be quite satisfied if his novels, especially those set in the past, taught his African readers that "their past—with all its imperfections—was not one long night of savagery from which the first Europeans acting on God's behalf delivered them" (1988, 45). In the essay "The Empire Fights Back," Achebe explained that *Things Fall Apart* was conceived as a response to the misrepresentations of Africa in some Westerners' stories. He mentions Joseph Conrad and Joyce Cary, whose stereotypical images of Africa forced him to "fight back." It is, therefore, the need to take back the discourse about oneself that constitutes the "overpowering urge to tell a story" (Achebe 2000, 38). The idea of taking back the discourse about oneself is, strictly speaking, no different from the need to "fight back." "The Empire Fights Back" may be designed to echo Bill Ashcroft, Gareth Griffiths, and Helen Tiffin's popular introductory postcolonial book *The Empire Writes Back* (1989). Chinweizu, Onwuchekwa Jemie, Ihechukwu Madubuike supported Achebe's theoretical approach in their collaborative work *Toward the Decolonization of African Literature* (1980). Its powerful Afrocentric impact effectively obstructed all other efforts to open a more diverse, postmodernist, all-inclusive discourse such as that anticipated by Kwame Anthony Appiah's *In My Father's House* (1992).

Another aspect of Africa's cultural discourses impacted was that of feminism. African feminism is often defined by what it is not; it is not European feminism. On the one hand, African women express the necessity for an African feminist discourse whose main goal will be to advance the condition of women throughout Africa. On the other, there is overwhelming pressure to walk the theoretical line established by Achebean modern African culture. Gloria Chukukere aptly captures the dilemma of African feminism:

> the liberation of women in Africa is linked to that of the entire continent from colonial and neocolonial structures. Western schools of feminism, such as Marxist, Socialist, and radical are part of the history of those

> countries' political development and reflect their concerns with class contradictions. This scenario is not exactly the case in Africa, in general, and Nigeria, in particular. For Nigerian women, ours is an anti-colonial, non-separatist movement. (1998, 137)

Chidi Amuta's widely reviewed *The Theory of African Literature*, which promised a radical, dialectical approach to African literature, amounted to no more than the same old Achebean "fight back" mantra, or what he calls "anti-imperialist poetics of African literature" (Amuta 1989, 77). Amuta's understanding of culture as the crystallization of social consciousness in different areas of historically conditioned material and ideational practices (78) is thoroughly Marxist, as is his understanding of the underpinnings of classes (79). His adoption of Marxist theory only "gave the anti-imperialist struggle in Africa" a more rigorous philosophical grounding. Amuta's lashing out against the bourgeoisie and the elite, and his vision of revolutionary pedagogy designed to liberate Africa, is ultimately no more persuasive than the Achebean historical role of narrative and its anti-imperialist world vision (117). It lacks a moral vision that would direct Africans' attention toward themselves or to one another.

With the exception of the writings of Wole Soyinka and Yambo Ouologuem, the African discourse on literature and culture has been shaped by the implicit presence of the West as an adversary to be fought. The African intellectual feels constantly frozen by the white man's scorching gaze, and his goal is to defend his people who are also victims of that gaze. Consequently, Africans are implicitly seen as a collective whose only goal is to defy that gaze. In this constellation, it becomes difficult for one African to consider another as a distinct individual to be appreciated for what he or she is. Referencing African feminist discourses, Gloria Chukukere has clearly demonstrated that the plight of individual women, who suffer under the burden of unfair patriarchal systems in many African societies, is secondary to their plight as (collective) postcolonial subjects.

Wole Soyinka gave ample warning against a solely anti-Western stance in African literature and its implicit collectivist shaping of African realities. In an address delivered at the Afro-Scandinavian Writer's

Conference in Stockholm in 1967, he argued that the writer needed to be released from the obsession with the past because it led to the "destruction of the will to action" and ultimately to "the total collapse of ideals, the collapse of humanity itself" (1988, 19). Soyinka was largely ignored, and African culture is the poorer for that.

The poverty of the African imagination is arguably demonstrated in the fact that Chinua Achebe's generation produced a discourse that froze the African world in a perpetual confrontational mode with the West. The African imagination is forced to engage in a futile search for, or an invention of, an African past that is inaccessible to the destructive eyes of the West. In this search, African reality is judged by the degree to which it relates to that imaginary, ostensibly true image of Africa. The resultant disconnect between Africa's reality on the ground and the urge to attack the West for the distortion of the African past recalls the type of fallacy that Karl Marx discovered in Hegelian and neo-Hegelian thinking. The neo-Hegelians, he charged, attempted to change reality by interpreting concepts. The "demand to change consciousness amounts to a demand to interpret reality in another way, i.e. to recognise it by means of another interpretation" (Marx 1978, 149). African culture, as it is interpreted in academia, has been much engaged in interpreting and reinterpreting the Western interpretation of African reality. It is fair to suggest that African intellectuals' preoccupation with Western epistemologies on Africa reduced their significance in the shaping of the critical imagination of their people.

African Literature in Search of a New Discourse Paradigm

Reviewing *The Education of a British Protected Child*, Ikhide Ikheloa aptly titled Achebe's endeavor "Lecturing the West in the Past Tense." Ikheloa analyzes the discourse paradigms of the book thus: "Missing is the Achebe who famously urged Nigerians to look inwards in *The Trouble with Nigeria* . . . Missing is the question: Why are things the way they are?" Ikheloa, in what can be understood as the frustrations of his generation, argues that "we must also engage in honest conversations among ourselves about our contribution to this mess. Those that rubbish Africa's name today are not just white folks; black on black carnage is the rage of the day in Africa. Our leaders are openly savaging Africa; let us turn our rage on them" (Ikheloa 2010). From the early years of independence, Nigeria has experienced numerous human catastrophes, most of which can be traced directly to the failure of Nigerians to view one another as human beings worthy of empathy. For example, from 1956 to 1966, thousands of Igbo, whose ancestral home was in the Southeast, were massacred in the North because they were of a different ethnicity (Obiwu 1996). Shortly after that pogrom, Nigeria experienced a devastating civil war in which millions of Igbo people perished. Since then, Nigeria has faced one brutal regime after another, violent riots, grizzly mass killings, the impoverishment of a whole populace, and many other atrocities, some of which are documented in books such as Karl Maier's *This House Has Fallen: Nigeria in Crisis* (2000). Given the disconnect between the African imagination and the reality on the ground, new paradigms for interpreting African literature must be examined. One such paradigm will be how Africans relate to one another without any reference to the West. The greatest question to occupy every interpreter of African experience should therefore be about how that particular work draws the African reader's attention to the human condition in Africa. If African literature had hitherto been occupied with addressing the misrepresentations of the African image, it is time that it engages in a thorough introspection in hopes of addressing African humanity.

Theodor Adorno declared that after Auschwitz and the horrors of twentieth-century Europe, philosophy can only be practiced "from the standpoint of redemption. Knowledge has no light but that shed on the world by redemption: all else is reconstruction, mere technique" (Adorno 1974, 247). Echoing Adorno, I argue that after the experiences of wars, genocides, and political oppressions in various independent African countries, the only literature worth taking seriously is one practiced from the standpoint of empathy, one that allows Africans to adopt the perspective of others while making judgments about them. The only literature worth taking seriously is one that turns our attention to ethics. When I speak of literature and ethics, I do not mean texts that prescribe specific moral codes. Rather, I refer to the means or techniques through which beauty moves toward the good in a text, and above all the good that impels an ethical response to the other. Generally speaking, literature touches people not through what it says but through what it does; and it anticipates a certain degree of responsibility, for the writer creates a world and expects this world to speak to the reader and affect aspects of the reader's life. Simply pleasing the reader can be within the bounds of ethics, particularly as understood by Michel Foucault in his "technologies of self" (1997, 227). There is much to be said about the ethical import of the pleasures of reading. However, my focus in this discussion is on how literature and the stories we tell about other people and places help us to connect with others and, in so doing, enrich our lives.

Literature involves a conscious reaching out to the world in a text. It is reaching out to relate. This is what Lawrence Buell draws attention to in "What We Talk about When We Talk about Ethics." He believes that ethics and literature meet in the relationship "between texts and readers" (2000, 6). Literary texts, however, speak to us in a peculiar way. They speak to us in a mediated form, through means we recognize as literary techniques: characterization, metaphor, dialogue, scenes, and plot development. Stories are always already mediated since what we experience in the text is already a reflected experience of the other, the author. Martha Nussbaum, in discussing the relationship between philosophy and literature, draws attention to the important connection between form and content and points out that "a view of life is told" (1990, 5). The writer carefully selects aspects of the world that she caringly (stylistically) deposits in the text with the hope that these aspects of the world will move the reader. The ultimate ethical question is which aspects of the world does the writer wish to disclose and what does the writer aim at in disclosing them?

The Role of Empathy in Literature

When Terry Eagleton announced the demise of literary theory in general, he singled out feminism as the one theory that has survived because it has always been consistently concerned with moral questions, with questions of how we relate to the other as decent human beings. For him, feminism "insists in its own way on the interwovenness of the moral and political, power and the personal" (Eagleton 2003, 144). He reminds us of the difference between moralism and morality. Moralism is narrow and "believes that there is a set of questions known as moral questions which are quite distinct from social or political ones." Morality, on the other hand, entails "exploring the texture and quality of human behaviour as richly and sensitively as you can." This suggests that one cannot talk about morality "by abstracting men and women from their social surroundings" (143). Feminism has always considered the texture and quality of human lives within their given social context. It begins by considering the body without which nothing functions. Not culture, not civilization, not politics. All moralities begin with the human body, ours and those of others. The aim of literature is to present a life that we can see, a life that we can relate to, once it has been seen; literature shows us the human face in unique ways that speak to us individually.

To flesh out what I mean by ethics or morality I will reexamine Aristotle's understanding of tragedy as a form of narrative that engenders ethics. For Aristotle, "imitation comes naturally to human beings from childhood (and in this they differ from other animals, i.e. in having a strong propensity to imitation and in learning their earliest lessons through imitation); so does the universal pleasure in imitation" (Aristotle 1996, 6). It is true, though, that other animals do imitate, and that contributes to their learning process. In Aristotle's understanding, humans raise imitation to the level of culture, to a thing that can be made (*poesis*) and that can be orchestrated for leisure and educational purposes. Humans are storytelling animals, and in stories we imitate actions. This is where Aristotle places tragedy, which he defines as "an imitation of an action that is admirable, complete and possesses magnitude; in language made pleasurable, each of its species separated in different parts, performed by actors, not through narration; effecting through pity and fear the purification of such emotions" (10).

Characters in stories, of course, are needed to carry forth or to dramatize or perform actions. Their performances follow an arc or plot that ultimately reveals how these agents fare and why we should relate to them. The plot that allows us to understand a story has to be complete; it must have "a beginning, a middle and an end" (Aristotle 1996, 13). Only in this constellation can it effect an ethical change in humans. As W. Hamilton Fyfe argues:

> The aim of a tragedy is to give the audience a peculiar form of pleasure such as no other art can give, and its success or failure must therefore be judged by reference to that aim. How does the tragedian achieve it? He arouses the emotions of his audience by re-presenting life to them. And this he does by staging a story. In any story there must be people, and they, as human beings, must have moral and intellectual qualities. (1940, xx)

Simply stated, narrative involves individuals (characters) to whom we relate. It is also correct to argue, as Aristotle does, that ethics, to the degree that we are wired to relate to others, is anthropological. This idea has been advanced by the renowned primatologist Frans De Waal, who argues that empathy is based on anthropology (2009, 66–71, 208–9). Humans and primates share the instinct to empathy, but humans tell stories, among other reasons, to enhance their innate propensity to relate to others.

It is also correct that Aristotle did not envisage tragedy as a mere strategy designed to engender fear and trembling just for the sake of horror. Indeed, he explicitly condemns such ploys. Rather, he is interested in realistic actions that might have unpleasant consequences for the agent, on the one hand, or pleasant outcomes that we can admire, on the other. Thus he rejects the intervention of gods in the actions of humans. It is in this regard that Aristotle argues that every well-told story has something to teach, and it does so by revealing universal aspects of the human condition in individual agents. In this respect, poetry is more philosophical than history.

The effect of the imitation of action in tragedy is that the audience experiences an immediate emotional thrill in the form of "pity and fear" through which the whole experience is purified in catharsis. Gerald Else argues in Aristotle's *Poetics* that catharsis "belongs to Aristotle's defense of the emotional side of poetry against Plato. The arousing of pity and fear is an integral part of the work of tragedy, at least, and something about that production is such that those feelings are, or can be made, beneficent rather than hurtful" (Aristotle 1967, 6–7).

I am interested here in the beneficent aspect of the imitation of the actions of agents within the framework of tragedy, and I interpret this aspect as a question of ethics because it concerns our relation to others. Humphrey House contends in *Aristotle's Poetics: A Course of Eight Lectures*: "Both pity and fear are derived from the self-regarding instinct, and pity springs from the feeling that a similar suffering might happen to ourselves. The objects of pity therefore should be like ourselves . . . This is the basis of the very possibility of sympathy—of the 'feeling with' somebody else" (House 1967, 101–2). In the same line of argument as House, Stephen Halliwell states in *Aristotle's Poetics* that pity and fear refer specifically to the "capacity to sympathize with the sufferer." He emphasizes that "Aristotle does not derive this sympathy from an undifferentiated sense of humanity: instead, he takes it to be rooted in a felt or perceived affinity between the subject and the object of the emotion." In that regard, tragic characters "have to be within the reach of an audience's compassion" (Halliwell 1998, 175–79). When we see actors perform on stage, we become direct witnesses to their fate. In narratives, the poet or novelist achieves the same effects by providing us with realistic details that bring the characters to life so that we can begin to know them.

Halliwell's discussion of Aristotelian tragedy is very close to Jean-Paul Sartre's understanding of the art of disclosure in a text. We sympathize with the world we know, with the world that has been presented to us in texts. In our sympathy, we are ethically challenged to act. Sartre, pointing to the need of communication, says: "The art of prose is employed in discourse; its substance is by nature significative—that is, the words are first of all not objects but designations for objects." In its significative function, Sartre goes on, prose reveals "an attitude of mind" (1988, 35). It equally calls for an attitude of mind of the reader. Sartre argues that the "prose-writer is a man who has chosen a certain method of secondary action which we may call action by disclosure. It is therefore permissible to ask him this second question: 'what aspect of the world do you want to disclose? What change do you want to bring into the world by this disclosure?'" (37).

Sartre writes from a Marxist-existentialist perspective. When he talks of engagement he means the Marxist sense of engagement as a revolutionary act aimed at changing society. I do not understand literature as a means to change society. My understanding is closer to Aristotle's definition of tragedy above. Yet there is an aspect of Sartre's understanding of engagement that merits a closer look. It is the engagement with the other as understood by Emmanuel Levinas. Levinas understands that the face is a place where ethics resides. In his conversation with Philippe Nemo, he maintains that "the face speaks," and in its ability to speak it commands the individual and "begins all discourse." Discourse is a call to engage, a call that the other's face initiates and that I am obliged to respond to. In responding to this call, the individual assumes "responsibility which is this authentic relationship" (Levinas 1985, 87–88). Discourse or engagement is the call to relate. For Levinas, the face is not merely the arrangement of facial features. "The best way of encountering the other is not even to notice the color of his eyes" (85). The infinite human complexities of a person standing before us are contained in that person's face. For Levinas, "the face of the other is destitute; it is the poor for whom I can do all and to whom I owe all. And me, whoever I may be, but as the 'first person,' I am he who finds the resources to respond to the call" (89).

For Levinas, the goal of all wars is to obliterate the face of the other. Literature is, in some ways, the opposite of war; it presents us the face of the other and urges us to respond. The relation to the other is to be seen as a template for our relation to the world. According to Levinas: "The interpersonal relation I establish with the other, I must also establish with other men; there is thus a necessity to moderate this privilege of the other; from whence comes justice. Justice, exercised through institution, which are inevitable, must always be held in check by the initial interpersonal revelation" (90).

Another idea that can help us understand the role of literature in ethics is Martha Nussbaum's definition of empathy as an "imaginative reconstruction of the experience of the sufferer," a "participatory enactment of the situation of the sufferer," which is always accompanied with the awareness that "one is not oneself the sufferer" (2001, 327). In Nussbaum's view, there is a deliberate switching of perspectives that, from the outset, acknowledges the humanity of the sufferer. To be sure, people do not always empathize with others who are in pain. Empathy can be blocked, for example, by the kinds of conditioning that Germans were subjected to during the Nazi regime. Other things can hinder people's ability to empathize with others. They include *ressentiment* or the feeling of anger caused by a hurt in the distant past, which cannot be redressed in the present. I have argued elsewhere that *ressentiment* engendered in the African by the discourse of colonialism tends to relieve the African of his responsibility toward his fellows. This is because the African, who believes that the West is responsible for the ugly state of affairs in Africa, does not feel directly and individually challenged to address the ills of his society. There is always the feeling that someone somewhere is responsible. Most corrupt African dictators such as Robert Mugabe of Zimbabwe or Sani Abacha of Nigeria have taken recourse in anti-imperialist rhetoric that effectively redirects people's attention to the evils of the empire and thereby prevents them from feeling the pain of their fellows. *Ressentiment* often finds expression in fierce anti-imperialist rhetoric.

In my understanding, the difference between contemporary African literature and the literature of Achebe's generation lies in the fact that the relationship between the reader and the text in contemporary literature is no longer mediated by the gaze of the white man. So when contemporary African writers refuse to write back to the center, and write to the self instead, they implore the African reader to engage with the African world as it is. A sampling of recent African narratives can help us demonstrate the general turn to ethics in African narrative.

Nigerian Writers and the Cry for Empathy

In an interview granted to R. Krithika, Chimamanda Ngozi Adichie says: "I am a happy feminist. I think all fair-minded people should be" (2009c). It is instructive that she uses the terms "fairness" and "feminism" in the same breath, especially considering how deeply mistrustful her African audience is of feminism. I interpret Adichie's linking of feminism and fairness as the willingness on her part to use the latter to enhance the understanding of the former in her African world. This understanding is particularly important since her feminism is understood primarily as the basis for the moral equality of men and women in society. Moral equality requires men and women to be accountable for their actions as adults. If one is to be a responsible adult, one must act without coercion. This, above all, implies that people should treat others the way they would want to be treated. The idea of fairness also implies putting oneself in the position of others. So the best thing that feminism can achieve in a man's moral world is to have men empathize with the women they are dealing with. This is not far from what she does in *Purple Hibiscus* (2003). The *in medias res* exposition leaves no doubt as to the locus of the issue against which all forms of resistance should be directed. "Things started to fall apart at home when my brother, Jaja, did not go to communion and Papa flung his heavy missal across the room and broke the figurines on the étagère" (Adichie 2003, 3). The indirect allusion to *Things Fall Apart* not only attempts to situate the narrative within an easily recognizable canon but also questions the historical thesis of things falling apart. It is no accident that things started to fall apart in the home rather than, for example, in the church or at work. Eugene, a re-creation of Okonkwo, single-handedly brings about the falling apart of his family. The figurines on the étagère should be understood as a metaphor for the members of the family breaking under the unbearable patriarchal pressure of Eugene's presence. Things fall apart when he beats his wife severely enough to cause her to miscarry. Things fall apart when he, believing that he is keeping his daughter from sin, pours hot water on her feet, "slowly, as if he were conducting an experiment and wanted to see what would happen" (194). Eugene's problems are many; the worst of them is his lack of empathy. He has what Baron-Cohen calls "zero degrees of empathy" or a single-minded focus of attention (2011, 10). He fails to imagine himself in the position of his wife and children. Were he fair-minded, as the author would judge, he would treat the members of his family with the same care required by the figurines.

What the protagonists in *Purple Hibiscus* could not imagine is lightly broached in Sefi Atta's *Everything Good Will Come* (2005): agency and moral responsibility. And responsibility seems to be what Atta demands of her readers in their response to the characters in *Everything Good Will Come*. There are a number of challenges to our moral sensibility, one of which concerns Sheri Bakare, who is gang raped as a teenager (Atta 2005, 69), a trauma from which she never fully recovers. Having been ravaged and traumatized, Sheri is understandably incapable of finding anything to affirm in her life. She is incapable of mustering any resistance against other subtle forms of oppression that afflict her. Sheri Bakare's experience of gang rape expresses the patriarchal oppression of women in its raw form, and this, of course, has nothing to do with the colonial intervention in African history.

Violence obliterates the face of the other. When Sheri is raped, her face is obliterated; she is seen not as an individual but as an object. Atta challenges us to see the face of this one individual, Sheri, who is metonymic for women of that society. She is metonymic in the sense that she is a part of a group that the system hardly recognizes as individuals with unique pains and pleasures. She also asserts her individuality when she chooses to respond to her experience in ill-advised ways. She indulges her body, not as a way of pleasing herself but of pleasing others. She would go on to "become part of the sugar daddy circuit in Lagos, hanging around senators, and going on shopping sprees abroad" (76). Sheri, a once-vibrant woman with her own mind, comes to be at the beck and call of a brigadier who collects ponies and women (157). Her situation should alert every morally conscious mind. It should make us aware of what happens to people on a daily basis when their individuality is crushed by violence. In that way, Sheri is also metonymic for all Nigerians.

Sefi Atta draws our attention to the horrors of a violent system and the necessity to change it. Informed by the moral consciousness that enables us to feel the pain of others, we feel the need to change the system that objectifies people. But more important, it calls for a response to the other. Enitan takes the lead in this regard; her happiness does not depend on what others think. Rather, she is ethically informed and, armed with her fearless intelligence, demands that whoever has a voice must use it "to bring about change" (259). Enitan believes that the ability to make a change in society begins with the ability to effect a change in the family, the ability for a woman to simply speak out as she does. The narrator is not interested in blaming men. Indeed, she goes beyond the male/female binary to expose the root of the problems. "We have all played a part in this mess, not caring enough about other people, how they live. It comes back to you" (228). Enitan's analysis of Nigerian society informs the reader with its incisiveness and candor. Dictators do not jump out of the heads of some gods as adults; they are groomed by the society that fails to nurture caring children:

> Teachers beat, neighbors beat. By the time a child turned ten, the adults they know would have beaten out any cockiness that could develop into wit; any dreaminess that could give birth to creation; any bossiness that could lead to leadership. Only the strong would survive; the rest would spend their lives searching for initiative. (131)

Sefi Atta's macro moral analysis of her Nigerian society calls for deep introspection on the part of the culture. She anticipates that empathy will emerge from that introspection. Atta poses the same challenge to every individual, one that could be traced back to the Socratic dictum: Know thyself. Taking up the challenge should provide the foundation for a truly fulfilled life as an individual and as a member of society.

Chris Abani's *Graceland* (2004) can be read as a plea for empathy; it is the wrenching sigh of a soul in pain. It is the story of Elvis Oke, a teenager who is enamored of the American musical icon Elvis Presley. Overwhelmed by the absurdities of life in Nigeria, he dreams of moving to the United States, where he believes he would easily realize his dream. Abani succeeds in the deployment of the image of the American Elvis within the discursive economy of the Nigerian cultural milieu. Oke's impersonation of the American legend is not gratuitous. His mother, Beatrice, had instilled in the young man the love of the American icon (Abani 2004, 42). The importance of the appreciation of other cultures is implanted in the young man. From the cradle, he is taught to cross boundaries and to realize that there are realities beyond those provided by his village and ethnic group.

Like his mother, Elvis's elementary school teacher also sharpens his transcultural appetite by teaching him to appreciate other cultures and the people that embody them. However, it is easy to fault *Graceland* as a concatenation of all that has gone wrong in Nigeria. There are all imaginable forms of violence: traffic in human organs, rape, incest, and child abuse. In fact, the narrative moves back and forth between Oke's life in Afikpo, the village where he was born, and Lagos, the Nigerian megacity.

What seems to link both places is the predominance of violence, which is part and parcel of Oke's life.

Those who know Nigeria understand that the reality of violence is often more bizarre than can ever be captured by fiction. It is perhaps better to understand Chris Abani's goal in this novel as a call for empathy for the many victims of casual, rampant violence in the country. Elvis holds a mirror to all Nigerians and urges them to put themselves in his position; he urges us not to brutalize him but to respect him as a human being.

Conclusion

In the introductory part of this article, I drew on the insights of the prominent African literary scholar Simon Gikandi to argue that Chinua Achebe invented modern African culture. Like Gikandi, we have to note that by "African culture," we mean the knowledge of Africa as it is discoursed in academia. Chinua Achebe was by no means the first African writer to write about the African condition as it was impacted by the West. Nor is it correct to believe that African culture has been solely occupied with a response to the West. However, it is true that his novel and its overwhelming acceptance helped set the tone for African, if not global, postcolonial studies. African culture has been predominantly understood within the paradigms of postcolonial discourse. I identify the culture born of this mindset as reactionary to the degree that it is absorbed with responding or reacting to impulses from outside the continent. It is my belief that this sort of African culture is dead. Binyanvanga Wainaina and Chimamanda Ngozi Adichie's popular attacks on the West's narrative about Africa could be seen as its last death throes. Chinua Achebe's death on March 22, 2013, to me, brings to a close what could arguably be called the age of Achebe in African literature. This age includes everything written before 2000 and that could be understood within the Achebean paradigm. It is the age of Achebe because before Achebe there had been nothing like postcolonial African literature, and after him there can only be a literature of introspection, one that largely ignores the gaze of the West. Introspectionism, by which I mean the simple act of self-observation, or the cultural act of looking inward with the goal of critiquing oneself in order to better relate to others, replaces *ressentiment,* which is largely other oriented. In the same vein, a community-oriented call for responsibility and empathy replaces angry, responsibility-evading, anti-imperialist rhetoric of the past decades. In the African age of introspectionism there will be voices that always hark back to the colonial experience with the goal of confronting the empire. But they will die out as the African imagination continues to confront its realities without accusatory reference to the West.

It is gratifying that Chris Abani, Chimamanda Ngozi Adichie, and Sefi Atta, among the most prominent names in the new generation of post-Achebe African writers, ignore the gaze of the West in their novels. Despite Chimamanda Ngozi Adichie's TED talk (2009b), most of her works of fiction share the same attitude as the works of her generation. If the Achebe generation rightly challenged the Western construction of the image of Africa in their narratives, this generation appears much more interested in disclosing the African condition. In disclosing it, they challenge us to respond to it. It is the job of literary critics, philosophers, and shapers of minds to take seriously the world that these writers draw our attention to.

Part Three

African Literature and Feminist Perspectives

7

Survivalist Autobiographies

The Struggles of African Muslim Women

GLEN BUSH

The collapse of Somalia, the genocide in Darfur and throughout Sudan, and the continued oppression of African Muslim women in Europe and the United States have ironically been a factor in the liberation of many women who had been voiceless. A good introduction to their struggles is the following excerpt from Abuk Bak's essay "Beyond Abeeda: Surviving Ten Years of Slavery in Sudan," which positions their plight in real world and theoretical perspectives:

> "My name is Abuk Bak." These are the words I said to Khiddir Ahmed, the Sudanese ambassador to the United States, when he came to Tufts University for a conference on Sudan in March 2004 . . ."As a child I was enslaved for ten years in Sudan," I told him, and handed him a letter I had written asking for reparations from the Sudanese government.
>
> "You are a liar," he said, looking straight into my eyes, "There is no slavery in Sudan." (2008, 41)

This brief excerpt illustrates the tip of the criminal iceberg that is the struggle of African Muslim women in Africa, the Middle East, Europe, and the United States. In 1954, when Mary F. Smith published her anthropological study of a Hausa woman from northern Nigeria, *Baba of Karo,* the West did not show very much "main street" interest in the text. However, since the Muslim genocide in Kosovo, the invasion of Kuwait and the Gulf War, and the 9/11 attacks, one sees an interest in African Muslim women and Islam in general growing enormously. The autobiographies *Desert Flower, Slave, Infidel,* and *Tears of the Desert* may well have been published without the 9/11 attack, but would they be as marketable as they are today? The common Westerner may not care about non-Western people and conflicts, but when the West is directly involved as a peacekeeping unit or as a military partner or a mediator, the interest increases. There is something at stake for the Westerner: sons, daughters, money, and political power. Unfortunately, the interest often takes on the aspect of voyeur more than concerned humanitarian. However, it is voyeurism that leads to the publication and sale of many of the African Muslim women autobiographies currently on bookshelves throughout the West. And that is the other side of the double-edged sword.

Collectively, these four autobiographies inform the Western reader of a lifestyle far removed from the plastic and comfortable life found in the West. The four women—Waris Dirie, Mende Nazer, Ayaan Hirsi Ali, and Halima Bashir—have set down on paper, with the help of Western associates, their stories of hardship and survival. The four tell their stories after they have escaped terrifying conditions and are living in Europe. In this sense, their autobiographies are narratives of escape and reinvention, for each one of them is able to reinvent her life away from the daily abuses common in the African Muslim world. Given the content of the autobiographies and the consequences of telling their stories, the term "survivalist autobiographies" will be used to describe their texts. As will be seen, other labels have also been applied to these and other women's autobiographies, such as life histories, life narratives, biographies, or life stories. However, in this case the term "survivalist autobiographies" serves both to denote and connote the life-threatening experiences of these particular African Muslim women.

All four books present the stories of African Muslim women living a life most Westerners would find, to put it mildly, horrid. In some ways one can relate these four to the classical Greek tragedies that set out to enlighten the audience through an Aristotelian catharsis. As one reads *Infidel* or *Desert Flower* or one of the other autobiographies, one is struck by the violence delivered on these women. The psychological and physical violence comes as calmly as a spring rain, but deals devastating blows to its victims. A six-year-old searching for water in the desert? Don't all children do this? It builds survival skills and communal loyalties. Female genital mutilation? Of course, all young girls are circumcised with a broken razor blade, and, yes, sometimes they bleed to death, but this is God's will. Rape? Why is she here without her father, husband, or brother? What does it say about the temptations of a seductive woman in the Qur'an? Questions such as these and their cultural male replies are common, the everyday. Is it any wonder these women want to escape their conditions? Theoretically, these four autobiographies are all examples of African nonfiction literature as well as feminist works.

A survey of the book reviews finds, not surprisingly, a general consensus of positive responses. In fact, Lesley McDowell's opening lines for her review of Halima Bashir's *Tears of the Desert*, written in *The Scotsman*, illustrates the issues (problems) that the reviewer has in reviewing the survivalist autobiographies of these African Muslim women: "How do you critique a book that is based on the survivor's experience of genocide? The short answer is: you don't. Because you can't" (2008). McDowell goes on to discuss the plot's vivid images of extreme abuse. This is the same approach countless other reviewers use when discussing these survivalist autobiographies. Often the ending of the reviews comes with an overwhelming sense of inspiration. Dirie, Nazer, Ali, and Bashir each tell a story that offers the reader a time to reflect. Perhaps that is the key to the academic connection as well. The scholar usually does not seek "inspirational autobiographies," for these are not generally considered academic texts; however, these texts most assuredly offer the scholar a venue for political posturing.

When one examines these autobiographies in this light, both as inspirational autobiographies and political conduits, it becomes apparent that the Africanness of the texts is not nearly as important as the political environment grounded in Islamic fundamentalism and the issues to be discussed later, that is, private/public self, truth-telling ("facts" and "everybody knows"), and author/coauthor roles. The four are African texts, but they are not anthropological studies, textual renditions, or autobiographies of what is often considered by Westerners as African life. These texts are political weapons designed to expose, rescue, and destroy.

Comparable to the pre-1865 slave narratives of the United States that set out to expose the truths about slavery, rescue those still enslaved, and ultimately destroy the "peculiar institution" of American slavery, these texts are contemporary slave narratives, survivalist autobiographies, with many of the same goals that seek to rectify the African Muslim institution of women's oppression. Collectively, these survivalist autobiographies bring these African Muslim women out of the shadows of a religious and cultural patriarchy and bring them into the global conflict for women's rights. Some of the book reviews surveyed mention the importance of human rights, but when these stories are put into the global marketplace, they become something else. They, the texts and the women, are weapons against Islamic patriarchy, Western colonialism, and historical injustices (injustices against voiceless women).

This essay discusses the struggle between four African Muslim women and their oppressors: the tension between the public and private self, the narratives as truth-telling complexes with a cultural opposition between verifiable facts and the accepted but unsubstantiated "everybody knows facts," and last, the author/coauthor (recorder) roles. Each of these themes merits an investigation of its own; however, collectively, they shed limited light on the cultural and religious entanglement these four lives experience.

The first tribulation that comes to view is the conflict between the public and the private self. Essentially, these women live a restrictive life that requires them to accept the duality of their existence, that is, the public woman who goes to the marketplace, engages in conversation with other women as well as children and males (on a very limited bases), goes to a madrassa for Qur'anic teaching, or goes into the field to work with the crops or livestock and her coworkers. The private woman is the one who lives in the home and only the home. She is part of the harem or *haram* (Arabic for "forbidden"). As part of the women's community within the home or compound, these women form their own close-knit community. In both forms, public and private, the women engage in an oral community. Speaking to one another as sisters, as women who "know" their male-defined world, they develop their language and narratives that differentiate them from the males and the children. In this sense, it is their orality that defines and makes them human. Essentially, what comes into existence here is the direct connection between the oral culture and the femininity of the four African Muslim women.

Gary S. Gregg writes about this female orality in his essay "Culture, Personality, and the Multiplicity of Identity": "Tradition reigns but liberation beckons . . ."(1998, 122). For the literary and cultural critic, this statement rings true. Many African Muslim women were restricted from autobiography by this simple phrase: "tradition reigns." Restrictions came (and come) in the form of Qur'anic law, Islamic and regional cultural parameters, and perhaps the most confining of all—forced orality. Arguably, forced orality is part and parcel of the other forms of restrictions, but it is also one that has its roots in ancient times, in pre-Islamic, pre-Christian culture. Traditionally, orality, throughout Africa, has been the sole means of passing on one's ethnic, communal, and individual knowledge. Men have had their oral cultures, women theirs, and then there is the joint oral culture best acknowledged by the role of the griot, the oral historian or storyteller. Margaret J. Daymond's comments concerning the two South African female writers Sindiwe Magona and Bessie Head on the role of orality among African women pertain quite nicely to African Muslim women's autobiographies. Daymond writes that "the [only] form of participation in the regulation of communal life that has been open to women in southern African oral cultures has been the telling of tales" (2002, 334). Furthermore, in this same segment, Daymond notes that the men were not, and did not, accept these tales as part of the village governance.

Oral cultures, although dying cultures, still have an important role in contemporary cultural analyses. They serve as the link to the past as well as the link to the present. African Muslim women, especially in areas such as Sudan and Somalia, are restricted from learning to read and write. Often their education is limited to memorizing the Qur'an in Arabic in a local madrassa. Although issues of having a voice and voicelessness can include colonialism and neocolonialism, this essay will limit the discussion to the conflict arising from Islamic and cultural oppression. One sees the complexity of oppression for African Muslim women as well as the difficulty in producing something as essential as an autobiography. Barbara Harlow attributes the changes in African women's writings and actions to "political repression and public resistance to it" (1986, 504). Harlow goes on to write that "African women are leaving the family structure to join forces in the beginnings, not always successful, of a new social order" (504). As evident from the increase in African Muslim women's autobiographies, Harlow's "new social order" definitely includes writing oneself into existence. This new existence is positioned outside both the male hierarchy and madrassa teachings. Instead, these women are divorcing themselves from their forced and arranged marriages, so that in the final product the reader finds the women not necessarily Muslim, at least not in the traditional sense of the religion, and philosophically not necessarily African anymore. As Harlow comments, "what they have in common . . . is their secularism" (508).

Although this essay focuses on African Muslim women, Nawar al-Hassan Golley's *Reading Arab Women's Autobiographies: Shahrazad Tells Her Story* sheds light on the Arab and Islamic influences common among African women, especially those from northeast Africa. Golley is committed to:

> using aspects of feminist narrative theories in order, first, to examine the ideological positions from which the writers/tellers of their stories write—to see whether writing these texts is part of a struggle against oppression; and, second, to explore other questions, such as: Are these women writing from within any kind of tradition, whether local or influenced by writing from other parts of the world? (2003, xi–xii).

As a feminist educated in both the Arab and Western world, Golley enjoys the opportunity to use postcolonial, feminist, and Marxist critical theories in her examination (2003, xi). Her position and her use of these theories are not only important for her exploration of Arab women's autobiographies, but important as well for other scholars who try to understand the complexity of dual existence, or as W.E.B. DuBois refers to this form of existence, "double consciousness." Golley writes, "I am using western critical theory to look at texts by and about women from Arab countries from a double stance. Many of these women, like myself, are under the influence of at least two different cultures" (xiii). Adding the term "African Muslim" to "Arab," one sees the similarity between the two goals. Furthermore, as stated earlier, African Muslim women cannot escape Arab influences. With the spread of Islam comes also the spread of Arabic influences and culture. Because of the theocracy that permeates much of the Middle East, especially Saudi Arabia, a country familiar to African Muslim women as a place of work for them or their male family members, Arabic culture and Muslim culture are intertwined in a ropelike fashion. Ayaan Hirisi Ali writes of her time in Saudi Arabia as one of the most restrictive times in her life:

> My mother also enrolled us in a local Quran school, although we spoke practically no Arabic. In Somalia, both school and Quran school had been mixed (boys and girls); here, everything was segregated . . . All the girls at madrassah were white; I thought of them as white, and myself, for the first time, as black. They called Haweya and I *Abid*, which meant slaves. Being called a slave—the racial prejudice this term conveyed—was a big part of what I hated in Saudi Arabia. The teacher didn't teach us to write, just recited to us from the Quran. We had to learn it, verse by verse, by heart. (2007, 42)

Many of the restrictions put on African Muslim women come either directly or indirectly from the conservative Saudi communities (*umma*). For example, Ayaan Hirsi Ali writes extensively on this topic in *Infidel*:

> Saudi Arabia meant intense heat and filth and cruelty. People had their heads cut off in public squares. After the Friday noon prayer you could go home for lunch, or you could go and watch the executions. Hands were cut off. Men were flogged. Women were stoned. In the late 1970s, Saudi Arabia was booming, but its society seemed fixed in the Middle Ages. (2007, 43)

It is also important to note that Golley's ideas on Arab women's autobiographies correlate with those of African Muslim women, remembering, of course, the matrix of customs formed by Arab, Muslim, African ethnic groups, and Western colonialism. For example, Golley contends that Arab women's autobiographies can often be better defined as "writing back" (2003, 15). Put into a larger context of marginalized women, "writing back" also applies to the African Muslim women's autobiographies in this essay.

Golley, like Ayaan Hirsi Ali and Waris Dirie, desires a collective changing of the political climate (Golley 2003, 15). With this change comes a reevaluation of not only the individual woman's role in her particular indigenous society, but also a political change that crosses gender, national, religious, and cultural boundaries. The matrix of customs that create historical and political traditions confine and restrict African Muslim women and are a contemporary form of enslavement, colonization, and imprisonment. Interestingly, though, whereas Golley, Harlow, and Daymond pass blame, either partially or wholly, on capitalism and imperialism, the African Muslim women autobiographers, Dirie, Nazer, Ali, and Bashir, argue that Islamic traditions (often warped by regional customs), cultural patriarchal traditions, and African traditions have imprisoned their minds more than capitalism and corporatism. This does not mean that colonization and imperialism have had no effect on African women, Muslim or otherwise, but it does mean that the Marxist microscope is not the only instrument worthy of analytical use.

From this line of thought, orality to writing to individual identity and existence, comes the case of the public and private self. The issue at hand is how does an African Muslim woman define herself when her environment is designed, historically and politically, to blur her very existence? The immediate discussion concerns the verification of the private self, that is, the private self in that the woman is restricted from leaving her physical and psychological confines without the authorization of a male "superior." In order to *become* a public self, she must have the ability and support to voice her opinions and ideas in a mixed community, one consisting of males, females, and children, regardless of ethnic, religious, racial, or sexual backgrounds. This is not an easy step, especially in many of the closed African Muslim communities. In an ideal world, the African Muslim woman would gain the support of other women in her cultural group, and together they would collectively voice—speak and write—themselves into the public sphere. Unfortunately, theirs is not a perfect world. One example of an African Muslim woman preparing and entering the public sphere is described by Halima Bashir. Her entrance, however, comes about while living in London, not Africa, and with the support of her husband, Sharif. Initially, though, Bashir is helped by two women gathering information about women in Darfur. Her conversation with the two women from the Darfur relief organization was contingent on her personal conversations with Sharif. In other words, the theory of transgressing one's predicament is not enough for Bashir; she needs the support of her husband, the male. Note, however, that it is not in the submissive role but as an equal that the vanquishing of her second-class status occurs. In the course of her actions, Bashir gains a certain level of confidence because of her male support.

Halima Bashir describes this transition in her life as "breaking the silence," and in the end she creates/talks/writes herself into existence in her autobiography *Tears of the Desert: A Memoir of Survival in Darfur*. Her narrative of growing up in Darfur among her people, the Zaghawa, takes the reader from the village to confinement by Arab raiders and slave traders and finally on to London and freedom. But it is the freedom period that ironically signifies the most demanding time for her. It is during this time, while awaiting English Home Office approval and living in a refugee hostel, that Bashir meets two women from the Aegis Trust who are documenting the war crimes and tortures committed by the Arabs in Darfur against the Zaghawa. At one point, Bashir notes that the women had only been able to collect the testimonies of six Zaghawa men but no women. It is here, at this point, that Bashir and Sharif agree that it would be appropriate for her to tell her story, *but only if she wanted to do so*. Thus, Halima Bashir slowly and painfully gains her voice:

> I called Sharif and asked him what he thought. He told me that if it was private, and if I wanted to, then I should go ahead. I asked the women what the information would be used for. They told me it would be given to powerful governments to expose the terrible abuses in Darfur. And the women's voice was a vital one.
>
> For a moment I thought about my father. I knew what he would have wanted me to do. He would want me to . . . speak out. It was good to be doing so knowing that my words might have an effect. Perhaps it gave some meaning to all that I had suffered. (2008, 287)

Would Halima Bashir have told the women interviewers her story without the support of her husband and the memory of her supportive father?

Perhaps. However, she may very well have ended up like some of the other refugees in the holdover hostels.

Instead of including a set of examples illustrating the transition from voiceless to voiced, an examination of truth-telling is more appropriate. Once one gains one's voice, one still needs to understand the dynamics of the words being voiced. Nothing is more perplexing than talking oneself into existence only to find that the existence has been manipulated by others, by males in religious, political, or social dominance, or their surrogates. Identity and voice must result in the truth. In postmodernist, postcolonial, Marxist, and feminist critical theories, the concept of truth is questionable. Yet, questionable or not, one must engage the philosophical and political importance of truth and truth-telling if one really wants to claim independence. Liz Stanley provides some insight into truth-telling in her discussion.

Stanley's contribution comes in the form of what she refers to as the "expert knowing" or the conventional wisdom measure of women's autobiography (1999, 3). Although Stanley focuses her research on European women's autobiographies, the same points apply here. She discusses the twofold "proof" often employed as the verification process: "This is fact" ("external material evidence") and "everybody knows" ("the coherence of public beliefs") (4). These two "reasons" for accepting a belief as "fact," as the truth, brings into play the cultural significance of those inside the culture as well as though outside the culture. For example, in the cases of the African Muslim women, one can see the role of authority figures within the culture as having a great deal to do with the actions and reactions of women in day-to-day activities. One may immediately assume that these actions are manipulated by the male hierarchy within the specific culture, but a closer examination shows that the males also are manipulated by the historical-political events that have created the culture. The spokesman/leader may say "do not do this," and expect the men to have the wherewithal to change, but cultural realities are much greater than a simple phrase, even if the words come from one in an authoritarian position. Case in point is the fourteen hundred years of Qur'anic teachings and interpretations that do not simply melt away even if the male cultural leaders want to change. They quickly find themselves victims of the same cultural processes that the women experience. For example, Ali writes in *Infidel* about her father's wish that she be educated so she could contribute to a new Somalia; however, he also finds it impossible not to follow the ethnic and religious traditions of the arranged marriage process. Ali's father is not portrayed as an ignorant nomadic herdsman trapped in his ancient culture but rather as an educated (both Western and Islamic educated) man anxious to build a new Somalia that can join the West. Ali describes the role of tradition in her father's world in this short segment concerned with her divorce from her husband (chosen for her by her father) by a council of Muslim elders.

Ali's father experiences Stanley's two "truths" in that the importance of an arranged marriage bridges both "this is fact" and "everybody knows." Of course Ayaan Hirsi Ali must submit to her father's wishes; this is a Muslim fact of life as well as an ethnic one that everybody knows is "fact." The actions by both Ali and her father follow the Qur'anic belief of male domination as well as the "everybody knows" belief of the ethnic group, perhaps an even more important belief since the survival of the group is dependent on cultural traditions such as arranged marriages between families so that the group remains strong and homogenous.

This review of Stanley's two truths illustrates the complexity of feminist criticism in that one simply does not challenge the status quo on grounds of patriarchal traditions but must also engage those institutions that have created the environments. It is at this point that Golley's arguments on the roles of the empowered Arab women intersect Stanley's contributions and simultaneously shed light on the African Muslim women autobiographies. If one follows both Stanley's and Golley's lines of thought, it becomes apparent that African Muslim women are not necessarily limited to a life of enslavement, as many Western news and social commentators claim. Nawar al-Hassan Golley writes, "The veil also has recently been considered a means of empowerment, rather than oppression, especially when worn as a personal choice" (2003, 25). Their empowerment comes in contrast to Western individualism and philosophy. Golley goes on to state that "Arab women's relationship to their bodies during the 1970s reflects the complexity of the sociopolitical situation of Arab societies at the time" (25). It is at this point that she acknowledges

Abu Odeh's work on feminism in Arab communities and the relationship between "capitalist" and "traditionalist" struggles (25). Truth-telling, with the insights of Stanley and Golley, equips one to appreciate the essence of the African Muslim woman's daily struggle. Political, historical, and religious issues overwhelm the woman, from whatever culture, in her bid toward self-expression, identity, and voice.

Heidi Gengenbach also addresses the issue of truth-telling in African women's autobiographies. Gengenbach specifically addresses Kirk Hoppe's analysis of these autobiographies or life history narratives, but her attention to the subject applies quite aptly to this discussion. Hoppe had earlier written in "Whose Life Is It, Anyway?: Issues of Representation in Life Narrative Texts of African Women" (1993) that the truth was brought into question because the African women were telling their stories to Western interviewers. Hoppe contends the African women were more concerned with the particular results of their stories, for example, he suggests that the African women survey the interview process and use the interview for their own agenda, resulting in employment, political validation, or eternal Christian salvation (Gegenbach 1994, 622). The result, according to Gengenbach, is that the African women's life narratives contain no truth, but do contain a truth about the Western interviewer's agenda and political position (622). The argument between Hoppe and Gengenbach is intellectually rewarding for readers today; however, it also brings to the forefront an important point, that is, are the women in this discussion, Dirie, Nazer, Ali, and Bashir, writing to tell their stories, their truths, and their histories, or are they more interested in their rewards, especially the rescue from horrid conditions and resettlement in a Western country that will afford them new opportunities—personal, familial, political? Gengenbach's and Hoppe's exchange moves the discussion of the African Muslim women away from the "facts" and "everybody knows" references and on to another avenue. Regardless if the "facts" are real or imaginary, now the issue is performance, action, and reaction. Truth-telling has now become even more complicated with political and cultural rewards becoming an active ingredient in the formation of not only the autobiography but also the autobiographer.

Furthermore, it is important to look at the reception of these autobiographies in light of recent political history, specifically the Islamist terrorists and their attacks and thwarted attacks on European, American, African, and Asian targets. Female mutilation, arranged marriages, slavery, gang rapes, honor killings, and genocide are not new to the world. However, today the victims of these actions have a venue that gives voice to previously voiceless women and children. Autobiographies and interviews in print, on video, and on the Internet are available throughout the world, including the Muslim and Arab regions that have in the past successfully suppressed incidents of terror. Once again, as readers and scholars, these texts, written or oral, must be examined for their "truth-telling." Is there political manipulation of these women? Or are these women attempting to manipulate some part of the cultural spectrum for their own benefit? These harsh questions need viewing, but this limited venue is not the proper place. Instead, though, one should not be afraid to ask how these examples of African Muslim women's survivalist autobiographies address cultural and feminist issues, especially those issues that focus on the public/private concept of self and on the factual accounting of their stories, that is, the facts, the "everybody knows facts," and truth-telling overall. Even this limited examination will not get the space it deserves in this discussion but will hopefully lead to still further academic exploration of African Muslim women's survivalist autobiographies.

Two of these autobiographies, *Slave: My True Story* by Mende Nazer and *Tears of the Desert: A Memoir of Survival in Darfur,* were told to the British journalist Damien Lewis, who also helped with the writing. Lewis is well known in the journalistic community for his work in Third World war zones. As a print journalist, documentary filmmaker, and fiction writer, he has gained the respect of a large cross-sectional community of readers and viewers. The question of public/private and truth-telling definitely becomes important in these two works. The third autobiography, *Desert Flower: The Extraordinary Life of a Desert Nomad* by Waris Dirie, was told to and cowritten with Cathleen Miller, a university professor of creative writing. Miller's work has been mainly travel writing but also includes biographical pieces. Thus, collectively, the coauthors, for that is what they are, do have a tremendous amount of input as to what is written and how it is written. Only Ayaan Hirsi Ali writes her own story in her own words, although she, too, has input and support from Western professionals and friends.

The following excerpt from "A Note from Damien Lewis" at the conclusion of *Slave* illustrates the problematic issue of authorship, translation, and literary/cultural purpose, one that is acknowledged differently from that of the writers, Michael Smith or Daryll Forde:

> I thought long and hard about how to get the best out of the writing ahead of us. Mende only spoke basic English . . . I spoke almost no Arabic, and my Nuba was nonexistent . . . She would need to trust me with her most difficult, painful memories and fears. I knew that having a translator between us would make that impossible.
>
> We agreed that working slowly in English, using an English-Arabic dictionary where necessary, we could make ourselves understood. (Mende and Lewis 2003, 337–38)

Here Damien Lewis, a seasoned writer with non-Western experiences, presents his rationale. His use of the phrase "I knew" three times shows his hard-felt knowledge of the task of writing, a knowledge that Nazer apparently lacked, or at least Lewis felt she lacked. A cynic may very well write that Lewis's assumption is exactly what feminists and other academics have argued against for at least forty years. Lewis, the Western, privileged white male, "knows" what is "best" for the African woman and how best to tell *her* story, *her* truth. Perhaps this is true, perhaps Lewis does position himself in the authoritarian role because he knows what is best. This is not the venue to examine Lewis's motives in cowriting *Slave* or *Tears of the Desert*, but it is the place to bring up the role of the African Muslim woman and her Western coauthor.

One may ask at this point, what exactly are these autobiographical/biographical texts doing? What, if any, is the common ground among these texts? What is the political agenda of the African Muslim woman in each text? What is the agenda of the coauthor? Are these autobiographical/biographical texts life stories or life narratives of women who want the world to know of their struggles and successes? Although often horrifying events may overwhelm the readers, is it this collection of horrid experiences that the African woman wants to tell, describe, and explain? Or have global political conditions and the Islamist terrorist attacks around the world, but especially in the United States and Europe, against a Western culture that embraces democracy, capitalism, and free speech fueled the conditions within the publishing marketplace that make African Muslim women and their narratives of female mutilation, slavery, rape, and mass murder commodities?

Just exactly who is using whom?

As a transition piece between the issue of author/coauthor and feminist autobiography, the following explanations of feminist autobiography by bell hooks and African women's autobiography by Marcia Wright are beneficial. First, hooks writes,

> The longing to tell one's story and the process of telling is symbolically a gesture of longing to recover the past in such a way that one experiences both a sense of reunion and a sense of release. It was the longing for release that compelled the writing but concurrently it was the joy of reunion that enabled me to see that the act of writing one's autobiography is a way to find again that aspect of self and experience that may no longer be an actual part of one's life but is a living memory shaping and informing the present. (1998, 431)

Marcia Wright adds to and defines autobiography, life history, and biography in the following way: "Autobiography implies the greatest degree of self-control; life history is often a mediated account composed by another person but retaining the perspective of the subject; and biography is a study of the focal person informed by many sources and external criteria of significance" (1989, 155). She explains her reference in connection with Christina Sibiya's *Zulu Woman*, an explanation that sheds light on the five texts discussed here by Dirie, Nazer, Ali, and Bashir.

> The life story of Christina Sibiya, I conclude, is to be placed on the side of autobiography; that is to say, the subject propels and shapes it more than the interlocutor-biographer. The personal narrative thus permeates the structure as well as the content of the published book. Without doubt, a

> lengthy life story of an African woman would not have been published, especially in its second paperback edition, were it not for its combination of power, sex, and drama. That the power was royal and tribal made it exotic. That the setting was South Africa in the industrial age made it accessible. (155–56)

This description illuminates the success of *Desert Flower, Slave, Infidel,* and *Tears from the Desert.* These four works definitely have power, sex, and drama. They are also very accessible to today's readers because of the enormous amount of media coverage that permeates global societies through such outlets as cable news channels, mainstream news documentary programs, the Internet, and film. A further look at women's autobiography and feminist theory also reveals another facet of the author/coauthor issue.

Brenda Daly, in "I Stand Here Naked, and Best Dressed in Theory: On Feminist Re-fashionings of Academic Discourse," writes: "As I know from experience, even when the occasion to speak out is provided by feminists, it is difficult for a survivor to strike the balance of self-disclosure and self-censorship, or between autobiography and theory" (1998, 15). She explains: "For, if a woman's reality is denied, it becomes difficult for her to assert her point of view with self-confidence. In other words, it is not only the reality that I was sexually abused as a child, but the fact that this reality was denied by my family, as well as by society, that for many years damaged my ability to speak or write with confidence" (23).

African Muslim women's experiences now begin blending with Daly's academic and feminist issues. The whole issue of self-identity and self-expression in Daly's examination is the same one that the authors and coauthors had to face when deciding what to write and how to write it. If one sees the African Muslim woman and the writing student within a similar paradigm, Daly's insights take on a formative role. The goals of Daly and the coauthors Mary Smith (Baba of Karo), Cathleen Miller (*Desert Flower*), and Damien Lewis (*Slave, Tears of the Desert*) merge in the following statement:

> To further stimulate self-analysis and theory building, I then ask students to exchange and compare their reading autobiographies . . . As

> Elbow says, "Often the best test of whether a student understands something is if she can translate it out of the discourse of the textbook and the discipline into everyday, experiential, anecdotal terms" (137). Elbow cites other authorities who advocate the integration of formal concepts with everyday experience: "Vogotsky, when he describes the need for what he calls `scientific' or `formal' concepts to become intertwined in the child's mind with `everyday' or experienced concepts; Bakhtin, when he explores the process by which people transform `the externally authoritative word' into `internally persuasive word' (137)." (Daly 1998, 17)

Brenda Daly's scholarship concerning autobiographical writing as an equal partner to theoretical writing corresponds not only to the author/coauthor issue but also to the earlier discussion of "facts," "everybody knows," and "truth-telling," especially as it relates to how the African Muslim women create their autobiographies. The role of the coauthors Smith, Miller, and Lewis, serve as the double persona of the academic professor urging and guiding the autobiographies as well as the television talk show host who sets the television stage for the "presentation which opens with emotional `confessions' by survivors . . . after which `the inevitable expert shows up; almost invariably a white man or woman with a middle-class and professional appearance, who, with a sympathetic but dispassionate air, explains to the audience the nature, symptoms, and possible therapies for such crimes of violence (277)'" (Daly 1998, 24).

This essay, and the women's autobiographies, begins and is grounded in the study of African Muslim women and the cultures that created them. As the exploration moves more toward textual analysis it clearly develops that the issues are far larger than just African Muslim women's issues. Not that those issues are minor or insignificant—they are not. However, at the intersection of global political events—such as 9/11, the wars in Iraq and Afghanistan, the European backlash to Islamic fundamentalism in European cities such as Paris, Geneva, and Hamburg, and the genocide that continues in Darfur even while Sudan's Muslim government pretends it does not exist—there comes a point that brings academic critical theory to the day-to-day events that are shaping real lives around the world. No one knows the effect of the Sudan elections or the recent political uprisings across the Middle East and North Africa. Theory is often just that, theory; but in the reading and rereadings of these autobiographies that have become life-story narratives and survivalist autobiographies, real women are suffering from genital mutilation, honor killings, and revenge killings because of the traditions that have created these situations. No better example exists for this statement than the murder of Theo van Gogh in November 2004 because his film company produced and distributed Ayaan Hirsi Ali's short film *Submission, Part 1*. The Moroccan man who murdered Theo van Gogh did so to protect Islam and Muslims from the infidels van Gogh and Ali. The concept of open debate, free speech, and intellectual reason does not exist in the world of Dirie, Nazer, Ali, or Bashir. Instead, there is total submission to authority (the translation of *Islam* is submission to God). Ali discusses the difference between the West and Islam:

> I didn't want any more imaginary guides telling me what to do, but I needed to believe I was still moral. Now I read the works of the great thinkers of the Enlightenment . . . and the modern ones . . . All life is problem solving, Poppers says. There are no absolutes; progress comes through critical thought . . . I wanted to be like Popper: free of constraint, recognizing greatness but unafraid to detect its flaws.
>
> Reason, not obedience, should guide our lives. (2007, 281–82)

Ali goes further and addresses a problem (more than an issue) that haunts Western universities:

> Many well-meaning Dutch people have told me in all earnestness that nothing in Islamic culture incites abuse of women, that this is just a terrible misunderstanding. Men all over the world beat their women, I am constantly informed. In reality, these Westerners are the ones who misunderstand Islam. The Quran mandates these punishments. It gives a legitimate basis for abuse, so that the perpetrators feel no shame and are not hounded by their conscience or their community . . . I wanted secular, non-Muslim people to stop kidding themselves that "Islam is peace and tolerance." (2007, 307)

Waris Dirie also comes to see the West as a place where conflicts can be fought and won with reason and law. However, unlike Ali, Dirie does not place as much blame on Islam as she does on the cultural traditions of both Islam and her fellow Somalis. As Ali gained recognition as a politician and political activist in the Netherlands, Dirie gained recognition as a supermodel in both the US and European fashion world. Her celebrity status opened doors for her not only as an individual but also as a voice for other Third World women, especially African Muslim women who had suffered similar hardships of violence and abuse. Female genital mutilation, female circumcision, is the focus of Dirie's war against women's oppression. Ali also has written about and discussed this subject in numerous texts and venues. Unlike Ali, Dirie's experiences in Africa and outside of Africa have not caused her to reject Islam; in fact, she praises her experiences, with the one primary exception—genital mutilation:

> Because I criticize the practice of female genital mutilation, some people think that I don't appreciate my culture. But they're so wrong. Oh, I thank God every day that I'm from Africa. Every day. I'm very proud to be Somali, and proud of my country.
>
> . . . Another benefit of growing up in Africa was that we were part of pure nature, pure life. I knew life—I wasn't sheltered from it. And it was real life—not some artificial substitute on television where I'm watching *other* people live life. From the beginning, I had the instinct for survival; I learned joy and pain at the same time. I learned that happiness is not what you have, because I never had anything, and I was so happy. The most treasured time in my life was back when my family and I were all together. I think of evenings when we'd sit around the fire after we'd eaten, and laugh about every little thing. And when the rains began and life was reborn, we celebrated. (Dirie and Miller 2001, 234–35)

Extending this discussion of abuse and voice, Halima Bashir, a medical doctor, tells her personal story of genital mutilation, rape, and war in her homeland, Darfur, Sudan. For her, it is not Islam the religion that is at fault, it is the Muslim Arabs and government officials. In reference to Islam and race, Bashir writes about the violence delivered by these officials. The account Bashir gives of being beaten and eventually gang raped by Sudanese Arab policemen and soldiers relates to the whole idea of silence, of voice and voicelessness:

> I was ordered to sit. The man in charge sat opposite me, while the others took up positions in the corners of the room. Silence again, as the man opposite just stared . . .
>
> It was me who finally broke the silence. "Why . . . Why am I here?"
>
> "SHUT UP! SHUT UP!"
>
> "SILENCE!"
>
> "KEEP YOUR STUPID MOUTH SHUT!"
>
> "NO QUESTIONS!" (Bashir and Lewis 2008, 185)

Then, to enforce the punishment of silence on Bashir, the police force her to *write* her silence:

> "Now, doctor, you have to sign this. This says you will never speak to a newspaper or anyone or anything ever again. You will never speak about anything. *Anything.* And if you disobey, then we will deal with you. You understand? Tell me you understand."
>
> I nodded. "Tell me!" he snarled. "I want to hear it."
>
> "I understand."
>
> He pushed the paper across the desk at me. "Now, sign!"
>
> "SIGN!" (187)

Bashir's sense of justice and rebellion led her to continue helping people as both a doctor and a spokeswoman. Her decision to break the silence, to put the signed document out of her realm of reality, causes further torture and abuse: "'Why did you do this? You signed a declaration. Or did you forget? You signed a declaration to keep quiet. You promised to'" (224). Imprisonment, torture, and gang rape are how the police dealt with Bashir.

Words—spoken and written—are extremely important to Halima Bashir's life. The stories told to her as a child by her elders, the words from the Qur'an and from medical school, the words of protest spoken and printed in newspapers, and finally the words of loss forced on her by her rapists, are the components of her mind and spirit. Eventually, fittingly, it is also words that help her break the feared, oppressive silence when her husband and she decide it is time to speak out for the victims of Darfur.

Mende Nazer, a Nuba woman from southern Sudan, epitomizes the silenced African Muslim woman. Of the women discussed in this essay, none of them were as voiceless as Nazer. Historically, Nazer's life story not only crosses but also challenges the very concepts of cultural and chronological boundaries. Nazer was a slave in both Africa and Europe. In the following paragraph she tells the reader the fear that comes with gaining freedom, gaining a voice, or at least a limited voice: "I was captured when I was still a child. I spent my teenage years and my early adulthood in slavery. For all that time I had no freedom. I was a non-person" (Nazer and Lewis 2003, 311).

As another form of torture and enslavement, Nazer experienced the loss of family. Finally, with the help of Damien Lewis in London, Nazer was able to contact her family in Sudan. This is when she finds that they too have been victimized by the Arab Muslim raiders and government officials. The idea, of course, was to destroy Mende Nazer's family ties and make the destruction look like the work of the Westerners and Christians, not the real culprits: "They were told that I was in England and that I had been kidnapped and sold to Christian extremists. They were told that I had been converted from Islam to Christianity and that I was in grave danger. They were told that my name had been changed from Mende to Caroline, a good Christian name" (317). Mende Nazer has been able to contribute not only to women's rights issues but to human rights issues as well. Furthermore, her work with antislavery campaigns and human rights groups in England has contributed to her new sense of self. However, with this new self, questions of identity and position arise. Interestingly, unlike the perspective of Ayaan Hirsi Ali, Islam is not seen as an obstacle. In fact, Nazer sees Islam as a supportive guiding light in her new world. Islam is Allah's word, not man's word, and it is Allah that offers a future:

> My dream is to take my parents on the Haj, the great pilgrimage to Mecca, in Saudi Arabia, Islam's holiest shrine. It is the duty of all Muslims wherever possible to make the Haj once in their lifetime, and I

> should like to enable my father and mother to do so. But I will have to be patient. And patience is a virtue I learned to possess in abundance when I spent all those years in slavery. Patience that I would escape, that I would take hold of my life again and that I would be free. Patience that I would see my family again one day. And, *Insha'Allah,* I will. A few of my new friends here in London have recently had children, and I am also dreaming about finding a partner and settling down to have a family. For me, that would be one way to rebuild the sense of family, identity and security that my years in slavery and exile have taken from me. (334)

In "Origins," the introduction to the feminist essays in *Interpreting Women's Lives: Feminist Theory and Personal Narratives,* the editors write: "The recovery and interpretation of women's lives have been central concerns of feminist scholarship from the earliest pioneering works to the present. Listening to women's voices, studying women's writings, and learning from women's experiences have been crucial to the feminist reconstruction of our understanding of the world" (1989, 4). The editors go on to explain the importance of experience and construction in the following way:

> These personal narratives illuminate the course of a life over time and allow for its interpretation in its historical and cultural context. The very act of giving form to a whole life—or a considerable portion of it—requires, at least implicitly, considering the meaning of the individual and social dynamics which seem to have been most significant in shaping the life. The act of constructing a life narrative forces the author to move from accounts of discrete experiences to an account of why and how the life took the shape it did. (Barbre et al. 1989, 4)

Elizabeth Fox-Genovese, in her discussion of African American women's writings, strikes on an important point that applies to the construction of the life narratives of the five women in these African Muslim women's texts. Although Fox-Genovese delves more into the historical aspect of African American life, such as slavery and Jim Crow, the essence of African American and African Muslim life is quite similar. The confinement of body and mind and the release from, the freedom from, that confinement finds itself in the words spoken and written by these women. "The autobiographies of Afro-American women have been written from within the cage. Frequently they sing with the voice of freedom, but always they betray the confinement from which that freedom is wrested . . . The self, in other words, develops in opposition to, rather than as an articulation of, condition. Yet the condition remains as that against which the self is forged" (Fox-Genovese 1988, 64). The condition in the present cases is the fusion of African traditional societies, specifically male-dominated societies, and Muslim societies dominated by the male interpreters of the Qur'an. As for Dirie, Nazer, Ali, and Bashir, they are products of a different time, the present. Interestingly, these four women find their freedom in the same way as the African American women, Zora Neale Hurston and Linda Brent, that Fox-Genovese writes about: they write themselves *into* freedom. Their autobiographies or life narratives articulate the conditions that in turn create the self, both individual and collective.

Another point that Fox-Genovese makes concerning African American women and their writing also applies directly to African Muslim women: "Autobiographies of black women, each of which is necessarily personal and unique, constitute a running commentary on the collective experience of black women in the United States. They are inescapably grounded in the experience of slavery and the literary tradition of the slave narratives" (1988, 65). African Muslim women in Africa are similar in that they are grounded in a literary tradition that embraces and fosters submission in the forms of African societal traditions, Islamic doctrine, and colonialism. In this sense, the slave narratives mentioned by Fox-Genovese become the autobiographies and autobiographical novels of Africans from around the continent. The struggle for selfhood is a key objective in African literature, a selfhood not unlike that desired in the slave narratives.

Fox-Genovese writes: "The myth or metaphor of the journey to selfhood is as old as culture, although it has carried a special resonance for Western Christian, notably Protestant, culture" (1988, 77). This statement recognizes the importance of "the journey to selfhood" not just for African American women but also for African Muslim women who must engage a society existing in, or on the verge of, war. The war is directly connected to their faith, Islam, which Fox-Genovese cannot claim in her comment on the role of Christianity or Protestantism. In this sense, Fox-Genovese opens the door for African Muslim women in much the same way she has for African American women, past, present, and future. Instead of "myth or metaphor of the journey," one should perhaps view these autobiographies as the "myth *and* metaphor of the journey." It is myth in the sense of the Jungian night-sea journey, that same myth Joseph Campbell writes about in *The Hero with a Thousand Faces,* the monomyth. This myth, the same as those in the Bible and the Qur'an, is what drives the participant forward. The metaphor *is* journey as selfhood.

8

Rebellion as a Narrative Strategy in Southern African Women's Writing

KANCHANA UGBABE

Feminist frameworks have in the process of redefining art provided new perspectives to situate women's writing. Gender, it has been established, is a fundamental category in literary analysis. The complex relationship between art and cultures goes back to Virginia Woolf's contextual theory of art as being attached to life (as in the case of the spider web) even if ever so lightly. Estella Lauter stresses the fact that "art is not 'objective' either in its production or reception" (1993, 28). Using the paintings of Frida Kahlo as an example in which the artist seeks to explore her pain and torment through visual symbols, Lauter concludes that rather than transcend everyday emotions of anger, frustration, and grief, women see art as the site for revealing them (29).

Women have a long tradition of rebellion and activism since the days of the suffrage movements at the turn of the nineteenth and twentieth centuries. Street protests, rallies, marches, and sit-ins have been part of their resistance strategies, their defiance against cultural oppression and social domination. In Southern Africa, the antiapartheid movement saw active participation on the part of women. In Nigeria, women participated in protest movements aimed at resisting the policies of the colonial government. Male writers' revolt against Westernization and against tradition has been amply documented in African literature.

Rebellion and protest have been used as instruments of self-definition in women's writing, both overtly and covertly. In North America, Europe, and Africa women's writing voices rebellion in numerous ways. The woman writer situates her discourse in a culture of resistance, appropriating genres that have conventionally been male domain, thus widening the angle of vision to embrace oppression in a variety of contexts—race, color, gender, and tradition. Rebellion comes at what may be called the edge of the precipice, the back against the wall, when the character, instead of a given set of expectations, resists the conventions of patriarchy and soars into the unknown. Alice Walker's Celie in *The Color Purple* is emancipated through rebellion, which offers her a new lease on life: "I'm pore, I'm black, I may be ugly and can't cook . . . But I'm here" (1982, 207). The novel itself can be read as a protest against the mistreatment of African American women in culture and society. It is the sisterhood between women that brings about change.

The novel as an embodiment of rebellion, or what may be called "protest literature," is a genre common to men and women writers. The writer in this context sets out with an agenda to draw attention to injustices or inequalities in society. The novels that deal with the Niger Delta (in Nigeria) and the rape of the environment by multinational companies are such protest novels.

Rebellion and protest in women's writing may be voiced through direct and confrontational modes or subtle means, a violent explosion of anger and resentment or an impenetrable muteness and silence. Alice Walker also maintains that women's silence may be intentional: "When women find their voices they know when to use it and when not to." Zora Neale Hurston's female hero defies tradition and convention in a powerful and eloquent way. Rebellion in Janice Crawford, the protagonist of *Their Eyes Were Watching God*, comes at the end of a series of dehumanizing thrusts that strike her to the core. Rebellion becomes a process that turns out to be a quest for identity—the pot of gold is not always to be found at the end of the rainbow, but the character, rather than being broken or crushed, transcends her limitations and attains self-definition. The communal voice is not supportive and is often a voice of censure.

"Pen and paper for women have transformed what otherwise might have been a sentence of solitary confinement," says Dale Spender (1989, 7). Over the centuries, women have overcome their sense of isolation and desolation by writing, sometimes diaries and journals, at other times fiction and poetry. Even if the writing is not published, or is published under a pseudonym, it provides a forum for the author to voice her fears and frustrations, to be in control of her characters and actions without inhibition or condemnation. "Words" and "books" have been women's weapons in the battle of the sexes. Mariama Ba said in a 1980 interview: "We cannot go forward without culture, without saying what we believe, without communicating with others, without making people think about things. Books are a weapon, a peaceful weapon, perhaps, but they are a weapon" (quoted in Makuchi and Abbenyi 1997, 148). The battle of the sexes in Europe during the modernist period was also fought with the pen as a metaphoric pistol, and with words as weapons claiming territory and authority. Sandra M. Gilbert and Susan Gubar trace men's and women's exchanges in the war of the words and the resulting gains for the woman writer in the twentieth century in the definitive study *No Man's Land* (1987).

Rebellion as a narrative strategy has enabled women writers to reconceptualize the bildungsroman and profoundly alter our vision of gendered reality. Individual narrative texts are organized from a feminine/feminist perspective using psychological, social, and aesthetic structures in innovative ways. Authorial strategies include the characterization of women as growing, changing, and developing in the female bildungsroman. It is a narrative strategy, among others, that is subversive of dominant patriarchy. Nnadozie Inyama draws our attention to the rebellious woman in Ama Ata Aidoo's *Anowa* and Efua Sutherland's "New Life at Kyerefaso" (Inyama 1992, 116). Society is ambiguous in its attitude to the woman who flagrantly violates accepted norms of behavior. She may meet with hardship, ostracism, or even death. Occasionally, she finds fulfillment in her new life. Inyama reiterates that the "the imposition of restricting codes on the life of the woman is ultimately to the detriment of society, since the woman's illuminating insights may be thus obscured. But when this freedom and insights are unfettered, the result could be a regeneration of an entire group" (120).

The feminine text besides being subversive in its narrative point of view undermines and demystifies patriarchal ideologies. The writer ventures into uncharted territories with a newness of vision and a zeal to tell a story. She is a metaphoric exile looking from the outside and trying to make sense of an inside world. The process of writing itself is an act of liberation, a rescripting of life and history. This is the impetus behind Flora Nwapa's *One Is Enough* and Buchi Emecheta's autobiographical text *Head above Water*, both feminine texts that transmute anger and frustration into structures of empowerment. Sometimes silence is used in women's texts as a form of rebellion, a conspiracy, a coded discourse that speaks more profoundly than words. Teresa de Lauretis, the feminist critic, comments that "strategies of writing and of reading are forms of cultural resistance" (1984, 7).

Women in Southern Africa have had to contend with imperialism and apartheid in addition to sexism and marginalization. Critics have pointed out the duality of oppression or the "double yoke" that women writers have had to contend with in the process of finding their voice. The works of Bessie Head (South Africa, Botswana) and Tsitsi Dangarembga (Zimbabwe) provide fresh perspectives on rebellion, protest, and the culture of resistance. Caught between boundaries, a nomad of sorts and a product of two societies, Bessie Head returns repeatedly to the state of exile in her novels. If Bessie Head were to write in the latter part of the twentieth century, perhaps her perceptions would have been altered. A post-apartheid society and one where being an exile is closer to the norm would have produced different types of texts. But writing as she does in the 1970s, it is the feeling of being dispossessed that is predominant. In *A Question of Power, When Rain Clouds Gather, A Collector of Treasures, Maru*, and *Serowe: Village of the Rain Wind*, she indeed draws a parallel between tribal and racial oppression and the subordination and brutalization of women by men. The title *A Question of Power* may suggest emotional outbursts of volcanic proportion but it is the author imbued with the spirit of Buddhism and Ghandian nonviolence that one encounters in the text. "Her women are invariably thrust into a hostile landscape from which they must grow and realize their identity (Ola 1986, 46).

This identity quest is carried out sometimes through quiet defiance, as one sees in Margaret Cadmore, a victim of sexism and racism in *Maru*. Galethebege in the short story "Heaven Is Not Closed" (*The Collector of Treasures*) is a strong and determined character whose rebellion is attitudinal: "He could see the protest on her face. She wanted to be married in Church according to Christian custom" (Head 1992, 9). She makes the sacrifice of marrying according to Setswana custom but on her own terms. Even her compromise is full of protest. "What you mean, Raloke, she said firmly, is that I must choose you over my life with the Church. I have a great love in my heart for you so I choose you" (11). But it is obvious that in the privacy of her heart Galethebege never forsook the Christian God that she worshipped. Heaven is closed to the unbeliever, according to the hypocritical missionary, but not to her.

Johanna in "Jacob: The Story of a Faith-Healing Priest" (*The Collector of Treasures*) is proud without being haughty and resists the condemnation of her extended family and the village gossip with her calm defiance: "I agree with all that has been said about me, she said, but I am a real woman and as the saying goes, the children of a real woman do not get lean or die." (Head 1992, 30). Her self-assurance earns her a home and the love and respect of Jacob.

The character Life, in the short story of that name, exemplifies a woman's strident assertiveness that breaks age-old taboos in society. Life's quest for identity takes her beyond the boundaries of social acceptance. Her philosophy of life is "live fast, die young, and have a good-looking corpse" (Head 1992, 40). Her violent death comes on the heels of her adulterous pursuits. In "The Collector of Treasures," Dikeledi, the woman "whose thatch does not leak" (Head 1992, 90), is violated by her husband, resulting in her gruesome murder of the man. Dikeledi's rebellion is not sanctioned by society as she serves out a jail term. More a victim of circumstances, she seeks refuge in friendships, "deep loves," which are the real treasures she collects.

Women in Bessie Head's writings are also lonely and uncertain of themselves; there is an incapacity to rebel against oppressive patriarchal forces at work in society. Head says in one of the essays: "If I were a fish in the stream, who knows, I might resist the current. I might try some way of evading, of disentangling myself from the pushing forces of the current. But I am only some of the water and move forward helplessly. Where all the water goes I must go (Head 1995, 128)." It is the same passiveness (powerlessness, vulnerability) that we see in the young woman called Mouse in *The Cardinals*. She works as a reporter for the newspaper *African Beat* and writes good stories. But it is her self-effacing nature and an inability to protest that prompts Johnny to ask, "What makes you conceal this aliveness behind a mask of death?" (Head 1995, 37). Women, however, are not all quiet defiance and self-abnegation. In "The Collector of Treasures," Dikeledi, who is deserted by her abusive husband and is subjected to further abuse upon his return, murders him.

Miriam Tlali, the first woman novelist to emerge from Soweto, is concerned in her novel *Amandla* and her short story "Point of No Return" with the realities of the racial situation in the explosive apartheid years. *Amandla* revolves around the events surrounding the Soweto uprising of 1976. Men and women are seething volcanoes, combative and confrontational in their rebellion but powerless in a society that treats them as less than human. Tlali's commitment to the women's cause and her consistent resistance to patriarchy find a prominent place in her writings. In *Mihloti* (1984) and *Footprints in the Quad* (1989), she writes about the sexual abuse of women, the subjugation of women in traditional practices and under apartheid, and women's struggle to take charge of their lives.

Tsitsi Dangarembga's engaging novel *Nervous Conditions,* set in the 1950s in rural and colonial Rhodesia, deals with the growing up and coming of age of fourteen-year-old Tambudzai, and is perhaps also a parable of the author's literary awakening. It is a novel about the passage of time and the process of growth rather than destination. Written in the first-person, the narrator-author is extremely sensitive to cultural configurations and assumes the rebellious posture of an adolescent on the threshold of womanhood. Rebellion and resistance work on several levels in the text, not the least of which is Tambudzai's desperate attempts to get a decent education in an environment that favors education for boys but not for girls. Her father's admonitions are prompted by his practical concerns: "Can you cook books and feed them to your husband? Stay at home with your mother. Learn to cook and clean. Grow vegetables" (Dangarembga 1988, 15). Her father and Nhamo, her brother, are preparing to travel to meet and bring home Babamukuru, the uncle returning from Britain. Tambudzai is all eyes and ears, but to her disappointment is once again put in her "proper place":

> My father called me aside to implore me to curb my unnatural inclinations: it was natural for me to stay at home and prepare for the homecoming.
>
> . . . I set about pleasing myself, which antagonized him even further. He did not like to see me over-absorbed in intellectual pursuits. (33)

Tambudzai complains again: "He thought I was emulating my brother, that the things I read would fill my mind with impractical ideas, making me quite useless for the real tasks of feminine living" (34). Naturally given to "excesses and flights of fancy," Tambudzai, like the female writer, is isolated from an intellectual milieu. Resistance for her is survival and a chance to harness her imagination and reinvent the world. Tambudzai feels "needed" in the camaraderie of the kitchen, making sadza in large drums. Her confidence receives a boost as the women praise her for her culinary skills. "Exclusion held horrors for me at that time because it suggested superfluity," says Tambudzai. "Exclusion whispered that my existence was not necessary, making me no more than an unfortunate by-product of some inexorable natural process" (39–40). Nyasha, on the other hand, is entirely self-assured and confident, seeking no reinforcement from anyone outside of herself. Tambudzai's rebellion expresses itself in her determination to go to school like her brother. She grows mealie meal and sells it to raise the money for her school fees. Later she is given a chance to leave the homestead and move to the mission compound where Babamukuru lives with his family. Her high school education is taken care of by her uncle, her liberation being the first of many that followed this transition.

No less practical and earthy, Tambudzai's mother advises her adolescent daughter with the traditional wisdom of one who has been there before:

> This business of womanhood is a heavy burden, she said. How could it not be? Aren't we the ones who bear children? When it is like that you can't just decide today I want to do this, tomorrow I want to do that, the next day I want to be educated! When there are sacrifices to be made, you are the one who has to make them. And these things are not easy; you have to start learning them early, from a very early age. The earlier the better so that it is easy later on. Easy! As if it is ever easy. And these days

> it is worse, with the poverty of blackness on one side and the weight of womanhood on the other. Aiwa! What will help you my child, is to learn to carry your burden with strength. (16)

Tambudzai flees the homestead where, if she remains, she would become yet another beast of burden, and opts for the enlightenment that education brings. With wide-eyed excitement she savors the newness of the world she migrates to—the world of the mission compound. Education, it is evident, enables the woman to rebel against superstition and against society's gender constructs.

Pauline Ada Uwakwe comments on the witty and ironic perspective of the narrator, Tambudzai, whose perspective is "necessary for our appreciation of the new insights she acquires about her experience as female in a patriarchal and colonial society" (1995, 75–84). Throughout the book *Nervous Conditions* it is evident that boys and men have a contribution to make in trivial and important matters. They shape their own destinies and decide those of the women in their lives. They represent power and authority. The needs of women on the contrary are incidental and not regarded as a priority. Nhamo and Chido from a very young age receive preferential treatment. Women and girls are expected to make sacrifices. This leads to rebellion from the women on all fronts—some like Lydia and Nyasha are volatile and refuse to be put down. Others like Maiguru and Tambudzai are subdued and sacrificial until they can take it no more. Uwakwe suggests three categories of women characters in the novel, namely, "the entrapped females" (Tambu's mother and aunt Maiguru), "the escaped females" (Tambu and Lucia), and "the rebellious females" (Nyasha).

Tambudzai's mother is "silently ferocious"; poverty and suffering have turned her into a cynical and bitter woman. Her nineteen years of marriage have been a litany of betrayal and suffering. She feels constantly done in, even by Babamukuru and Maiguru, who try to give her children a head start and thereby lift her out of her wretched state. She describes her daughter Tambu as "willful and headstrong" (24).

Katharine Frank sees the New Woman in Africa as wavering "helplessly between her allegiance to her culture—her African identity—and her aspiration for freedom and self-fulfilment" (1987, 17). These female protagonists in novels written by women are in a transitional phase between cultural affiliation and modernity, which comes with freedom of choice and empowerment. Tambudzai's father does not believe in women's education or enlightenment. The by-product of these patriarchal and societal attitudes is one of exclusion. Tambudzai is torn between guilt and a determination to succeed when she is taken to the mission compound. Rather than feel grief at her brother's death, she silently rejoices at the opportunity for education it has given her. She feels guilty that she is not sufficiently grateful to Babamukuru for his generosity toward her and her family. Her final act of rebellion comes when on the day of her parents' wedding (a comedy, as she describes it), she categorically refuses to be part of it and feigns illness. She wished to scream and create a scene, but "my reverence for my uncle . . . had stunted the growth of my criticism," she says (Dangarembga 1988, 164). From there the rebellion takes her one step further—her quiet and firm decision to accept the admission and scholarship to the Young Ladies College of the Sacred Heart. Tambudzai is mentally and materially emancipated. As a punishment for defying Babamukuru's authority, she is given fifteen lashes and asked to take the place of Anna the housemaid for two weeks.

Nyasha's rebellion in the novel is directly related to her cross-cultural upbringing. Raised in England and transported to colonial Rhodesia, Nyasha refuses to submit to the authority of her parents. She is intelligent, boisterous, reads *Lady Chatterley's Lover*, smokes, and stays out late with friends. Nyasha is sensitive to the way Shona women are treated in her society as opposed to the rights and privileges enjoyed by Western women. She has no strong affiliations with her own culture and tradition. Nothing anchors her to her society. She is aware that her father is disappointed in her. She even tries to see things from her father's perspective while being conscious of the fact that nobody makes the effort to understand her. She becomes a victim, unreasonably, of the female condition when her father calls her a "whore." Not only does Nyasha hit out (literally punch her father in the eye), but she retreats into depression as well and becomes bulimic. Tambudzai's comment is appropriate: "But what I didn't like was the way all the conflicts came back to this question of femaleness. Femaleness as opposed to, and inferior to maleness" (116).

Maiguru's rebellion comes as a surprise to the readers and the characters in the novel. Maiguru, a woman with a master's degree, exposure to British culture, and a good salary, submits entirely to the wishes of her husband and the unending demands of his extended family. She is courageous, accommodating, and deferential as a wife, mother, and woman. But deep inside her is a festering sore, which is related to being a voiceless female in a male-dominated society. Maiguru's outburst is accompanied by a decisive act. She leaves her home and goes to live with her brother until she is brought back by Babamukuru after five days. "I am tired of my house being a hotel for your family," she declares, "I am tired of being a housekeeper for them I am tired of being nothing in a home . . . I have had enough!" (172).

Finally, Lydia also rebels. She resents the fact that the men gather together and decide her fate while she is not given a chance to defend herself or narrate her own version of events. She barges into the meeting and sets things right. She becomes visible on account of her ability to speak, to rebel, to articulate her grievances in the company of men. Florence Stratton identifies the literary convention of using the "paired women" in fiction by successive generations of female writers (1994, 97). In African American women's writing, it appears as a "sisterhood," a bonding between women as opposed to the isolated individuality of the male character. Janie Crawford and Phoebe feature in Zora Neale Hurston's *Their Eyes Were Watching God*, and Celie and Shug in Alice Walker's *The Color Purple*. The familial or social juxtaposition of two female characters (as friends, cousins, sisters) is also found in Flora Nwapa, Mariama Ba, Tsitsi Dangarembga, Chimamanda Adichie, Chika Unigwe, and Sefi Attah. It is a feature that is peculiar to women's writing and reinforces the connectedness of women and their dependence on one another. The paired women may complement each other, they may be kindred spirits, as Stratton points out, or stand in antithesis to each other.

Tsitsi Dangarembga in *Nervous Conditions* and *The Book of Not* presents the power configurations in society. Men are the custodians of culture and tradition. Women constantly defer to men. Communication is not a two-way process. Yet the women in the novel are not willing slaves. They may seem like victims of male "put downs" but they do not give up without a fight, and sometimes they do not give up at all. Nyasha's reaction to her mother's rebellion sums up the woman's dilemma: "So where do you break out to? You're just one person and it's everywhere. So where do you break out to? So what do you do? I don't know" (Dangarembga 1988, 174).

It is as if the fire of rebellion and resistance had gone out of Tambudzai in the sequel to *Nervous Conditions, The Book of Not.* A victim of circumstances (racism, colonialism, the struggle for independence), Tambudzai becomes bitter and cynical, more like her mother, who sees a negative outcome to every situation. As one of the few black girls in the prestigious and predominantly white Young Ladies' College of the Sacred Heart, Tambudzai sets out to prove to the world and to her family that she could excel. However, it is evident that her star is on the wane. She gets the best O-Level results in the school but the trophy goes to the white girl, Tracey. Sister Emmanuel's comment on the report card reads: "Tambudzai has a complex . . . Constantly she wears a supercilious expression" (Dangarembga 2006, 89). The message is that if she was not "happy" in the school, she could be taken elsewhere. The same message is given to Tambudzai by Mrs. May, the matron at Twiss Hostel: "If you're that unhappy here . . . I'm sure you could find somewhere else that suits you" (243–44). She meekly and sacrificially accepts her lot that her battle with Sacred Heart was on the "scale of struggle similar to David and Goliath," that her dreams were smothered in rubble and ruin (163).

Babamukuru is suitably disappointed with her A-Level results. She graduates from university with a low-class degree in sociology and gets a job as a copywriter in an advertising company. Her small measure of success in the company has a lot to do with her love of words:

> Words—you could do so much with words. You could maul them and twist them and tear them, but if you did they would not dance. Yet words were forgiving. You grappled with them and sweated and when you were tired became gentle, and the words leaped for you, streaked with healing powers from depths, as it is said of dolphins. So I loved words . . . how I could make the language leap and spin and dance, how like a soul in and out and round and round in rhythm I could twist it! (220–21)

Even in the "lowly" profession of copywriting, Tambudzai felt she had achieved some success and was going to be rewarded for it. But her confidence in herself was short-lived, as her success is stolen from her by her colleague, Dick Lawson. Rather than break out in a rage (as she might have previously done), Tambudzai resigns from the company, giving the false excuse that she was about to be married. All along she ponders the existential question of *unhu*. In the end it seems to be the supreme virtue of tolerance bordering on martyrdom (unhu) that gives her the feeling of being a complete woman. The strength and determination seen in the character Tambudzai in the earlier novel are sadly absent in the latter.

It is evident from women's art and writing, both within and outside of Africa, that rebellion does not come easy and is not without consequences. Where a woman character is not given the chance to rebel or voice her anger and frustration, she becomes a victim figure. Charlotte Perkins Gilman's protagonist in "The Yellow Wallpaper" gradually descends into insanity. Her creativity is suppressed and it seeks release in acute neurosis. Burdened with guilt (as in the case of Gilman's protagonist), women suppress and distort what they are unable to express freely. They fear deeply the consequences of telling the truth, which may be patriarchal disapproval, exile, imprisonment, or even death. Kate Chopin's protagonist in *The Awakening* has to bear the consequences of nonconformity and rebellion—suicide. In "The Story of an Hour" Chopin's protagonist "mourns" for the "death" of her husband while being aware of the freedom from repression his apparent death has brought her. Her outer self conforms while her inner self rebels, a condition and a conflict she is unable to live with for long. She dies quite suddenly—"of joy that kills," as the doctor's diagnosis puts it. Death seems to be the only way for the author (and the character) to deal with the conflict between the outer and inner lives. Marianne Hirsch draws our attention to the fact that in fiction of this nature, the plot traces a circular path rather than a linear development. "Faced with the break between psychological needs and social imperatives, literary convention finds only one possible resolution: the heroine's death" (1983, 26, 27).

Gendered spaces have never been so avidly contested before as in the twilight years of the twentieth century and the first decade of the twenty-first century. Women are on the cusp of change in both the Western world and in Africa. Women's roles are being rehabilitated in literature as women's position in society becomes multifaceted, and women move from the margins to the center. Zaynab Alkali, Buchi Emecheta, Ama Ata Aidoo, and the writers of the 1990s emphasized the importance of education for women. This is beginning to yield results as the current crop of African women writers write as "professionals" rather than as "women." The gender-related hierarchies, particularly with reference to women's education (as seen in Tsitsi Dangarembga's novels), are less and less evident in urban African societies. Even when women are "behind the veil," literally or metaphorically, they use the veil as an instrument of subversion. There is a combination of restraint and daring in Zaynab Alkali's women characters. Women's education is not an issue to be debated in the twentieth century. Chimamanda Adichie's women characters in *Half of a Yellow Sun* are academics: Ifemelu in *Americanah* has a fellowship at Princeton;, Bolanle in Lola Shoneyin's *The Secret Lives of Baba Segi's Wives* is a graduate, and Sefi Attah's protagonist in *A Bit of Difference* is a professional woman who works for an NGO. They are all assertive women who take charge of their lives.

9

Rewriting Human Rights

Gender, Violence, and Freedom in the Fiction of Chimamanda Ngozi Adichie

HEATHER HEWETT

Human rights activists and scholars have frequently voiced disappointment in the failure of the human rights community to prevent, address, and redress violations on the African continent. Others have raised questions about the validity of human rights ideals as they are currently defined and deployed by international governmental and nongovernmental organizations. For example, scholars such as Makau Mutua fault human rights frameworks for limitations ranging from an "unrelenting focus on individualism" to their failure to "address economic powerlessness and the scandalous international order," arguing that their Eurocentric origins and ideological alliance with a "free market vision of political democracy" have prevented human rights from being useful to postcolonial African states (2008, 34, 35, 31). In response, other scholars point out that many African states have participated in the human rights legislative process, authoring human rights declarations and conventions such as the African Charter on Human and Peoples' Rights. As the scholar Fareda Banda observes, the founding documents of organizations such as the African Union suggest that a human rights ideology "appears to have been voluntarily embraced by African states" (2005, 3).

The author wishes to thank the Rutgers Institute for Research on Women for the opportunity to participate in its 2008–9 seminar "The Culture of Rights/The Rights of Culture," which provided much of the groundwork for this article.

The topic of human rights becomes even more complex when we consider the images and stories about Africa disseminated globally by the news media, particularly in the United States and Europe. While Africa has experienced more than its fair share of human rights violations, it has also witnessed more than its fair share of news stories focusing on human rights atrocities and humanitarian crises, often to the exclusion of any other news. The writer Binyavanga Wainaina shows the irony of these stories and their accompanying stereotypes in his article "How to Write about Africa":

> Among your characters you must always include The Starving African, who wanders the refugee camp nearly naked, and waits for the benevolence of the West. Her children have flies on their eyelids and pot bellies, and her breasts are flat and empty. She must look utterly helpless. She can have no past, no history; such diversions ruin the dramatic moment. Moans are good. She must never say anything about herself in the dialogue except to speak of her (unspeakable) suffering. (2005, 93)

Wainaina's description suggests how images of passive and suffering Africans are frequently gendered: The Starving African is a mother, a homeless and historyless refugee who is unable to care for her children without outside help. Centuries-old narratives about "saving" Africa inform this particular image, which, in turn, performs the cultural work of "proving" the need for such missionary impulses and the need for benevolent Westerners—thus constructing the binary of voiceless victim and the humanitarian savior. This binary informs many narratives about Africa, including, Mutua argues, human rights. Indeed, Mutua indicts human rights discourse itself for its dependence on Western missionary ideologies, arguing that the "grand narrative of human rights" is marked by the "damning metaphor" of the "savages-victims-saviors" triad: although the human rights movement originated in response to the atrocities of the Holocaust, its "theoretical underpinnings" can be traced back to Western colonial attitudes that viewed Africans as either savages or victims, and in need of saving by Western saviors (2001, 202, 213).

The Nigerian-born writer Chimamanda Ngozi Adichie has written directly about these Western stereotypes of Africa, pointing out that early twenty-first-century stereotypes of Africa as "sex[y] and hip" presents a "new 'afro-fashion . . . based in part on the stereotype of the poor starving African in need of salvation by the West" (2008, 44). Adichie argues that fiction provides a way to combat "simple stories" about Africa and to present, instead, a complex picture that moves beyond stereotypes (45). As she puts it, "literature is one of the best ways to come closer to the idea of a common humanity, to see that we may be kind and unkind in different ways, but that we are all capable of kindness and unkindness" (46). As a result of giving voice to multiple stories, Adichie's fiction delves deeply into many of the issues and debates surrounding human rights in Nigeria. In stories such as "The American Embassy" and novels such as *Purple Hibiscus* and *Half of a Yellow Sun*, the author critiques the "grand narratives of human rights" by complicating our preconceived notions about who is a savior, a victim, or a perpetrator. These texts simultaneously claim and question human rights ideals as they have been defined and practiced in the twentieth century, performing a kind of ideological human rights work in the realm of the imaginary and the fictional. The resulting critique resonates with the political work of many African feminists, womanists, and women's rights advocates who have sought to redefine and expand human rights ideals and practices to include and address the needs and concerns of all Africans, including women and girls.[1]

Making Visible the Invisible: Gender, the Private Sphere, and Human Rights Regimes

Adichie's critique of human rights begins in her first novel, *Purple Hibiscus* (2003), a young girl's coming-of-age story. Fifteen-year-old Kambili Achike suffers under the domination of her father, Eugene, a successful and dogmatic newspaper publisher who fights against political tyranny and corruption in Nigeria. State-sponsored violence and intimidation provide the backdrop to Kambili's story, as an unnamed Abacha-like dictator seizes power in a military coup and serves as the target for the prodemocracy editorials and reportage of the *Standard*, Eugene's newspaper. Early

1. See Tripp, Casimiro, Kwesiga, and Mungwa 2009; see Banda 2005.

in the narrative, we learn that Eugene has received a human rights award from *Amnesty World*, and his editor publicly thanks him for being "a man of integrity, the bravest man I know" (Adichie 2003 42). Yet the novel charts the distance between his public and private persona, revealing this brave man to be domineering and physically abusive at home. Despite the high walls that protect Kambili's home, these walls do not keep her safe: she is physically abused by her father and suffers from an inability to speak (Hewett 2005, 85–86). Juxtaposing the violence outside and inside her home, the novel exposes the parallels between military rule and Eugene's abusive authoritarianism, rooted in the abuse of the colonial missionaries who educated him.[2] Furthermore, his domestic despotism produces effects similar to that of Nigeria's ruler. Just as the father abuses and silences his daughter, the government terrorizes and finally kills the newspaper editor, Ade Coker.

While Adichie's critique suggests the parallels between domestic violence and state-sponsored violence, it simultaneously reveals how the human rights movement has not always viewed the victims of domestic violence, or violence against women and girls, as part of its agenda. Part of the problem emerges from the fact that human rights instruments and institutions did not originally define or practice "human rights" in a way that considered the "larger socio-economic web that entraps women" (Bunch 1990, 488). As Charlotte Bunch points out, "The narrow definition of human rights, recognized by many in the West as solely a matter of state violation of civil and political liberties, impedes consideration of women's rights" (488). Rather than jettisoning the system of human rights altogether, many feminists and women's rights activists have claimed human rights ideals for women at the same time that they have critiqued the human rights regime for its inattention to gender as well as other intersectional components of identity.[3] Thus many feminists around the world

2. As Andrade points out, *Purple Hibiscus* uses "ironic juxtaposition" to illustrate the parallels between "family repression and national repression": "the public, philanthropic Eugene is very different from Papa, the private, family monster" (2001, 96).

3. For example, see Imam's (2005) exploration of how to claim and critique human rights in service of women's reproductive and sexual rights in Nigeria.

have worked to expand definitions of human rights to consider not only a much broader and interconnected range of economic, cultural, and social rights but also to make visible the range of ways in which women's rights can be denied or violated. As Banda argues in her examination of women and human rights in Africa, "the lives of women are lived out largely in the private sphere, where violations against women are more likely than not to be committed by non-state actors," often in the name of custom or tradition (2005, 43). Indeed, one such domestic violation—violence against women and girls—only became an international agenda item in the 1980s; as Margaret Keck and Kathryn Sikkink document, for much of the twentieth century, violence against women was "on the agenda of neither the women's movement nor international human rights groups" and did not become a priority for these groups until the mid-1990s (1998, 166). In many African states, women's organizations and networks "have spearheaded initiatives to build support for [human rights] treaties and protocols" (Tripp 2009, 7) and have brought global attention to violence against women as an important issue (Banda 2005, 159–206). In a narrative strategy that parallels that of many transnational and African feminists, *Purple Hibiscus* makes visible the invisibility of domestic violence by revealing how a human rights discourse focused solely on the state's abrogation of civil and political rights cannot see or address the full extent and range of violence that entire families can suffer at the hand of an all-powerful patriarch.

Adichie extends her critique of the limitations of human rights discourse in her short story "The American Embassy," first published in *Prism International* in 2002 and subsequently included in the collection *The Thing around Your Neck* (2009d). "The American Embassy" locates a story of personal trauma within a society suffering from the military violence of the Abacha regime: we are introduced to the unnamed protagonist, a woman waiting in a long line outside the embassy for a US visa, while a soldier flogs a man across the street. The story makes clear both the everyday nature of such shocking violence as well as the powerlessness of Nigerian citizens through its description of the casual commentary of the other visa applicants: "'Our people have become too used to pleading with soldiers,'" observes the man standing behind the protagonist (128).

The woman's personal tragedy provides a feminist critique of human rights activism that makes visible the unseen victims of state terrorism, allowing the story to pose questions about the price of prodemocracy work when women and children become the targets of retaliation and revenge. The woman's husband is a prodemocracy journalist at *The New Nigeria*, lauded for his bravery in a manner reminiscent of the praise surrounding Eugene Achike. The day after her husband writes one of his articles for the paper, the "BBC carried the story on the news and interviewed an exiled Nigerian professor of politics who said her husband deserved a Human Rights Award. *He fights repression with the pen, he gives a voice to the voiceless, he makes the world know*" (136). But his wife knows how he allowed his work as a journalist to feed his ego; she understands that his motives are neither selfless nor altruistic. In a flashback, she remembers his behavior after he returns from being interrogated:

> She remembered her husband's expression, that look of the excited messiah, as he talked about the soldier who had given him a cigarette after beating him, all the while stammering in the way he did when he was in high spirits. She had found that stammer endearing years ago; she no longer did. (134)

The phrase "excited messiah" captures his inflated view of himself as a redeemer, thus obliterating any idealized image of a victim of human rights abuse. The protagonist also knows that "fear" and self-preservation led him to flee the country, leaving both her and their child, Ugonna, behind—the child for whom she gave up her own career as a journalist, and who subsequently becomes a victim when soldiers come looking for her husband. When the man standing behind her wishes for more newspaper editors "with that kind of courage," she thinks: "It was not courage, it was simply an exaggerated selfishness" (135).

By narrating these events from the wife's perspective, the story powerfully and unflinchingly examines the unseen victims of human rights activism: a child made vulnerable because of his father's surfeit of self-involvement and lack of foresight; a woman left alone and bereft, traumatized by her own "fail[ure]" to protect her son (133). It pierces the rhetoric of public human rights talk, particularly the valorization of courage and self-sacrifice that can mask and obscure male privilege. Just as soldiers whip civilians with impunity—indeed, just as soldiers kill children, betraying the pleasure of their own power with their "glower" and "swagger" (130)—so too human rights activists can fight against tyranny without full consideration of the consequences and reverberations of their struggles. Those within the private space of domesticity are not protected by international human rights regimes but are, instead, rendered vulnerable to state-sponsored violence and its psychological effects. Ugonna's story will never appear in the newspaper; the depth of his mother's own trauma will never be recognized; and more likely than not, neither will be connected with the activism of her husband. Their lives contain unspoken truths and agonizing realities beyond the orbit of official human rights discourse: "She had the urge to ask the visa interviewer if the stories in *The New Nigeria* were worth the life of a child. But she didn't" (139).

In refusing to speak about these matters to the visa interviewer, Ugonna's mother chooses to keep her own story private, outside of the official diplomatic discourse governing amnesty applications. This official discourse requires applicants to perform a particular identity for diplomats, translated to her by the other applicants in line as well as her friends who have been helping her: "Make Ugonna real. Cry, but don't cry too much" (133). She refuses to perform her own mourning for a stranger or to tell the story that is expected of her; but unlike the narrator in *Purple Hibiscus*, her silence signals resistance and agency, not powerlessness. With this silence, the story indicts the mechanisms of an international system set up to help victims of human rights violations—victims who must provide "evidence" of their suitability for political asylum to diplomats seemingly unaware that military violence regularly takes place across the street from their own embassy (139). Ultimately Ugonna's mother rejects this system entirely by refusing to "hawk" her son's story in exchange for her own safety (138). If she has somehow failed him as a mother, she refuses to leave Nigeria as her husband did.

Taken together, both *Purple Hibiscus* and "The American Embassy" expose the failings of human rights ideals when they participate in, and reproduce, larger systems of gendered inequity. They reveal that the focus of human rights regimes—the abuse of civil and political rights—does not address all forms of violence. Put another way, these stories explore how human rights discourse can participate in the illusion that the private space of domesticity provides a safe haven from the violence of a patriarchal and militaristic state; on the contrary, the brutal acts that can take place behind closed doors not only terrorize but also destroy. Furthermore, each narrative's use of imagery suggests an understanding of the depth of this destruction in ways that resonate with Elaine Scarry's understanding of the "dissolution" of a prisoner's world during torture (Adichie 2009d, 38). For example, in "The American Embassy," the protagonist cannot understand the blood on her son's body, initially misinterpreting it as cooking oil: "the splash on his chest so red she wanted to scold him about playing with the palm oil in the kitchen" (Adichie 2009a, 128). In this moment of violence, which ends her son's life and destroys her own illusions—that she can protect her son, and that they are safe at home—she mistakes the evidence of his death as an everyday ingredient of cooking and nourishment. Her confusion signals the way her life has been undone; one wonders whether she will ever see palm oil in the same way again. Conversely, in *Purple Hibiscus*, domestic objects become weapons: Eugene uses household objects in his physical abuse of his daughter—his belt, boiling water from a kettle poured into the bathtub—thus converting these everyday objects into objects of torture. As Scarry argues,

> The de-objectifying of the objects, the unmaking of the made, is a process externalizing the way in which the person's pain causes his world to disintegrate; and, at the same time, the disintegration of the world is here, in the most literal way possible, made painful, made the direct cause of the pain. That is, in the conversion of a refrigerator into a bludgeon, the refrigerator disappears; its disappearance objectifies the disappearance of the world (sky, country, bench) experienced by a person in great pain; and it is the very fact of its disappearance, its transition from a refrigerator into a bludgeon, that inflicts the pain. (1985, 41)

Indeed, Eugene's abuse of Kambili destroys her ability to speak, in the way that Scarry understands the "world-destroying" power of torture to obliterate the "created world of thought and feeling" that "gives rise to and is in turn made possible by language" (Adichie 2003 30).

At the same time, both stories challenge the missionary rhetoric present in many Western narratives about Africa: that African women are powerless and in need of saving. Both Kambili's and Ugonna's mothers exhibit strength and agency through claiming their own voice (in the case of *Purple Hibiscus*) or rejecting human rights discourse altogether (in the case of "The American Embassy"). However, if both narratives bear witness to stories not normally seen or heard by official human rights regimes, each offers a slightly different perspective. Whereas "The American Embassy" seems to reject human rights regimes completely, *Purple Hibiscus* suggests, if only fleetingly, the possibilities of reclaiming and reconstructing human rights frameworks. This possibility lies in Kambili's self-authorship and claiming of her own voice, thematic trajectories that fundamentally constitute the genre of the bildungsroman.

In making this argument, I draw on Joseph Slaughter's contention in *Human Rights, Inc.* that the bildungsroman "is the novelistic genre that most fully corresponds to—and indeed, is implicitly invoked by—the norms and narrative assumptions that underwrite the vision of free and full human personality development projected in international human rights law" (Slaughter 2007, 40). Historically, the bildungsroman has served as "the predominant formal literary technology in which social outsiders narrate affirmative claims for inclusion in a regime of rights and responsibilities . . . the *Bildungsroman* continues to serve—as Marianne Hirsch and others have recognized—as 'the most salient genre for the literature of social outsiders, primarily women or minority groups'" (Slaughter 2007, 27). Slaughter further observes that while contemporary postcolonial bildungsroman reimagine this literary form, they also perform similar cultural work to their "nineteenth-century European counterparts" in the ways that they "make legible the inequities of an egalitarian imaginary" (39).

In *Purple Hibiscus,* Kambili lays claim to her own "inclusion in a regime of rights and responsibilities" symbolized by the Amnesty World award given to her father. She does this primarily by telling her own story, but the novel suggests a larger frame within which she tells her own story: an African diasporic history of resistance against slavery and oppression. Within the intertextual universe of the novel lie several narratives of struggle, including the story of Jaja of Opobo, the "defiant king" who resisted the British (Adichie 2003 144); mention of "culturally conscious" musicians, including Fela Kuti, the Afrobeat musician and human rights activist (151); the abolitionist autobiography *Equiano's Travels, or the Life of Gustavus Vassa the African*, recommended by her Aunty Ifeoma (143); and finally, Chinua Achebe's novel *Things Fall Apart*, which chronicles the struggle of its Igbo characters against Christianity and colonialism and which *Purple Hibiscus* revises and rewrites in multiple ways (Hewett 2005, 79). This intertextual universe locates Kambili's own struggle for human rights—for a voice and a self, for physical safety from abuse, for her brother's release from prison at the end—within an African diasporic tradition of resistance. Thus *Purple Hibiscus*, like Adichie's subsequent novel *Half of a Yellow Sun*, makes the case for an expanded human rights framework situated within a long history of African and African diasporic political and social justice struggles.

Narrating Biafra: The Limitations of Human Rights in *Half of a Yellow Sun*

Adichie continues this examination of human rights in *Half of a Yellow Sun* (2006), an expansive historical novel that revisits the Biafran secession from Nigeria, the massacres and violence leading up to it, and the human tragedy and massive fatalities of the Nigeria-Biafra War of 1967–70. The novel positions the calamity of this war within Nigeria's colonial past and, as Susan Strehle argues, the "inevitable failure of the nation created by British colonialism and grounded in the Western myth of the nation as a single family of those born (*natio*) to a homogenous clan" (2011, 652). Building on Strehle's argument that the novel articulates a "broad interrogation of nationalism" itself, I suggest that the novel's exploration of war and human rights abuses suggests further shortcomings of international human rights discourses tied to national identity and citizenship.

Adichie has called her novel a "love story" as well as a "war story" because of its focus on the lives of individual characters and "what it means to be human" (2008, 53, 51). The novel follows the interconnected stories of several main characters: two twin sisters, Olanna and Kainene; a British expatriate, Richard, who is Kainene's lover; and Ugwu, the houseboy of

Olanna's lover Odenigbo, a professor. Elements of the novel suggest other genres as well; for example, Amy Novak identifies *Half of a Yellow Sun* as an example of trauma fiction "because of its focus on the massacre of the Igbo, the ensuing civil war, and the death and starvation of a million or more Nigerians and because of its exploration of the difficulty of recounting and voicing that trauma" (2008, 33). Novak argues that the novel not only explores the traumatic experiences of each of its main characters but also the ravages of postcoloniality: the "traumatic legacy of colonialism" that repeats itself in the "ethnic and political strife" of postindependence Nigeria (234). It also brings attention to the failure of humanitarian ideals to stop the trauma and violence of war.[4]

Novak's insightful analysis of the novel focuses on questions related to speaking about trauma on a global stage as well as the politics surrounding the representation and distortion of traumatic events in the Western media. She points out that it is nearly impossible for Richard to present an alternative view of the war in Biafra when British newspapers insist on reporting about "ancient tribal hatreds" and mistranslate Nigerian pidgin English, or when editors ask for stories about "tribal incantations" and cannibalism (2008, 166, 167). This inability to hear anything other than narratives about Africa as "an indistinguishable, violent, disease-ridden, uncivilized, and unknowable presence in the Western imagination," as Novak puts it, silences counterstories and thwarts Richard's attempts to bear witness to what he sees (40).

The novel juxtaposes these media narratives with the experiences of its Biafran characters, who struggle and starve while the world watches—aptly captured in the title of Richard's unwritten book, "The World Was Silent When We Died." As Novak argues, the eight fragments that comprise pieces of this book, scattered throughout the novel, disrupt the "more conventional narrative flow of the novel as a whole" (2008, 40). Written in the present tense, they describe various moments of the author writing

4. Many critics charge that the food aid sent by Western countries inadvertently prolonged the conflict and resulted in far more suffering and death among Biafrans (see Gourevitch 2010).

"The Book." By the final fragment, we learn that the author is actually Ugwu, not Richard, thus "marking the exit of the Western subject from narrative control" (40). These book fragments thus open up a heteroglossic space within the novel. As Novak writes, "The introduction of these fragments into the narrative economy of Adichie's novel and the shift of speaker from Richard to Ugwu represents a significant disruption of the Western addressee's interpretive privilege" (42). They open up a space that allows the novel to voice an alternative narrative about Nigeria, one focused on Biafra and the tenuous nature of a national identity imposed by England during the colonial era; at independence, the third fragment observes, Nigeria is made up of "a collection of fragments held in a fragile clasp" (Adichie 2005, 155). Taken together, these fragments provide an example of both a "reconstitution of lost subjectivities" and a calling forth of "new narratives of affiliation and belonging" that complicate nationalist narratives about Nigeria (Schaffer and Smith 2004, 32).

Written as exposition and argument instead of narrative, this fragmentary book-within-a-book recounts the story of Biafra within a longer history of British colonialism. The unnamed author begins with evidence of the horrific violence of massacre: a small child's head in a calabash, carried by her mother—a moment that Novak identifies as Olanna's experience of trauma (2008, 46). (The horror of the calabash resides in its transformation from an ordinary domestic object into a repository of death, much like the palm oil in "The American Embassy.") After tracing the history of colonialism and independence, the writer identifies the 1966 massacres as the catalyst for Biafran identity in the fourth fragment: "What mattered was that the massacres frightened and united the Igbo. What mattered was that the massacres made fervent Biafrans of former Nigerians" (Adichie 2006, 205). In the fifth fragment, we are told that the author focuses on the war's human rights violations and the world's response:

> He writes about starvation. Starvation was a Nigerian weapon of war. Starvation broke Biafra and brought Biafra fame and made Biafra last as long as it did. Starvation made the people of the world take notice and sparked protests and demonstrations in London and Moscow and Czechoslovakia . . . Starvation aided the careers of photographers. And

> starvation made the International Red Cross call Biafra its gravest emergency since the Second World War. (Adichie 2006, 237)

The identification of Biafra as a victim of human rights violations (because of the Nigerian blockade of Biafra) and the ensuing humanitarian crisis continues in the seventh fragment, a poem written by the book's author that directly implicates the reader in the silence around Biafra. After mentioning the photos in the "gloss-filled pages of *Life*," the speaker asks the reader: "Did you see? Did you feel sorry briefly,/Then turn round to hold your lover or wife?" (Adichie 2006, 375). These fragments examine the way that Biafra was represented in photographs and probe the impact of these images on readers outside of Nigeria; as Madelaine Hron comments, images from this war provided the first introduction of the world to "the mediatized image of starving children with bloated stomachs, suffering of kwashiorkor" (2008, 44). The fragments suggest that Western viewers responded with a sense of urgency as well as passivity.

As the fragments suggest, the global response to Biafra included humanitarian assistance, mainly provided in the form of an "air bridge" coordinated by NGOs, whereas most of the international community refused to intervene in the war, even when Nigeria used starvation as a "weapon of war"—prohibited by the 1977 protocols to the Geneva Conventions (Gourevitch 2010, 102).[5] Although the book fragments skirt other contested human rights claims (namely, the charge that Biafra represents a forgotten genocide), they create a counterhistory that advances the case of Biafra against Nigeria; as Strehle puts it, Ugwu's book "constitutes an act of resistance against a triumphant Nigerian nation" (2011, 668). As he claims subnational rights, he contests the formation of human rights based on existing nation-states such as Nigeria with their British colonial origins.

This fragmentary book-within-a-book also signals the novel's preoccupation with the act of writing. Each fragment begins with a variation of the same construction: "he recounts" (Adichie 2006, 82), "he discusses" (115), "he writes" (155), "he argues" (204), "he writes" (237), "he writes" (258), "he writes" (375), and finally, "Ugwu writes" (433). Taken together,

5. The United Kingdom supported the Nigerian blockade of Biafra.

they serve as a metatextual meditation on authorship, culminating in the naming of the author, Ugwu—who follows in a long line of writers (as does Adichie herself) who have tackled the difficult and controversial subject of Biafra. Adichie signals this tradition with the epigraph of *Half of a Yellow Sun*, which quotes several lines from Achebe's *Christmas in Biafra and Other Poems*, in addition to an end-of-book list of thirty-one titles that she used in her own "research" (434).

Unlike many of these earlier writers—indeed, unlike the fictionalized Ugwu—Adichie did not live through the massacres or the civil war. As a member of the next generation, her authorship—and her novel—can be described with the concept of "postmemory," in the way that Marianne Hirsch defines it:

> Postmemory describes the relationship that the generation after those who witnessed cultural or collective trauma bears to the experiences of those who came before, experiences that they "remember" only by means of their stories, images, and behaviors among which they grew up. But these experiences were transmitted to them so deeply and affectively as to seem to constitute memories in their own right. Postmemory's connection to the past is thus not actually mediated by recall but by imaginative investment, projection, and creation. (2008, 106–7)

Adichie describes her relationship to Biafra in similar terms: "May we always remember," she writes at the end of the author's note to *Half of a Yellow Sun*, including herself in the "we" of her family who experienced the war and must prevent this history from being forgotten (2006, 435). In "Truth and Lies," she comments on her own compulsion to write about Biafra: "I wanted to write—I had to write—about this period because I grew up in the shadow of Biafra, because I wanted to take ownership of a history that defines me" (2006b). In fact, the "shadow" of Biafra, a still-unresolved experience of trauma, compelled her to write several stories about the war before *Half of a Yellow Sun*.[6] As Hawley argues more broadly about Nigeria:

6. These include a play, *For Love of Biafra*, and three short stories: "That Harmattan Morning" (2002), "Half of a Yellow Sun" (first published in *Literary Potpourri* in 2002), and

> In the Nigerian context, no similar forum [like the Truth and Reconciliation Commission in South Africa] has been found to refashion a nation after the horrors, self-inflicted and nurtured from abroad, that tore the country apart so soon after supposed independence. Contemporary fiction, though, suggests that time, and art, may by default have become the only effective means to digest the poison of the past, and to slowly heal from within the damage that has been done. (2008a, 16)

Hawley compares Adichie's postmemory cultural work to other examples of contemporary fiction that also attempt to forge a coherent narrative about the traumatic past in order to enable healing.

As a member of the post-Biafran generation, Adichie possesses an understanding of this era that comes not only from familial stories but also from the many narratives written about it; her postmemory is thus "mediated," in the way that Hirsch describes mediation, "by broadly available public images and narratives" (2008a, 112). As Adichie explains in her author's note, *Half of a Yellow Sun* is "based" on the events of war but her "intent is to portray my own imaginative truths and not the facts of the war" (2006, 434). In this way, *Half of a Yellow Sun*, like the many other narratives about Biafra, represents an effort to "wage" a "struggle for justice in legal, emotional, and cultural terms" (Goldberg 2007, 26). In other words, the novel participates in the project of (re)writing Nigeria's history, with particular attention to how this history might fit into the larger story of struggles for human rights.

At the same time that the novel rewrites national history, it narrates the story of how Ugwu claims authorship and writes himself into history, suggesting how these two projects are intertwined. Ugwu's story follows the trajectory of a bildungsroman in the way that it charts his individual education and development. Literacy enables Ugwu to refashion himself from an uneducated village boy to a liberated, educated citizen who not only authors himself but also the story of Biafra. This trajectory toward freedom and self-realization through language is underscored by Ugwu's

---

"Ghosts" (first published in *Zoetrope* in 2004 and subsequently included in *The Thing around Your Neck*).

favorite book, *Narrative of the Life of Frederick Douglass*, which he discovers after he is conscripted into the Biafran Army:

> He sat on the floor and read. He finished it in two days and started again, rolling the words round his tongue, memorizing some sentences: *Even if it cost me my life, I was determined to read. Keep the black man away from the books, keep us ignorant, and we would always be his slaves.* (Adichie 2006, 360)

Douglass's *Narrative* forcefully argues for the connection between emancipation, literacy, and the power of the "black man" to tell his own story, and it becomes intertwined with Ugwu's experience of the war, perhaps because it provides a hopeful model for a boy confronted with "the casual cruelty of this new world in which he had no say" (Adichie 2006, 359). Later, when Richard asks Ugwu whether he was "afraid" during the war, he answers "sometimes," but immediately adds, "I found a book at our camp. I was so sad and angry for the writer" (396). Douglass's narrative furthermore provides a template for Ugwu's own literary ambition; he first settles on the title "Narrative of the Life of a Country" for his own book project (424). More than the classic British books he had previously read at Odenigbo's house in Nsukka—*The Mayor of Casterbridge* (126), *The Pickwick Papers* (175)—Douglass's *Narrative* provides Ugwu with a form and a language for claiming liberation and authorship for Biafra as well as himself.

Douglass's narrative also helps to construct an imaginative pan-African horizon that contextualizes and historicizes the many interlocking narratives of *Half of a Yellow Sun*. For example, among the many reading materials at Odenigbo's house are periodicals such as *Drum*, the South African magazine that played a role in the antiapartheid movement, as well as the British *Socialist Review*. Before the war, the poet Okeoma, modeled after Christopher Okigbo, performs his poetry regularly at Odenigbo's house. On these nights, he and other academics discuss a wide range of global issues: decolonization; race, science, anthropology, and the Holocaust; and the civil rights struggle in the United States (51). Ugwu does not understand these discussions at the time, but they suggest the outlines of a larger African diasporic history within which his own personal growth unfolds. As Slaughter argues of postcolonial bildungsroman more generally, "many contemporary postcolonial *Bildungsromane* (like few of their European predecessors) translate . . . scenes of reading to construct literary genealogies that situate readers (both the novel's protagonists and its real readers) in an international imaginary" (2007, 32). These "scenes of reading" both enable the protagonist to participate in a public sphere and produce an "imaginary topography" of an "international literary public sphere" that imagines and prefigures what Slaughter calls a "human rights' imagined inter-nation" (33). In *Half of a Yellow Sun*, this "imaginary topography" and "international literary public sphere" centers on Douglass's *Narrative* and African diasporic struggles for liberation and human rights. By so closely aligning Ugwu's narrative with the Biafran narrative, and comparing both to Douglass's narrative, the novel provides an expansive framework for understanding the specific historical events of Biafra.

At the same time, the novel complicates Ugwu's journey toward self-authorship and self-emancipation. While writing contains the power to heal and liberate—"the more he wrote the less he dreamed" about the "dreary bleakness of bombing hungry people" (398)—it does not heal all traumas. For while Ugwu can write about many of the war's victims, he cannot write about one: the girl he gang raped with other soldiers. This memory, which haunts him, remains unwritten in his own text, much like the "silence" that descends around the character of Kainene at the end (Novak 2008, 46–47). With this unnamed female victim, the novel suggests that Ugwu's own narrative agency depends on another act of violence, another silencing. Ugwu realizes this himself, at the very moment when he begins to consider a new title (ironically, Richard's working title) for his book:

> Later, Ugwu murmured the title to himself: *The World Was Silent When We Died*. It haunted him, filled him with shame. It made him think about that girl in the bar, her pinched face and the hate in her eyes as she lay on her back on the dirty floor. (396)

Thus we circle back to the exclusions and silences contained within human rights discourses: even a book such as Ugwu's, a book that narrates a forgotten and misrepresented history—a book inspired by Frederick Douglass himself—does not give voice to this girl. Ugwu knows this, and he is ashamed. Yet this girl remains outside his narrative, and her silent image haunts her perpetrator's successful claiming of authorship and freedom. The unnamed girl functions in a similar fashion to the unnamed wife and mother in "The American Embassy," reminding us that girls and women also suffer from human rights abuses, sometimes from perpetrators who are fighting for liberation. As the categories of "victim," "perpetrator," and "savior" blur into one another—as they often do in war and conflict—the reader is faced with the messy truths and imperfections of human beings, even as they strive for liberation and freedom.

Part Four

African Literature and Cultural Aesthetics

10

Dialogism, African Poetics, and Contemporary Nigerian Poetry in English

SULE E. EGYA

The basic argument in this article is that contemporary Nigerian poets, that is, the younger generation of poets that emerged on the Nigerian literary scene since 1988, produce poems that are primarily artistic *utterances* aimed as responses to, or are anticipating responses from, the sociopolitical conditions that parallel their thematics. Far from merely reflecting the social realities of the time, the poetry is a historicization that offers a discourse that is both alternative and dialogic. The figuration of the poet as an individual, of the poem as an emplotted event, and the intentionality of the poetic discourse as an outcome of an act—a radical, cultural, nationalistic act—is fundamental to the conception of the poem as an utterance. In this context, I want to argue that the poets recognize themselves as Nigerian writers, living in Nigeria, versifying about the Nigerian condition, especially the issue of military oppression; and that the poets locate their artistic energies in the literary tradition laid out by the poets that emerged immediately after the Nigerian civil war, prominent among whom were Odia Ofeimun, Niyi Osundare, and Tanure Ojaide. As a matter of fact, this literary tradition, that is, the Nigerian literary tradition that naturally admits dialogism, goes beyond post-civil war poetry and is firmly rooted in African orature; it is from this traditional aesthetic conception that poetry is first recognized as an utterance made by the poet to his/her audience or community. Whereas the concept of "dialogism" is inherent in African poetics, the epistemological formation of dialogism in Western thought as appropriated in contemporary discourses in the West started with the work of the twentieth-century Russian scholar and theorist Mikhail M. Bakhtin. I intend to discuss Bakhtin's concept of "dialogism" as well as the concept of "dialogism" in African poetics, and propose how contemporary Nigerian poetry can be read as a dialogue. The poems, in spite of their diverse artistic garbs, are utterances in a process of communication that occur either between the poets and the state, the oppressor, or between the poets and the ordinary people, the oppressed.

Bakhtin's Dialogism

Bakhtin, whose work became prominent after his death through the publications of poststructuralist thinkers such as Julia Kristeva, is perhaps the greatest theorist of what one may call literary communication at a time when Russian formalism and the Anglo-American new criticism reigned supreme over literary scholarship.[1] In many ways, Bakhtin's thought on language, especially the language of literary works, the novel in particular, portrays him as a dissident thinker at the time he lived and worked. In his insistent railing against what he calls the "impersonal and sacrosanct tradition" of poetry (Bakhtin 1981c, 16), an implied reference to the dominant and dominating formalism of his time, which, like structuralism, sought to disengage literary criticism from political or moral issues and focus exclusively on objective formal properties of the text, Bakhtin seeks to divert attention to the vital but neglected linguistic energies of the novel. In his essay "Epic and Novel," Bakhtin challenges formalism thus: "[the] utter inadequacy of literary theory is exposed when it is forced to deal with the novel" (1981c, 8). What Bakhtin calls "literary theory" could have been the self-assertive formalism of the time and its rather allied structuralism. To challenge the discourses of formalism and struc-

1. Kristeva, in an interview with Margaret Waller, speaks of Bakhtin's influence on her work: "Personally, I had found Bakhtin's work very exciting . . . I think that my interpretation [of his work] remains, on the one hand, faithful to his ideas, and demonstrates, on the other, my attempts to elaborate and enlarge upon them. Whence the concept of intertextuality . . ." (Waller 1989, 281).

turalism, Bakhtin positions the novel in opposition to poetry, privileges what he regards as the many-languagedness of the novel, and expounds a theory of communication that does not restrict itself to, or prioritize, historicity, the author, the reader, or the literary work. For Bakhtin all of these elements are implicated in the heteroglossic amplitude of the novel. In "Discourse in the Novel," an essay that most powerfully orchestrates his theoretical grounds, Bakhtin maintains that "[the] novel orchestrates all its themes, the totality of the world of objects and ideas depicted and expressed in it, by means of the social diversity of speech types . . . and by the differing individual voices that flourish under such conditions" (1981b, 263).

The essence of Bakhtin's theory of the novel or, rather, of literary language in the novel is the synchronic coexistence of voices ("many-languagedness") in a work of art, principally the novel. The novel contains many voices, that is, the voices of the characters, of the author, even of the (anticipated) audiences, and, implicitly or explicitly, of the society. Hence the novel is heteroglossic and polyphonic, more so because these voices are not just *silent* voices, but are engaged in interaction, in a dialogue. In contrast to this dialogism in the novel, the poem is, according to Bakhtin, only the systematized language of the poet, that is, a crystallization of metaphor, of a single voice; the poem lacks the amplitude to contain any languages or voices beyond the *static* language of the poem. This is how Bakhtin puts it:

> In poetic genres, artistic consciousness—understood as a unity of all the author's semantic and expressive intentions—fully realizes itself within its own language; in them alone is such consciousness fully immanent, expressing itself in it directly and without mediation, without conditions and without distance. The language of the poet is his language, he is utterly immersed in it, inseparable from it, he makes use of each form, each word, each expression according to its unmediated power to assign meaning . . . , that is, as a pure and direct expression of his own intention. (1981b, 285)

This theory is not far from the formalist conception of the language of poetry, and it is in fact germane to say that Bakhtin is, in his thoughts on poetry, influenced by the formalist's extrahistoricistic conceptualization of it. Unlike the poet, the novelist or the prose writer, according to Bakhtin, besides creating characters with *visible* idiolects, "attempts to talk about even his *own* world in an alien language (for example, in the non-literary language of the teller of tales, or the representative of a specific socio-ideological group); he often measures his own world by alien linguistic standards" (1981b, 287). What Bakhtin seems to be implying in essence is that the prose writer deploys language in a more nuanced way than the poet.

But this is often not the case, and that is why a number of scholars (Jacob Blevins, Kimani Njogu, Donald Wesling, Walibora K Waliaula, among others) have deployed Bakhtin's own theory of dialogism to demonstrate that a poem too can be polyphonic, heteroglossic, and dialogic. Such studies, that is, the transcoding of Bakhtin's key terms to ascertain the nuanced use of language in poetry, is surely not aimed at opposing Bakhtin's far-reaching thoughts on the language of the novel. They rather reveal the capacity of Bakhtin's theory of dialogism to embrace other genres of not only literature but also popular culture. For instance, in a study entitled *Intersubjectivities and Popular Culture: Bakhtin and Beyond* (2008), Esther Peeren transcodes Baktin's terminology into the study of films and television series. Both Jacob Blevins's *Dialogism and Lyric Self-Fashioning: Bakhtin and the Voices of a Genre* (2008) and Donald Wesling's *Bakhtin and the Social Moorings of Poetry* (2003) argue, quite convincingly, for the linguistic energies of a poem, be it epic or lyric, to realize the phenomenon of heteroglossia and polyphony. These studies attempt to free poetry from, in Donald Wesling's words, "[the] mythos of poetry as a singular or sacred language, suppressing conflicts in its own history and suppressing the presence of other-languagedness" (2003, 22).

Bakhtin, in his theoretical deliberations, seems to anticipate the recent studies that deploy his theory to investigate the dialogic essence of other genres of literature and popular culture. Although privileging the novel over other genres, he concedes that other genres too may be able to realize other-languagedness. Bakhtin admits that heteroglossia is not "completely shut out of a poetic work" (1981b, 286). But he strongly argues in "Epic and Novel" that for any literary genre to be heteroglossic, polyphonic, and dialogic, it has to be novelized, that is, it has to acquire the linguistic nuance, many-languagedness, or multiple voices that the novel naturally has:

> What are the salient features of this novelization of other genres suggested by us above? They become more free and flexible, their language renews itself by incorporating extraliterary heteroglossia and the "novelistic" layers of literary language, they become dialogized, permeated with laughter, irony, humor, elements of self-parody and finally—this is the most important thing—the novel inserts into these other genres an indeterminacy, a certain semantic openendedness, a living contact with unfinished, still evolving contemporary reality (the openended present). (1981c, 7)

It appears clear here that the thrust of Bakhtin's theory of dialogism is language in a speech situation, that is, *parole* as opposed to *langue*.[2] Dialogism recognizes an utterance, located in a particular situation, spoken by a particular subject, either as a response to another subject's utterance or as an initiation of a dialogue that anticipates response(s). Intersubjectivity underlines the concept of "dialogism." Such intersubjectivity is complex and may transcend the boundary of self and other or binary opposition—it emphasizes the performativity of discourse, in which case issues of self-reflexivity and self-referentiality are incorporated. This informs Bakhtin's delineation of what he calls internal dialogism as opposed to external dialogism. Internal dialogism, which theoretically caters for the phenomenon of monologism, soliloquy, and the perceived singularity of subjectivity in lyric poetry, takes advantage of word context, the relation of one word to another in a phrase, a sentence, a passage. Beyond that the semantic mapping of each word is not only determined by the word next to it but also by the psychological domain both words share. Internal dialogism,

2. In explaining Bakhtin's theory of dialogism as a philosophy of language, Michael Holquist, in his introduction to *The Dialogic Imagination*, writes: "Language, when it *means*, is somebody talking to somebody else, even when that someone else is one's inner addressee" (1981a, xxi). Here the emphasis is on language in the context of usage.

according to Bakhtin, offers the subject the wherewithal to "overshadow the object" (1981b, 282). The subject who appears to be speaking to himself may be speaking to another subject that is simply implied in the overshadowed object. Or in the superficially monologic voice of the persona in a lyric poem, there may be embedded in the dynamism of the deployed words and imagery a dialogism structuring the relation between the poet and the persona, the persona and his or her *other* (in the postcolonial sense of self and other), or the persona/poet and the society or, rather, the immediate environment that claims a strong connection to the poem.[3]

Dialogism in African Poetics

It is perhaps not a large claim to say dialogism, in its barest form as an interpersonal phenomenon, is inherent in African oral poetics. The performance of African orature, whether epic, song, or narrative, is an anthropocentric condition that emphasizes the presence of a performer and an audience. Most scholars of African oral performance have focused on the interactions between the performer and the audience during a performance.[4] Such studies have shown that the interactions between the performer and the audience is generally at the dialogic level. The immediacy of the performance atmosphere only heightens the mood of interaction; it not only relativizes the interpersonal contact but also validates the very orality of the performance. Integral to this performer-audience interaction under the immediacy of the performance atmosphere is a certain perceived accord between the audience and the performer, an accord that is cosmic, epistemological, cultural, social, and political. This becomes the nexus of the communication at the heart of each oral performance: each word, image, or expression that comes from the performer

3. The dialogic connection between the poem and its environment is predicated on the contention that "[the] artist creates from a socio-historical milieu of which he or she is a product and, similarly, the addressee is a social product also informed by the socio-historical events with which he or she is in contact. The literary piece, in turn, reshapes the history of the place and time in which it is received" (Njogu 2004, 10).

4. On the topic of oral performance in Africa, I find the studies collected in *The Oral Performance in Africa* (Okpewho 1990) quite insightful and useful.

gets understood at the point in which this harmony is established. In their contributions to the classic *Oral Performance in Africa*, Isidore Okpewho and other scholars such as Edris Makward, Ropo Sekoni, and Enochs S. T. Mvula stress, in diverse ways, the dialogic interactions between the performer and the audience-participants. In spite of the epochal and technologically driven changes affecting oral performance in Africa, the scholars in their empirical studies seem to agree that oral performance in Africa remains, in Ropo Sekoni's words, "a communication system in which a social discourse takes place principally between a narrator/performer and an audience" (Okpewho 1990, 139). The audience here is of course understood as the entire community to which the performer belongs, to which he or she addresses, and from which he or she gets responses.

The metacommunicative or paralinguistic devices available to the oral performer, used by him or her without restrictions, are not only to embellish the performance but also to intensify addressivity and enhance intersubjectivity. Paralinguistic strategies aim to supplement the inadequacy of bare words, no matter their semantic intensity; they amplify and reinforce the contextuality of words. The words depend on the paralinguistic features for their effectiveness.[5] The point of interest here is that the paraverbal devices may help activate dialogism in the minds of the audience-participants, or broaden or perspectivize it in a way that the words alone cannot do. The response of an audience-participant to an oral artist's performance may solely depend on the gestures that accompany the words of the artist; at least the audience-participants' imagination is sure to be enhanced by the gestures he or she sees from the performer. Whereas some gesticulations are individualistic, that is, the creation of the individual artist, some are not, especially those of the esoteric performers. Masquerades, for instance, have patterned paralinguistic features.

Oral African artists, in most cases, not only establish a dialogue between themselves and their community, that is, their audience-participants, but they also establish dialogues with their ancestors. Oral

5. For more on the place of paralinguistic features in oral performance, see Okpewho's *African Oral Literature* (1992, 46–51 and passim).

performers, whether esoteric or not, do realize that their artistic activities are in a continuum. They know that what they are performing has been performed before or, at least, that they are toeing a familiar path. Most oral performers come on stage chanting their lineage, their precedence, the accomplishments of their precursors; they leave the stage chanting the dreamed achievement of their progeny. In his seminal book *Reading Poetry as Dialogue: An East African Tradition*, which is a sustained study of dialogism in oral poetry from Kenya, Kimani Njogu hits this point when he says: "Any given performance is a re-telling of previous performances. It is also a response to possible performances" (2004, 96). Each oral performance, from this point of view, is multidiscursive and intertextual, a strength that oral performers harp on to validate their performance. Whereas in written literature there is often talk of imitation and (negative) influences on writers, oral artists thrives within influences and imitations, and proudly so. If what they perform is descended from their ancestry, the wish is to perform as skillfully as their ancestors, although oral artists must take into cognizance the contemporary sociocultural atmosphere.

From the point of view of thematics, the oral performer, like the Akan parabolic bird Santrofi Anoma, in spite of being (overwhelmingly) loved by the community, questions institutions, interrogates complacency, and does not shy away from topicalizing the moment of performance or, at their sober moments, reflecting on, critiquing, and criticizing the issues raised in the performer's thematic concerns.[6] The oral performer may feel compelled to return to the same issues in his or her next performance, in which

6. In a popular Akan myth, Santrofi Anoma is regarded as a dilemma bird liked by the people for its aesthetic song, but disliked for its downright critique of the society. The Ghanaian poet Kofi Anyidoho explains the dilemma of Santrofi Anoma thus: "Endowed with mysterious treasures of the mind and voice, Santrofi is both a blessing and a curse. Santrofi is a blessing for the clarity of its vision and for the transforming beauty and power of its gift of song. But Santrofi is also a curse for its irritating and irrepressible urge to expose the unsavoury side of the society . . . Society is blind without Santrofi's visionary guidance, but it stands forever condemned by Santrofi's persistent accusations of improper conduct" (1997, 5). There is a sense in which every oral artist in Africa, or each of the poets I have identified in this essay, is a Santrofi Anoma.

case the dialogue continues between the performer and the community. Making reference to the Yoruba proverb: "We say half a word to the wise; when it gets inside him or her, it will become whole," Karin Barber points out that "audiences make the meaning of the text 'whole' by what they bring to it" (2007, 137). Barber also posits that the entire society, beyond the presence of the audience-participants, is implicated in this dialogism. In her view, "oral performances also convene an imagined audience, often exceeding the people actually present, and hail them *as* a particular kind of listener, offering them a standpoint from which to secure uptake of the utterance" (138). This sense of addressivity, the infusion of an imagined voice in one's literary expression, or the longing to realize and accentuate the absent voice of the other, is what today can be discerned in the dialogization of the written contemporary poetry in Nigeria.

Contemporary Nigerian Poetry

Contemporary Nigerian poetry here refers to the poetry that emerged since 1988, first anthologized under the very suggestive title *Voices from the Fringe: An ANA Anthology of New Nigerian Poetry*, edited by the poet and scholar Harry Garuba. The context in which this poetry is new is one that is not clear-cut in matters of theme and style or obvious paradigmatic shift; it is not that the new poets stylistically or thematically deviate from, or challenge, the existing matrix of the social moorings of Nigerian poetry.[7] In the late 1980s, Garuba had noticed what he called "significant literary renaissance . . . especially in the genre of poetry" in Nigeria (2005, xv). Being the coordinator of the famous Poetry Club of the University of Ibadan, Ibadan, where undergraduates who wanted to become poets rubbed minds with their teacher-writers, such as Niyi Osundare and Femi Osofisan, Garuba had his keen eye on the "youngmen [*sic*] and women

7. It is important to point out that some of the poets today classified as "third generation poets," that is, the post-1988 poets, have challenged this matrix. Notable among them are Maik Nwosu, who appropriates myths at a time that mythopoeia increasingly wanes under the pressure of the post-civil war poetry. The tendency to deviate from the norm is also latent in Uche Nduka's early collections and explodes through his subsequent collections published in exile.

. . . writing and becoming increasingly frustrated by their inability to find publishing outlets for their works" (xv). It is thus such young men and women, those voices confined to the fringe, who form the contents of Garuba's anthology. The poetry therein acquired the nomenclature "new Nigerian poetry" because the editor chose (for him it was rather "imperative") to exclude any poet who had already published an individual collection (xvi). But what Garuba had seen as a significant renaissance in poetry in Nigeria actually began just after the civil war. It was indeed after the Nigerian civil war (1967–70) that Nigerian writing, perhaps in all genres, witnessed a certain renaissance due to the urgent desire of writers to challenge what they saw as the worst inhumanity to hit Nigeria and the alarming ease with which politicians and businessmen, including privileged writers and intellectuals, profited from the situation.[8]

The poetry in *Voices from the Fringe* is not new in the manner that the poetry of the trio Odia Ofeimun, Niyi Osundare, and Tanure Ojaide, placed against the poetry of Christopher Okigbo, J. P. Clark-Bedekeremo, and Wole Soyinka, may be considered new, or in the sense that the very polemical *Towards the Decolonization of African Literatures* argues for a new poetry.[9] The anthology does, however, introduce unknown poets who later turn out to be fairly productive in the 1990s and at the turn of the new millennium. One fundamental factor in any mapping of the poetry of

8. Scholars such as Olu Obafemi, Nesther Alu, Chidi Amuta, and Obi Maduakor have identified the Nigerian civil war as that critical juncture in which Nigerian poetry in English not only flourishes but also refocuses its artistic energies toward issues that affect the well-being of Nigeria.

9. The poet and literary scholar Funso Aiyejina, in his quite influential essay "Recent Nigerian Poetry in English," announces the emergence of Odia Ofeimun, Niyi Osundare, and Tanure Ojaide, rightly projecting them as the voices of a new generation of poets, subtly lauding their poetry for its concern with the condition of the masses. Perhaps what is most remembered of Aiyejina's essay today is the subtitle: "An Alter-Native Tradition." The essay, as the subtitle attempts to show, announces not only what it considers a new theme but also what it considers a new style. Although in my view it is true, as Harry Garuba insists, that in all phases of poetry in Nigeria there has been a concern with the well-being of the nation (2005, 51–72), I consider Aiyejina's contention that the trio of Ofeimun, Osundare, and Ojaide revolutionized poetry in Nigeria germane (1988).

these new voices from the fringe, and of their post-1988 poetic production, is the sociopolitical tension under which they all labored. It does seem that Garuba relies heavily on this factor to make a case for his generational shift in the introduction to his anthology. Insofar as one focuses on the intensity of the tension, and here I mean the disparity in degree, not in change, that is, if the understanding that the oppressive regimes of the late 1980s and of the 1990s (the twin regimes of Gen. Ibrahim B. Babangida and the late Gen. Sani Abacha) are considered, the poetry of the 1988 poets, which I would prefer to call the military-era poets, yields a shift in the paradigm of sociopolitical discourse in Nigeria's literary landscape. But here too the issue is problematic, and has indeed been problematized by scholars such as Titi Adepitan (2006, 124–28), who think the new poets may have emerged laboring under sociopolitical anxiety but that they may not have responded more than, or in a different way from, earlier poets such as Osundare and Ofeimun. Nevertheless, any characterization of this poetry must, in my view, focus on a historicism that fuses this poetry with the intense militarization of Nigeria during the regimes of the aforementioned dictators. This fusion should seek to erase any gap between text and context (in the sense in which early Marxists think of base and superstructure), for any such gap only undermines the energies of this poetry to historicize or produce its own discursive voice in the welter of other voices. Here I would accept Tony Bennet's conceptualization of context as a dynamic phenomenon, "a set of discursive and intertextual determinations . . . which bear in upon a text not just externally, from the outside in, but internally, shaping—in the historically concrete forms in which it is available as a text-to-be-read—from the inside out" (2005, 71–72). The claim then is that this poetry does not merely reflect or represent the events of military oppression in Nigeria of the 1980s and the 1990s but that it constructs its own military oppression, seeks to establish its own narrative in order to contest other existing narratives such as the rhetorical narrative of military messianism in Nigeria. I am of course here thinking along the lines of Jerome J. McGann's thoughts on the "performative aspect" of poetry elaborately presented in his book *Social Values and Poetic Acts: The Historical Judgment of Literary Work*. He argues for the consideration of poems as "literary works," as against "non-dialectal" texts, "[which] continue to live and move and have their being" (1988, 125). The notion of a poem as an act implies that factors surrounding its production should be put into consideration. Who produces the poem? Under what condition is the poem produced? What is the publishing history of the poem? A poem does not just happen to be, it is not a disembodied text. The processes of writing, publishing, distribution, even consumption, have a way of shaping the life and the narrative of the poem. McGann writes, "The options that writers choose in the areas of initial production, as well as in printing, publishing, and distribution—the options that are open to them in these matters—locate what one might call the 'performative' aspect of the poetic: what poems are doing in saying what they say" (1988, 74–75). Contemporary Nigerian poetry seeks to be studied against this background. It is a poetry that chooses to scream its existence even in a society where poetry reading is near-zero percent. This you will encounter in the anthology (*Voices from the Fringe*) that introduces it, and the individual collections that have bodied forth from it: Uche Nduka's *Flower Child*, Emman Usman Shehu's *Questions for Big Brother*, and Chiedu Ezeanah's *The Twilight Trilogy*, among others. It is a poetry that announces itself, asserts its existence, and forces its dialogic narrative on the consciousness of the society. The stridency, desperation, and anguish of this poetry are visibly metonymic of the crisis that confronted the entire society in the 1990s.

Along with the poetry of this tortured generation there have emerged narratives in politics and sociology that capture the intensity of the military oppression in the Nigeria of the period. Journalists such as Kunle Ajibade and Chris Anyanwu who were incarcerated during this military oppression have produced memoirs that vividly reveal those years. In Ajibade's *Jailed for Life: A Reporter's Prison Notes* and Anyanwu's *The Days of Terror*, the authors succeed, in spite of their emotional excesses and impassioned tones, in replicating some of the horrible incidents of the condition of despotism in Nigeria in the 1990s. But perhaps a more dispassionate representation of that condition in a nonfictional mode is Karl Maier's *This House Has Fallen: Nigeria in Crisis*. Maier is a British journalist who reported on Nigeria in those years of military tyranny. He offers an interesting metaphor when he says: "abused by army rule for three-quarters of its brief life span, the Nigerian state is . . . a battered . . . elephant staggering toward abyss with the ground crumbling under its feet" (2000, xx). I am aware of poststructural theories, especially those of Hayden White, that seek to collapse the boundary between history and fiction and pose the disturbing question: Just whose story is being told?[10] The journalists of course are telling their stories, in the same vein that I am trying to argue here that the poets too tell their own stories through poetry, formulating a unified dialogic discourse that tells the story in the form of addressivity. The mettle of the poets in troping the events that are so manifest in their poems is figural realism, that is, the construction of the phenomenon of military oppression in Nigeria in figural language. The poets—and this has been the crux of my argument—do not just *figurally* construct what they saw of military oppression at the point at which they versified, but do so with certain intentionality that permits dialogic structuring. The poet emplots in the poem a discursive narrativity, many voiced and polyphonic; the poem contains voices that often reveal themselves in the form of subjectivization and objectivization, a way of fulfilling its goal of intersubjectivity. To read this poem as a dialogue is to (following Bakhtin) recognize it literally, literarily, as an utterance. The ensuing voices that cause it to be an utterance often stand against each other (subject voice and object voice), as in when the poet addresses the oppressor-figure, or in agreement with each other (subject voice with subject voice), as in when the poet addresses a fellow poet or anyone he or she considers a fellow victim of military oppression.

This reading of the poem as a dialogue, then, is primarily, crucially, predicated on its thematization of military oppression in Nigeria. But how does one know the poem is talking about military oppression in Nigeria? This is one question that confronts an outsider, unlike me, who may not have known of the military regimes in Nigeria. But it is a question that

10. Since his famous *Metahistory: The Historical Imagination* (1975) and in *Figural Realism* (1999), Hayden White has sought to stress, underscore, and demonstrate what he calls "the literariness of historical writing and the realism of literary writing" (1999, ix), which basically projects the figuration and imagination immanent in any kind of narrative. The

gets increasingly neutralized when one keeps assembling and reading poems written from 1988 to 1999 and thereafter. The emplotted events in these poems, even in other genres such as fiction, betray any form of figural realism, and in fact raise other questions that may ginger historical and sociological research.[11] If you read the poems in Remi Raji's *Webs of Remembrance* (2001), if you read the poems in Idris Amali's *Generals without Wars (2001)*, if you read the poems in Chiedu Ezeanah's *The Twilight Trilogy (2005)*, even if you penetrate the turgidity and mythopoeia of Maik Nwosu's *Suns of Kush* (1998), you are confronted with a tripartition of imagistic essences dramatized in the voice of the poet, the voice of the oppressed figure, and the voice of the oppressor figure. This is also contained in some of the post-1988 anthologies, notable among which are Steve Shaba's *A Volcano of Voices* (1999), Toyin Adewale's *25 New Nigerian Poets* (2000), and *Camouflage: Best of Contemporary Writing from Nigeria*, edited by Nduka Otiono and Odoh Diego Okenyodo (2006). In the end, the question of whether the poems are dealing with military oppression or not will be dispelled, and as to the question of whether the reference is to the military oppression in Nigeria or not, the poems themselves consciously attempt to address oppressor figures both in and outside Nigeria.[12]

11. Beyond the poems of this era, the works of fiction often amply emplot the phenomenon of military oppression, thus betraying their organic connection with the history of Nigeria of the 1990s. In almost all the novels written since the 1980s by Nigerian writers there is always an overt or covert representation of the oppressor figure, mostly in the form of the military dictator. I am thinking of novels such as Maik Nwosu's *Invisible Chapters* (2002), Helon Habila's *Waiting for an Angel* (2004), Akin Adesokan's *Roots in the Sky* (2004), Sefi Atta's *Everything Good Will Come* (2005), and Chimamanda Ngozi Adichie's *Purple Hibiscus* (2003).

12. Some of these poets, even while they are thematically burdened with the political crisis of their immediate environment, their nation, they also stretch their artistic concern to embrace humanitarian issues in other African countries, such as apartheid in South Africa and civil wars in Liberia, Sierra Leone, and Somalia, among others. Read, for example, Emman Usman Shehu's "The Chilling Game" (in *Questions for Big Brother*, 1988), Maria Ajima's "For Woman—For Winnie" (in *Poems of Sanity*, 2000), and Maik Nwosu's "Ballad of the Peace-Keeper" (in *Suns of Kush*, 1998).

One obvious sign of addressivity in the contemporary Nigerian poem is the pronouns the poet often deploys. Most poems contextualize and dialectize the pronouns "we" and "them" or "I" and "you." Any handful sampling of these poems yields an overwhelming example of the dialectical dialogue that exists between the voices realized in the poems. It is pertinent to point out that although the mere construction of "we" and/versus "them" or "I" and/versus "you" results in dialogism, to fully fathom dialogization one has to go beyond the syntactic structuring or its equivalent semantic mapping. The aim of an inquirer in this line is to possibly ascertain the poem's historicism, which will help to account for the dialogic tension between or among the voices contained in the poem. As Njogu points out, "Dialogue is a relation characterised by tension" (2004, 2). This tension only surfaces when the poem is situated in a time and place, for it is under the pressure of time and place that the voices in the poem emerge, some distinct, some indistinct. If you situate the poems in a time and place, the "we" versus "them" construction naturally accentuates the poem's anthropocentrism. The dialogic tension then becomes the defining factor of conflict in the poem. In contemporary Nigerian poems, flora and fauna, nonliving objects, even deities, are anthropomorphized often to dramatize the beastly, extrahuman, and uncontrollable features of the oppressor figure, on the one hand, and the naivety, cowardliness, and undue paraplegia of the suffering masses, on the other hand. Denja Abdullahi's "The Silent Stool," for instance, anthropomorphizes stools, that is, the objects humans sit on, it classifies the victims of the oppression as the silent stools (in which case "stools" appropriate the pronoun "we"):[13]

We of the earth are the stools
That bear the malodorous weight of farting rumps
We of the earth know the Secret
Hidden in the deceptive frown of fattened anus

13. Abdullahi's "The Silent Stool" is taken from *A Volcano of Voices*, ed. Steve Shaba (Lagos: Kraft Books, 1999). Reprinted here by permission of the publisher.

Daily we smell the faeces of their revelry
Daily we host the after-fumes of feast
To which we are never invited
Ours is to silently await the return
Of the prodigal deposits of our stifling masters

Who remembers the silent stool
When the family gruel is being prepared?
Who cares for the comforting settee
When Executhieves negotiate their bloated contracts?
Who knows if the chair has a nose
When the journey from the pit-latrine is made?

The masses (the poet sees himself as one of them) are the silent stools. It is on these silent stools that the oppressors with their "malodorous weight of farting rumps" return to (sit on) after spending all the day partying with the public funds. This poem is an utterance from the poet persona who addresses the oppressors on behalf of his fellow victims; the first line alone sets the clue: "We of the earth are the stools" (Abdullahi 1999, 2). Characteristic of poems that address the oppressor figure, there is an embedded voice that speaks not to the oppressor figure, but to voices beyond, reaching to providence in the understanding that only the supernatural powers can set the victims free from the wrath of the oppressor figure. The wide gap between the powerful few ("Executhieves") in the ruling class and the masses is dramatized and dialogized, foregrounding the pitiable condition of the latter.

Musa Idris Okpanachi's "We Give You This Country" is one such poem that the embedded voice echoes all through the lines.[14] While the poet persona on behalf of the masses addresses the oppressor figure, the "you," he is also addressing providence; each image that emphasizes the helplessness of the people also subtly stresses the availability of supernatural powers that may rescue the oppressed. And when in Ogaga

14. Okpanachi's "We Give You This Country" is taken from his collection *The Eaters of the Living* (2007). Reprinted here by permission of the publisher.

Ifowodo's poem "Greed Will Kill the Beast" the poet persona seems to be addressing, placating, his fellow victims from a philosophical point of view, he is in fact asserting the presence of eventuality hinged on the concept of redemptive demiurge.[15] For the poet, this is the end of the oppressor figure:

> Greed will kill the beast
> In his roaring lust, fastened
> On a child. Deafened by his sirens,
> Blinded by a habit of defiance.
>
> He will not let go his flesh
> And flee the wrath of poisoned arrows
> Shooting from every eye,
> Greed will kill the beast. (1998, 45–52)

This eventuality is presented after the beast, the oppressor figure, is projected as a superhuman being—he is extremely cruel and tramples on any beings on his way ("he paves his way with loaded rifles," 19). The beast and his acolytes are cast in a dialogic relation with the ordinary people he brutalizes, maims, and kills—among them children and women. The beast is of course a military officer, a general, whose raiding is heralded by "sirens, guns and tanks" (31). In this poem the voice of the beast is vivid, the voice of oppressed masses is also vivid, and between them is the voice of the poet, which, by its insistent tone, is on the side of the oppressed.

There is, then, a sense in which the contemporary Nigerian poem, seen as an utterance in a dialogue, encompasses at least three voices: the voice of the persona, often the poet persona, the voice of the oppressed masses (which easily aligns with the voice of the poet persona), and the voice of the oppressor figure (the many beastly "yous" of contemporary poems). These are voices that are or can be obvious. Other voices can be found embedded in poems. For instance in Maik Nwosu's poem "Ballad of the Peace-Keeper," one first encounters the voice of the poet persona, who

15. Ifowodo's "Greed Will Kill the Beast" is taken from his collection *Homeland and Other Poems* (1998). All excerpts from this volume reprinted by permission of the publisher.

obviously emerges as the addresser, then the voice of the soldier Shantali, first as an addressee and later as an addresser. Shantali, as an addresser, addresses Mairo and Malumfashi, two embedded voices, the knowledge of which requires, even if in small measure, a certain historicity. In the voice of the poet persona and in the voice of Shantali there is embedded the voice of the oppressor figure, whose knowledge too requires extratextual engagement. Take this passage:

> home at last was where the shadows
> overtook my flight
> at first in the weighty silence
> among the welcoming throng
> and finally in the confirmation:
> "private umoru shantali, bereaved
> in the cause of peace"
> . . . .
> *malumfashi, where is mallama*?
> where the life i left behind
> in your slittery marrows?
> death is a treachery, mairo
> . . . .
> i have combed the inner regions
> of the north
> hooted through the dense zones
> of the south
> an echo voiceless with loss
> a howl pitchless with sorrow
> now i hear your voice also
> in the shoulder of the corn-woman
> see your dimples in the bosom
> of the milkmaid
> hear your injunctions in the desideratum
> of the mullah. (Nwosu 1998, 12)

In Shantali's voice is not just the voice of Mairo, his lover, and Malumfashi, the man to whom he entrusts her, but also the voices of innocent ones affected by the war, or the business of peacekeeping, in both the northern and southern part of Nigeria. The anguish here is that of people who lost persons and properties as a result of the war. I would go as far as to say that in the voice of Shantali, toward the end of the poem, there are embedded the voices of the suffering people of Mogadishu, of Sarajevo, of Johannesburg, of Kigali, of Gaza. Clearly this poem is multivoiced. And all the embedded voices stand against the somewhat overpowering voice of the oppressor figure who, in the eyes of many, devises the war and sends soldiers to war to keep peace.

In contemporary Nigerian poetry, one other voice, whose intrusion is really mild, is the voice of society, and here I am referring to the often unexpressed spirit or governing philosophy of a people, of a community, which may come from no concrete place but would exert a certain control over human behavior. For instance, when one character in Sefi Atta's novel *Everything Good Will Come* says, "[it] is amazing that privileged people in Nigeria believe that doing nothing is an option" (2005, 263), she is indeed referring to a dominant voice of the nation. Of course, this voice is not that of the masses, it may not even be that of the privileged in the society, but it is a voice that has come to rule over thinking along the lines of political action.

Conclusion

While making a case for the lyric poem as a polyphonic text capable of embodying dialogism, Jacob Blevins opines that "[the] underappreciation of the complexity of lyric discourse is often the result of such a characterization of lyric as a kind of readerless genre, a mode of expression that is the equivalent of private confession or simply the romantic valorization of the individual" (2008, 12). I would add that any reading of a Nigerian poem (with "Nigerian" here *uncompromisingly* contextualizing the poem), especially the poems I have periodized under the stretch of military oppression in Nigeria, as a "private confession" or celebration of individualism amounts to a misreading (which of course I am aware could be valid). Even when the persona of the poem is, as it were, inwardly and outwardly "I," or ostentatiously silent, the polyphony is there, only realized beneath the seeming formalism of artistic energies. Kimani Njogu points out that "the speaker [i.e., the persona or the poet persona] can be both a subject and object of discourse insofar as he or she is capable of distancing the inner self from the outer self" (2004, 10). A reading of contemporary Nigerian poetry as dialogue, apart from the clues often provided by the semantic structures, entails a number of factors. The poem should be recognized as an atomized realization of the social discourse existing in Nigeria that started not from the beginning of Nigerian literature written in English or other European languages but from deeply rooted orature. In spite of Niyi Osundare's criticism that the younger Nigerian poets have been infected by what he calls the "CNN syndrome," that is, have uprooted themselves artistically in the quest to function on the global stage, most of these poets are in fact trying to connect themselves to the roots, though perhaps not in the way Osundare is noted for (Osundare 2005, 21). My point here is that contemporary Nigerian poets, following the interventionist role of the oral artist, still see themselves as oracles that must speak up in the face of sociopolitical difficulties, and in doing so they *intentionally* set out to address characters and issues. The poet should be located communally. Although this may verge on the "biographicality" of the poet, it requires the inquirer to first recognize the poem as an utterance, and to seek to know who makes the utterance, what even prompts the utterance, to whom is the utterance made, under what condition is the utterance made, and what kind of response the utterance anticipates. For the poets I am dealing with here, for instance, one cannot dismiss the fact that most of them were born before or during the civil war, grew up witnessing the oil boom mostly as minors or teenagers, saw the oil doom of the 1990s either as undergraduates or as graduates who were often rendered worthless by the acute hardship and collapse of structures. Most of their poems (such as the collections and anthologies I have mentioned above) were written at that period of hardship and inhumanity. Most of the poets considered it a duty to engage in antimilitary activism, and some of them, such as Ogaga Ifowodo, suffered incarceration. Indeed, the personal travails of the poets often constitute the subject of dialogic poems such as Toyin Adewale's "Safari," written as a dialogue between the poet and her fellow poet Ifowodo when he was imprisoned (Adewale 2000, iii–v). Knowledge of the social realities, of how the poem gains its life and its publishing history (that, for instance, the publishing houses rejected poetry manuscripts during the production of these poems), shapes the status of the poem as a dialogic utterance.[16] The foregoing implies that, against the formalist conception of a poem as a superior form of discourse, a poem is in fact a figural discourse, just like any such discourse, and is amenable to any pragmatic objectives. It is indeed this understanding that underscores the idea of a poem as an utterance, a linguistic phenomenon, just like others, aimed at addressing a people or a society. This is, arguably, naturally so in African orature. In contemporary studies we should begin to see the poem, especially the poems I have identified here, as requiring a Bakhtinian theory of dialogism, or any other such theory, to unravel its connection to its society. I recognize of course that this is just one form of reading among other existing forms of reading, but it is one that, in my view, would be more fruitful than others.

16. For details on the dearth of publishing outfits in Nigeria and how this affects the evolution of contemporary Nigerian poetry, see Garuba's introduction to *Voices from the Fringe* (1988), and Adewale's introduction to *25 New Nigerian Poets* (2000).

11

Confronting Politics through History

A Reading of the Historical Novels of Ayi Kwei Armah and John Edgar Wideman

DUL JOHNSON

Politics can be defined not only as that profession devoted to governing affairs or opinions about politics but also as the understanding of the prevailing social order that regulates or shapes the writer's world, and his conscious efforts to positively influence it. We define history in the traditional sense, as a record of events of the past, whether the records are written or oral, although we do not see it as something locked in the past. The interplay between politics and history is what determines social structures of every society, and what gives direction to its future. History, then, is a growing, unending chain that is created from present social activities taking their roots in those of the past and defining those of the future. By these definitions we submit that politics is both a by-product and the driving force of history and vice versa. Therefore, the terms "history," "politics," and "social order" will be used interchangeably in this essay.

Literature, history, and politics can hardly be separated. But not all writers commix them in the same way and the same degree. There are different reasons for this. Some histories are quiet. Some are turbulent and some are triumphant. Some are an admixture of all of these characteristics. Africa's history has been a turbulent and painful one, and this history, with all its turbulence and pains, has dogged people of African descent wherever they are. It is the history of slavery, of the exploitation of its wealth and people by Western and the Arab world. It is also the history of colonization by the same forces, but more effectively by the West. The African American is still struggling to gain the acceptance and respect that the civil rights movement of the late nineteenth century fought for, although certain gains have been made. For as long as imperialism, new forms of slavery, and racial segregation continue to exist, committed writers will use their works to try to bring about change.

What is the function of literature? This is a well-worn debate that bears invoking here. It is an important question for all committed writers, but one that Ernst Fischer resolved for us when he submitted that art, by which he meant literature also, "is necessary in order that man should be able to change the world" (1970, 14). Literature, by this declaration, then, is a lesson—a lesson in the sense in which history or stories told by fathers and grandfathers to their children and grandchildren are lessons. And if all literary works are lessons, then the historical novel is more than a lesson; it is (or can be) a manual for political action. For Ayi Kwei Armah and John Edgar Wideman, as it is for many—even if not all—African and African American writers, literature would be no use if it did not seek to change the society in a positive way.

Armah and Wideman

For these two writers it is history itself that brought them to the decision to write what they write. Look at the coincidences of period and circumstances: Armah was born in 1939, Wideman in 1941. Ghana's struggle for independence was in the late 1950s, which coincided with the youthful period of Armah's life when events easily make a lasting impression on the mind. This was also roughly the period when the civil rights movement in America that led to the beginning of the emancipation of America's blacks—another form of independence—was attaining feverish levels of activism, and Wideman was growing up in a predominantly black neighborhood of Pittsburgh. Armah had left for America at the same time, and so he and Wideman, probably unknown to each other, had their minds shaped by the same experiences.

For Armah, these struggles for basic civil rights in America were the motivation for his revolutionary ideas and dreams of emancipation for his country, Ghana, and for Africa as a whole. This was also the period of intense agitation for independence among many African nations. Independence was supposed to dismantle the yoke of colonialism and change the course of Africa's history. On his return to Ghana, however, Armah found out that all hope for social emancipation with the coming of independence had been dashed and the course of Ghana's history (and Africa's) was not going to change. Wideman too was discovering in America what Armah was discovering in Ghana—that the promised changes were only a façade. Wideman was full of hope. Armah, on the other hand, was full of despair. Thus the two writers began their careers on separate notes of hope and despair, each earning something of a label for his stance. Armah was described by his fellow African writers and critics as a "pessimist" (Kibera 1979, 71; Lindfors 1992, 268). Wideman was perceived in some circles as a person who avoided commitment to some tendencies of the civil rights movement. And, as Hill points out, considering the period in which the two writers came of age and began to write, Frantz Fanon's revolutionary philosophy was bound to have influenced their political and social imagination (Hill 2011, 134).

Armah's disappointment was not simply with things not working the way the people had expected or because hopes were dashed. It was because, under colonial subjugation, the spirit and identity of the people was either denied or at best diminished. And when the opportunity came for this situation to change, the very people who should have made the change happen betrayed them. For Wideman, an abiding faith in the integration of the black race into the mainstream American system was failing; he witnessed staggeringly high statistics of violence against black people, rising levels of poverty and deteriorating living conditions, segregation and mutual suspicion among the races. One of the fallouts of this lower quality of life for black citizens was increasing crime and violence among black youth, with attendant repressive measures from law enforcement agencies.

History and the Issues

For both Armah and Wideman, the literary response to the social problems of their people would take the form of history itself. Thus they adopt a historical approach to their prose rather than use history merely as raw material, creating characters that engage us with the important social ne human contents, problems, and movements of their time (Gikandi 1992, 315). They differ in style, in their methods of deploying historical material, but they arrive at the same point and deliver the same message—that the conqueror cannot write the history of the conquered truthfully and accurately. And in spite of Wideman's unsure steps at the beginning, their works are among the boldest attacks on Africa's postindependence neocolonial state and America's post-civil rights situation. Both of them give us a sense of hope at the end of their excursions through history, drawing strength from the knowledge of a past that, although not blameless, was true and provided direction and powerful examples of individual as well as collective strength. This sense of hope replaces Armah's initial sense of gloom and futility and redeems Wideman's image of an alienated African American.

The novels we are concerned with are Armah's *Two Thousand Seasons*, *The Healers*, and *Osiris Rising*, and Wideman's *Philadelphia Fire*, *Fatheralong*, and *Brothers and Keepers*, even though the latter is nonfiction. There are two reasons *Brothers and Keepers* is considered here. It engages with the fundamental historical issues that Wideman deals with in the other novels. But he treats the issues in an interpretive manner rather than the historian's methodology, giving the book the quality that makes fiction enjoyable. The second and more important reason is that Wideman's style—his handling of historical material—in the other two novels suggests that, for him, there is little or no difference between fiction and reality, especially when that reality is a historical matter. Armah, on the other hand, is completely historical, both in form and content.

Armah's Historical Novels

Kofi Anyidoho asserts that the creative mind behind Armah's work "is one engaged in a continuing dialogue with Africa's tormented history" (1997, 34). Gbemisola Adeoti has also observed that Armah is a writer "who has grappled with the trajectory of the continent's history" (2005, 4). An important point to note, though, is that Armah started with the history that was being made, contemporary issues, dipping his pen in the ink of pessimism as a result of his disappointment with the social order at the time. His replacement of the initial sense of despair with hope in his historical novels therefore makes a significant point that history is a healing balm. This hope is most strongly expressed in *Two Thousand Seasons*, where, as it is in medicine, the healing process begins with diagnosis. Armah's diagnosis is that Africa's present problems have their roots in her history. The novel, narrated by an all-knowing communal voice using historical facts, lays out the origins of the problems, with the hope, as Hugh Webb puts it, of articulating the "values that will enable the African peoples to move forward, collectively and fruitfully" (1980, 24).

The struggle to move forward is not an easy one. It requires faith. But it also requires a mental journey into the past. Many Africans are as daunted by the enormity of the problems as the earlier Armah was. But, as *Two Thousand Seasons* assures us: "Endless our struggle must seem to those whose vision reaches only to the end of today. *But those with ears connected to our soul will hear a message calling us to a better life, to a life closer to our ancient way*, to a preparation for the best, the only living way (1979, 194, emphasis added). Armah suggests that the loss of spiritual contact with the past is responsible for the problems of contemporary Africa and that African writers should work toward reconnection. His position is consistent with Fanon's on what the colonized writer ought to do: "The colonized man who writes for his people ought to use the past with the intention of opening up the future, as an invitation to action and a basis for hope. But to ensure that hope and to give it form, the writer must take part in (the) action and throw himself body and soul into the national struggle" (Fanon 1967, 157). Armah himself has stated: "My first adult decision was to work in a liberation movement. I was ready to give up everything for it including my interest in writing" (Igwe 1987, 12). But how could he when writing remains a very important weapon in the war against imperialism?

For Armah, the writer has the task of healing the race by reconstructing its genuine history and bringing the people to its knowledge. The importance of this cause is announced in the prologue to *Two Thousand Seasons*: "The linking of those gone, ourselves here, those coming; our continuation, our flowing not along any meretricious channel but along our living way, the way: it is that remembrance that calls us. The eyes of seers should range far into purposes. The ears of hearers should listen far into origins . . ." (1979, xiv). As part of the search for a cure for Africa's leadership problems *Two Thousand Seasons* gives more of its energy to explaining the causes and the manner in which the carnage took place. In a way this novel is the history of Africa's encounter with Arab predators and white destroyers, an experience that spanned over two thousand seasons. Important to this novel's purpose is the refutation of the distorted history of Africa as seen and recorded by and through the eyes of predators and destroyers. Armah sees this distortion as part of a scheme designed to warp the African mind.

Robert Fraser has said that Armah's mind "is of a historical order, not in the ways applicable to the historian or even the historical novelist proper, but rather as one whose mind dwells on tracts of human experience in search of a clue to the depredation visited on his people" (1980, 2). In other words, Armah is a novelist who concerns himself with a special aspect of history, to which he reduces everything. In a folkloric manner, Armah describes how the peacefulness of fertile times and the absence of any anxiety or danger made men withdraw from their duties and allowed women to do virtually everything that kept their societies going, so that when danger struck, first from the desert, the people were helpless. The questions Armah raises (whose answers are the prescribed cure for Africa's disease) are: How and why did we stray from the way, which is life? How can we get back onto it? The answers emphasize "connectedness" and the unity of all black people. Like the griot or folk storyteller, his answers are rendered through witticisms, paradoxes, aphorisms, and anecdotes. And, typical of a folktale, one is expected to learn from another's or one's own mistakes.

Armah has explored this idea of uniting African people (through their common history) even in his earlier novels, especially in *Fragments* (1969) and *Why Are We So Blest?* (1969). But it is in *Two Thousand Seasons* that the idea takes the center stage, promoting connectedness as the way and warning against unconnectedness, which is death: "The disease of death, the white road . . . the broken reason that thinks only of the immediate paths to the moment's release, that takes no care to connect the present with the past events, the present with the future necessity" (1979, 8). The desert images this destruction and death. Hence it is the natural drought, the invading desert from the north that the people had to fight first. The Arab predators who set in with the carnage that scattered the people coastward are represented in the dry barrenness of the desert before they make their real appearance. But the scattering would not have occurred if the disease of "social division did not exist." Unfortunately, in their flight coastward where they are to meet worse destruction, the people do not leave behind the deepest causes of this disease—the chiefs and royals with their "unconnected sight" and "fractured vision."

Religion is probably the strongest weapon both the Arabs and the Europeans used in their destruction of Africa, the subtle weapon of imperialism that destroys the mind before the body is taken captive. In *Two Thousand Seasons*, Armah ridicules these religions in order to make the point that Africans have always known and experienced God as "a great force in the world, a force spiritual and able to shape the physical universe, but that force is not something cut off, not something separate from ourselves"; that force is "an energy in us, strongest in our working, breathing, thinking together as one people; weakest when we are scattered, confused, broken into individual unconnected fragments" (1979, 96). This is a God of unity and creation, not one of division and destruction. This belief system is useful in uniting the people, unlike the religions of the West or the Arabs, which divide by their very sectarian nature.

In Armah's view, a successful rejection of the forces of destruction and entrenchment of the right way will come with visionary leadership, the kind Isanusi provides to the youth who collectively form the hero of the novel. Armah uses Isanusi's revolutionary, inspiring leadership and the successful revolt of his initiates against the system to prove that change is possible and will come some day. The story also demonstrates the possibility of Africans coming together to end their destruction. The group's task is to reassert the people's culture, purify their internal politics, and put an end to foreign domination of their economic, social, and political life. By awarding victory to them (a group of twenty), Armah has been criticized for making trite a very serious racial and historical event. What the critics fail to realize is that the "healers," as Armah demonstrates in his next novel, are a select few who are morally superior to the rest of society. Such people, though spiritually connected to the rest of the society, must physically withdraw from the general rot so as to be able to pursue their vocation.

If *Two Thousand Seasons* identified the disease by taking recourse to history, then it is possible to find the cure through history. *The Healers* (1979), aptly subtitled *An Historical Novel*, is Armah's prescription for the cure. The disease, as we have identified earlier, is unconnectedness, which has led to a myriad of sociopolitical problems. In *Two Thousand Seasons*, it was social division that weakened the society and made way for Arab predators. The holocaust experienced by the Asante people and the fall of their previously impregnable capital city Kumasi (a historical reality) did not happen merely because whites had powerful destructive weapons. It was more the result of the division in the leadership. It was the Queen mother herself that was responsible for the fall, for the royals were interested in power for themselves. She would rather have been a slave under the whites than a free citizen under a powerful soldier who was not a royal: "if what should be done now was to yield a bit to the whites, better that than to lose all power to an upstart general" (1979, 291).

Armah believes that social divisions must be fought, and collectively, not through individual or unconnected and therefore meaningless struggle. The point is clearly stated by Damfo during a conversation with Nyaneba concerning Asamoa Nkwanta, the General: "If we the healers are to do the work of helping bring our whole people together again, we need to know such work is the work of a community. It cannot be done by an individual. It should not depend on any single person, however heroic he may be" (1979, 270). An aspect of the disease of social division is individual heroism, something that is alien to the African people. A perceptive and politically potent leadership acts from a collective rather than individual consciousness. Armah believes that individual struggles are important and necessary. But he does not think the individual should act alone. He is only the mover of the larger mass but not a replacement for it. This is why, for the healers, "the restoration of health to individual bodies is integral but subordinate to the healing of the whole society (Amuta 1992, 15).

Historically speaking, *The Healers* is a time bridge between *Two Thousand Seasons* (1979) and *Osiris Rising* (1995), although *Osiris* itself goes further back into the past. The panoramic view of African history in *Two Thousand Seasons* does not specifically bring up the past to link with the present. It brings it up to the era of slavery. *The Healers*, although not neglecting the era of slavery, deals with the historical dawn of colonialism, which is the time most African and "Third World" nations lost their political independence. The importance of history in the healing process is revealed to Nkwanta as Damfo tries to connect him to the past as part of the therapy:

> "I also know the idea, but it goes so far into the past," Asamoa Nkwanta said, "a mind going after it may get lost in the past."
>
> "Minds don't stay in the past," Damfo said. "They can find the truths of the past, come back to the present, and towards the future. That's not getting lost. The present is where we get lost—if we forget our past and have no vision of the future." (1979, 176)

Complete healing means reuniting the people, not only the Akan people but the African people as well—all black people. Nkwanta cannot see that far, does not believe such unity is feasible. This unity is in the mainstream of Armah's political philosophy, which is here articulated by Damfo, who believes (as Isanusi before him) that this reunification is possible: "If the past tells you the Akan people and the black people were one in the past perhaps it also tells you there is nothing eternal about our present divisions. We were one in the past. We may come together again in the future" (1979, 176).

It is difficult to miss the note of hope on which Armah ends *The Healers*, as poetic justice is served in the trial and conviction of Buntui and Eja Ababio, the usurper king and beneficiary of the murder of Prince Appiah. This hope is also evidenced by the reunification of the healers—young and old, male and female—amplifying Armah's message of collective action (by a united people) as the only way to end Africa's scourge. This is why in this novel, as well as the ones before and after it, Armah turns away from the idea of the lone individual hero (who is often also an artist) battling against the larger society, which always overpowers him.

Critics who may still be in despair at the end of *The Healers* can breathe a sigh of relief after reading *Osiris Rising*, a novel that is both a rehash and refinement of all the themes of Armah's previous novels—political ineptitude, materialism, neocolonial mentality, cultural alienation, the distortion of Africa's history, unbridled corruption, and so on—all of which beset Africa as a result of the disease of unconnectedness. These are the issues that have dominated all his previous works, including the nonhistorical ones. In *Osiris*, they are given a greater and deeper historical meaning. It is this novel that very clearly defines Armah's political ideology as Africanism, if African socialism (or African democracy) seems vague or difficult to accept. But it is not merely Africanism; it is Africanism anchored in, and informed by, authentic African history as passed down or recorded by Africans themselves and not the truncated tales by Africa's predators and destroyers or their local agents.

Quite appropriate to Armah's desire for the centrality of the knowledge of Africa and African history in solving Africa's problems, the progressives in the school in Manda, where molders of future minds are being trained, argue for "making Africa the center of our studies . . . shifting Eurocentric orientations to universalistic approaches as far as the rest of the world is concerned . . . (and) giving our work a serious backing in African history" (1979, 104). The contents of the proposed extensive changes to the curriculum as midwifed by Asar—Armah's spokesman and a revolutionary—leave no reader in doubt as to what Armah thinks should be the content and focus of the curricula of African universities, particularly the Departments of African Studies, History, and Literature.

If Asar is Armah's spokesman and a revolutionary, then *Osiris Rising* is a manual for historical research and revolution, *the* manual for African revolutionaries. It is at once a prescription for how to study African history, culture, and literature and how to prosecute a meaningful and result-oriented revolution. In summing up the novel, Akhuemokhan sees Armah to be saying that for Africa to witness a successful revolution the mindset of the people must change: "The (African) race must learn to think for itself if it wants a permanent remedy to its lingering social ills. It is pointless to hope that the remedies of outsiders will one day yield dividends; even in fiction" (2009, 70). The change in mindset is imminent in the formation of a workers' cooperative, an organization that works as a pressure group under cover. Then there are the students of Manda College, who have begun to demonstrate their ability to resist official intimidation and the muzzling of freedom of expression. These are the results of the efforts of Asar and the other revolutionaries. It is important that the movement is based in a teacher-training institution. Isanusi, Araba Jesiwa, and Damfo too are teachers as well as seers and healers.

It is the teaching profession that unites the revolutionaries in the novel—Asar, Ast, Neta, and Ama Tete and Armah himself—those who implant ideals and ideas: those who are "mid-wives for the coming ones . . . born to bring Africa together" (Armah 1995, 78). But from the outset Armah makes it clear that the real teachers are not those found in the institutions and classrooms. The real teachers are the ancestors, the possessors of native knowledge—represented in the book by grandmothers (the traditional storytellers, who are also the historians). Thus, it is Ast's grandmother, Nwt, that fires her interest in history (Egyptology in particular) and the shaping of her revolutionary zeal. These are symbolically introduced through the Ankh—the Egyptian symbol of life and creativity. She tells Ast that the symbol comes from "home," meaning Africa, even though they are African Americans living in America. Her sojourn to Africa is in search of truth, knowledge, creativity, love, and life. And she is able to find them.

This is one of the truths that Armah reveals in *Osiris Rising*, urging the reader, the researcher, and Africans as a whole to turn to ancient Egypt for proof of the kind of civilization Africa gave to the world before the destroyers came. It is important that Ama Tete, the fountain of knowledge, Asar and Ast's teacher and mentor, is the one to reveal these facts. Also, and symbolically, she is the one who gives life to Asar and Ast, not just in uniting them as husband and wife but also in seeing (and spiritually midwifing) their offspring. Having been taught by her grandmother, Ama Tete, though young, is grounded in history and vast in knowledge. She is the modern version of Araba Jesiwa (or even Nana in *Fragments*) and the female version of the characters of Isanusi and Damfo. Ama Tete teaches the truth about Africa, present and past, and Asar, though a teacher by profession, is glad to be her student. This is because the knowledge Asar possesses is not the knowledge of history, which Ama possesses. The artist-revolutionary needs the historian-revolutionary, both as teacher and as partner.

The society of the ankh goes back a thousand years into the past—"our past," says Ama—recruiting its members from all walks of life, sharing the common goals of creativity and industry. "Because it was devoted to life, its chosen symbol was the oldest of Africa's life signs, the ankh" (261–62). Armah contends that such order, such unity, existed in Africa until the destroyers came. He admits that the system was not perfect; there were always selfish and greedy individuals, especially among the royalty. This is what Apo represents in the story and what Cinque, his descendant, seeks to perpetuate. As Ama explains to Cinque:

> It started as a group committed to our people and afraid for us . . . The friendship of the ankh wanted to preserve only the best of our values . . . The seers saw disasters ahead *if we did not fill the gulf separating creative ancestors and hedonist descendants with working values*, if we divorced consumption from production . . . it was to work against such continuous disasters that the companionship of the ankh was born . . . (261, emphasis added)

Osiris is an Egyptian pharaoh-god. As a pharaoh he was said to have been compassionate, to have refined and educated his people—the kind of leader Armah would urge African rulers of today to be. Sadly, Osiris's life was cut short by his own greedy and wicked brother, Set (or Seth), who chopped Osiris's body into fourteen pieces. That Asar is the modern Osiris and aggregate of the revolutionary spirit of the cult, and Seth (SSS) the aggregate of the forces of destruction of "the way" and life, is evident in Seth's murder of Asar into "fourteen starry fragments" (305). But the similarity does not start and end there. *Osiris* foreshadows the future as well, revealing the action plans that are on the ground and suggesting imminent success. The revolutionaries have won the more important intellectual battle both symbolically and practically in the school and by the workers' group. Besides, Ast not only replaces Asar but will also mother future revolutionaries. Thus, although Asar is physically eliminated, no sense of despair prevails, as in the previous novels. Nor does

SSS, or any of the agents of the forces he represents (Cinque and his group and the conservative professors), enjoy any sense of triumph.

Armah's dream of a united Africa also materializes, literarily speaking, in Ast. By her international status—an African American now come to Africa—she becomes the representative mother of the future Africa. It will not be a dull, bleak future. It will not be a dark, illiterate, and directionless future. It will be a dynamic and revolutionary Africa, bringing up and completing the building and healing work of the Isanusis, Jesiwas, Damfos, and the society of the ankh. When that African unity that will bring about the revolution comes, the revolutionaries will not come from one place but from all over Africa, bearing such names as Abena, Mokili, Ashale, Kamara, Manda, Ulimboko, Kimathi, Soyinka, Umene, Chi, Mpenzi, Nandi, Ngazi, Irele, Akolo, Kakra, Nsa, and so on.

Wideman's Historical Novels

We have defined history as a growing, unending chain, created from present social activities taking their roots from the past and defining those of the future. In effect, both in the individual and collective lives of people and communities, actions and decisions are constantly being influenced by history. This being the case, we have a strong reason to start the discussion of Wideman's work with *Brothers and Keepers.* Although the events of *Brothers and Keepers* are historical, they also contribute to the evolution of Wideman's and African American history and shape future events.

An even more important reason for including and beginning with *Brothers and Keepers* is that Wideman gives us not only the recorded history but also the real history that he and his people have experienced daily—the living history of the African American, the one he was living without knowing he was part of it: Wideman's, and his brother's, and their family. In the narratives we get to see the Wideman family, know who they were, where they lived, and who their neighbors were. We get to feel the relationship between black people and their white neighbors, and between the black people and the whites in the country. *Brothers and Keepers* also lays the foundation for the other historical novels.

In his youth Wideman had a fairly comfortable life. He had loving parents who provided for all his needs even if his father showed little emotion. This was not so for most blacks. His brilliance assured that he went to good schools, which also could not be said for most of his people. He may then have been one of those people Armah describes in *Why Are We So Blest?* as "an African rarity . . . (and) hero of his race" (1969, 101). Such rarities are regarded with a sense of awe and may never experience the roughening that others get. Yet he could never escape the history growing around him, the history he was growing up with.

But Wideman was also growing up when hope was in the air. There were the efforts to integrate African Americans into mainstream America and the gains the NAACP was making in that direction. He had personal ambitions and the promise of success, and the American Dream must have been a reality for him then. These factors must have led the young Wideman to respond to the events of the time less radically than would be expected by most people. His neutrality led ultimately to a feeling of alienation from his own people. But this was not to last for long. Adult experience and the reality of history were bound to make a change.

In the 1985 article "The Language of Home," Wideman writes:

> I was once a paperboy . . . I had to climb Negley Avenue Hill . . . Because white people resided at the top . . . the climb was almost worthwhile. They tipped royally, compensating me . . . the enormous distances separating their houses . . . The turf atop Negley Hill remained foreign. *Immense houses of stone and brick, long curving driveways, sculpted trees and shrubberies, lawns cleaner than most people's living floors* (my emphasis).

Some of the stark realities were the life term his brother Robby got, the circumstances that led to it, and the truncation of justice he and his brother experienced in the attempt to get a retrial and bail. The events of *Brothers and Keepers* are a watershed in Wideman's transformation from the individual to the connected, roots-conscious man, a Wideman who would seek "through family . . . the strength to bear the weight of lives shattered by loss, the ability to shape rather than be shaped by experience (Roark 2002, 180). Accordingly, his search begins with the awareness of responsibility to family, a basic human right that America denies its black compatriots. Here is the scene when he and his family walk into the prison:

> They're with me. I'm responsible. I need to say that, to hang back and preside . . . aware of the weight, the necessity of vigilance because here I am, on alien turf, a black man, and I'm in charge . . . (and) prepared to make anyone who threatens them answer to me. And that posture, that prerogative remains rare for a black man in American society. Rare *today*, over 120 years after slavery and second-class citizenship have been abolished by law. (2005, 44)

As he finds out, the law abolishing slavery and second-class citizenship was made by whites, who were themselves above it. It was made for blacks, who could not enforce the law. In effect, the law did not seem to exist as far as the treatment of African Americans was concerned. The denial of freedom and dignity resulted in resistance and revolt, especially among the black youth. This was also the reality for Wideman, but he did not recognize it, or rather, it was not obvious to him. He confronted the facts head-on early in his career while teaching Afro-American literature. At the time, "Robby was living through the changes in black culture and consciousness" that he, Wideman, was reading about. Amiri Baraka's *Black Fire*, the book Wideman read, was full of "black rage and black dreams and black love" and described young black men "walking the streets . . . with dynamite growing out of their skulls (111). Somehow Wideman did not fully appreciate that Robby was actually one of those so described until their encounters in prison revealed it.

Encounters with the reality of history in the experiences relived in *Brothers and Keepers* may not have changed Wideman's belief in the excellence of the individual spirit. But he realized that an individual could never function properly outside the community, which begins with the family. His alienation may not have been unconnected with this inherent knowledge, which he later reveals in *Fatheralong* (1994). It is this knowledge that leaves him confused when his parents could not forge a common philosophy of family. But the time would come (it had to come for him) when the fundamental questions of "who am I?" and "what am I?" would have to be answered.

As he relives an intimidating scene between him and a white schoolmate, Wideman enlarges the picture, showing us the power of being white against the powerlessness of being black in America. The scene reveals his impotency then and his regret now over having been so powerless.

> Why did that smartass white son of a bitch have so much power over me? Why could he confuse me, turn me inside out, make me doubt myself? Who was I? What was I? . . . Four hundred years of oppression, of lies had empowered him to use the music of my people as a weapon against me. (31–32)

As Wideman confesses in this same passage, "Twenty years ago I hadn't begun to comprehend the larger forces, the ironies, the obscenities that permitted such a reversal to occur." Now he is beginning to understand the dynamics of his society, the reason Robby was forced to do what he did and why he could not get a fair hearing. Experiences that he might have neglected in the past take on new meanings. The Wideman we encounter in *Brothers and Keepers,* and in the subsequent novels, is an angry man, angry at the way society has treated his people, at the way society has treated his own family. He is the Wideman who can draw our attention to the fact that "blacks have no rights which the white man was bound to respect" (187). This Wideman is rooting for a change in the treatment of America's black population, a change in the course of America's history.

The necessity for *Brothers and Keepers* was to find expression and connection, and, it was hoped, freedom for Robby. But that was John the individual thinking. Once the project began, the artist in him took over, a sense of commitment crept in, and the book's purpose broadened. It became a comment on national and even universal historical issues, and drew attention to a system that "encourages violence and perpetuates another very old American habit—old as slavery in Europe's New World colonies—the habit of embodying in some stigmatized, segregated other those incriminating desires, fears, and deficiencies we deny in ourselves" (xii). Every society has its criminals, and blacks do commit crimes just as whites do, whether they are in the United States or in Nigeria. Prisoners seem to get a raw deal everywhere in the world. Wideman's book would not have been worth the attention if it was simply about Robby or crime and the horrors of incarceration. Assuming fictional (and therefore representative) characters, both John and Robby comment on America's legal system and its unfairness to black citizens. Every society has its first-class and second-class citizens, defined by social status and attained in a relatively egalitarian arrangement, except in caste systems. An egalitarian system is what America claims to be. Yet a whole race is condemned to a second-class position by the dictates of skin color.

Given this situation, resistance or revolt is inevitable, and America's history is painted with the evidence. By John and Robby's submissions, it is the system that creates the monsters. Robby illustrates this with the case of one of his friends who, out of neglect, becomes a walking corpse before he gets any attention, too late. "What else can they do, John? Sometimes I can't blame them. No jobs, no money in their pockets. How they supposed to feel like men?" (68). As Robby relives his youth, he realizes that his whole life has been shaped by his relationship (or the lack of it) with whites, within whose neighborhood he grew up. While he does not absolve himself of the crime for which he was convicted and even regrets it, he knows that he was essentially a good boy turned bad by the system. "I know that had something to do with it. Living in Shadyside with only white people around . . . I got a thing about black. See, black was like the forbidden fruit (84)." Robby saw the life that whites were living—as grand as kings and queens—while he and his ilk were condemned to suffering and serving whites. He does not want to end up like the rest of the black young men. "No way Ima be like the rest of them niggers scuffling and kissing ass to get by. Scuffling and licking ass till the day they die and the shame is they ain't even getting by (152)." Unfortunately, this is the reality of being black in America, a fact of history that Wideman did not recognize for a long time. After he comes to terms with it, Wideman wonders if he has prepared his children for life in their society, if he has "taught Dan and Jake enough about their history so that they'll recall auction blocks and professional appraisers of human flesh? (186)."

It is the narrative of *Brothers and Keepers* that gives the book its historical value. John and Robby not only relive their own experiences, they also comment on the experiences and the history of America's African population as far back as slavery, on their situation as of 2005, and on their situation to come. They do this by citing historical events, by romanticizing with the past, and by commenting in words, actions, and even silence. *Brothers and Keepers* is more than a memoir, more than the story of the two brothers and their family, more than the story of prisoners and their brutal keepers. It is the story of African Americans. It may not have achieved its goal, but that is not because of its inability to convincingly evoke the history and present social order that are responsible for the turn of events in their lives. In any case, asking for a reason will amount to begging the question because the book is also about why it could never achieve its goal.

Both *Philadelphia Fire* (1990) and *Fatheralong* (1994) take on specific issues that Wideman explicated in *Brothers and Keepers*. For *Philadelphia Fire*, it is the disregard for the life of a black man. The incident of the Philadelphia bombing of 1985 provides the overall motif through which Wideman examines several key issues in the experiences of African Americans in their country. Earlier in *Brothers and Keepers*, Wideman made the point that about 50 percent of American jail inmates were blacks. And this is a country where they are in the minority. He argued that if the situation were reversed, if a white boy had killed a black boy, things would have been different. If blacks "have no rights that whites are bound to respect," then the lives of blacks do not count at all.

On May 13, 1985, 6221 Osage Avenue in West Philadelphia was bombed by the police after all efforts including bullets, water cannon, and high explosives failed to dislodge the occupants. The building housed a resistance organization known as MOVE and had nearly three 300 black people living in it. Eleven of them were killed and over 260 people were rendered homeless. Although there were investigations, the law absolved its agency from any blame for what Wideman refers to as "the holocaust" (2005, 7). The question that Cudjoe, the novel's protagonist, and Wideman ask is whether this could have happened to a white settlement. Cudjoe, a journalist, teacher, and writer is fascinated with the story of a young boy's escape through the fire, a scene he had seen on television. He wants to meet the boy, to hear his story, but no one seems to know exactly where Simba is. Cudjoe goes to Margaret Jones, a former member of the group whom he had known closely before he went into self-exile. His desire is to write a book "about the fire. What caused it. Who was responsible. What it means" (2005, 19). What Cudjoe gets is much more than what he was searching for. Margaret is a storehouse of information on the incident; in fact, she is the history itself, and Wideman uses her to give us a bigger picture of African American history. She is reluctant to give any lead to Simba because she believes that living history is more important and considers the book a mercenary engagement. "Don't need a book. Anybody wants to know what it means, bring them through here. Tell them these bombed streets used to be full of people's homes" (19).

Margaret tells him that Simba has disappeared but that she knows someone who had seen him. He never gets a concrete lead, but the search does not end here. In fact, the search itself is the real story, Wideman's and Cudjoe's main story. It is through the search that we get vignettes of the experiences of blacks in America. As Rosemary Bray puts it, Wideman uses this search to take "his readers on a tour of urban America perched on the precipice of hell—a tour in which even his own personal tragedy is part of the view" (1990). In fact it is difficult to separate Cudjoe from John and John from Cudjoe, and Wideman, it seems, does not want us to separate them. The search itself assumes greater significance when taken for what it really is—a search for identity. Therefore it is neither Cudjoe's nor Wideman's alone. It is every black American's search.

The modern world takes cases of holocaust seriously, and acts of genocide or ethnic cleansing attract international condemnation and investigation. The United States is often in the forefront of human rights issues. How is it, Wideman seems to ask, that a case of holocaust, of ethnic cleansing, is carried out in America under the apparent sanction of the legal agency that ought to protect and ensure the rights of every individual American, and it goes unnoticed? And why is the world silent about it? As Margaret Jones puts it, "Nobody cares. The whole city seen the flames, smelled the smoke, counted the body bags. The whole world knows children murdered here. But it's quiet as a grave, ain't it?" (Wideman 2005, 19). This indifference and silence becomes the most important question in the novel and every vignette of history we get from then on, both at the collective and individual levels, are attempts to answer this one question or its variants.

Margaret Jones was an ardent follower of King, the leader of MOVE, before he was killed. Her question is therefore a rhetorical one and she expects Cudjoe and everybody else to know the answer. Cudjoe's questions too are quite unnecessary, she thinks, because, again, everybody knows the answers. But if Cudjoe or others choose to pretend, she throws the answers right in their faces. This she does in different situations, for example, when she expresses concern about her own children and the lack of security for them: "You think the police do anything about it? Hell no. Not till one these little white chicks slinking around here ODs and turns up dead, then they'll come down on that corner like gangbusters" (32). Everybody knows what caused the fire, who was responsible, and what it meant. And if everybody is quiet about it, it is because nobody cares. But the victims still live with the answers, and they know too, as O.T. says, that the black mayor cannot do anything about it. "Bull-shit. You think they'd let him burn down white people's houses? Sheeit. He be hanging by his balls from some lamppost. Mayor's not in office to whip on white folks. Nigger control. That's what he's about" (41–42). This shows that the mayor, ironically named Goode, has no powers of his own; he is only a tool in the hands of the system that put him there. Cudjoe learns this much from Timbo, the mayor's assistant, who claims that the bombing incident is no fault of the mayor's. When Cudjoe wonders why the mayor had to do anything at all, he gets an answer we know is not Timbo's but the official position he has to echo: "They were embarrassing, man. Embarrassing. Trying to turn back the clock" (81). The pressure group was a big threat to the system, as were its predecessors in the days of the civil rights movement such as Martin Luther King Jr.

Martin Luther King Jr., although a political activist, leader, and mobilizer, did not encourage violence as the way forward. Margaret's accounts of King and MOVE's activities and the demise of King himself clearly show that we are dealing with the historical Martin Luther King Jr. As African Americans and the whole world asked when King was killed, Wideman's Margaret asks Cudjoe: "What King and them be doing that give anybody the right to kill them? Wasn't any trouble till people started coming at us. Then King start to whoofing to keep folks off our case . . . Just talk . . ." (17). This suggests that MOVE was not a violent organization, though it operated underground. But the system was paranoid about organizations (not individuals). That is why the likes of J.B. are not a problem to the system. "No one notices a funky derelict emerging from an almost invisible wedge between two buildings . . . (after all) if you stink bad, the cops don't like to touch you" (180). Organizations may pose no apparent danger but they possess the potential.

The search may not have produced Simba, but it is more than rewarding, and perhaps it is as well that he was never found. After all, was the search itself not for self-identity? At some point, Cudjoe tells us that Simba is his son, and then his brother, a part of him. But the reader sees beyond that relationship and can see that Simba is also Wideman's son who is serving a life sentence. Indeed, at another point we are convinced that Simba is both Cudjoe and John Wideman. When the search becomes one for his son, Wideman is palpably drowning in emotions as he asks: "How does it feel to be inhabited by more than one self?" And is his son "doomed to come apart no matter how hard he struggles at constructing an identity, an ego, a life . . ." (110). It seems that in their circumstance blacks have to live through a double identity in order to get by. This is the lesson we get through the double character of J.B., who has to adopt another identity, another self, like Athol Fugard's Sizwe Bansi in *Sizwe Bansi Is Dead* (1972). There is no way out. As one of the characters tells Cudjoe: "We're victims . . . Stuck playing roles we have been programmed to play. You never had a chance; neither did I. We've turned out the way we were supposed to" (175).

Not finding Simba, his unsure identity or his disappearance into the crowd serves a number of purposes. It makes his character representative of every black man. It is also a survival or coping mechanism for the hunted man. It further illustrates the invisibility of the black man, which Ralph Ellison eloquently demonstrates in his novel *Invisible Man* (1952) decades before. This invisibility plays out at the scene of the memorial service for the victims of the bombing incident. Seeing nobody in the square, Cudjoe populates it with ghostly images from history, from 1805 when blacks, descendants of slaves from 1684 who had come to celebrate freedom—America's Independence—were brutalized and pursued by their howling fellow countrymen. The significance of this recollection is that nothing has changed:

> Cudjoe hears footsteps behind him. A mob howling his name. Screaming for blood. Words come to him, cool him, stop him in his tracks. He'd known them all his life. *Never again. Never again.* He turns to face whatever it is rumbling over the stones of independence Square. (199)

Through all of this, Cudjoe emerges a supremely different person, as does Wideman. These are the very last words of the novel, signifying Cudjoe's resolve to face the known (and even the unknown) squarely. There is no running away from one's history. At best, what we can do is right it by writing our own version of it. Tracie Guzzio puts it succinctly:

> The past and the present meet when Cudjoe "hears footsteps behind him . . . The "fever" that caused the incident, the racism and hatred that spurred it on, has followed Cudjoe all his life. The burden of that history has always been the "footsteps behind him," but now Cudjoe is ready to confront history no matter how painful. "Never again will he run away from who he is or from his history." (2006, 187)

Philadelphia Fire (1990), as Stephen Casmier aptly puts it, is "a story of the struggle between spoken testimony and official history" (2006, 197); the one lived and talked about by the African American and the one manufactured by the authorities. The burden of that history has always been with Wideman, with every black man in America. The realization is important, but the decision to face it is even more so. Perhaps it was this decision that caused Wideman to write his next historical novel, *Fatheralong* (1994).

The search for Simba in *Philadelphia Fire* (1990) takes us into *Fatheralong,* which also concerns the search for identity and in an even more historically conscious manner. The general opinion about *Fatheralong* seems to be that it is about fathers and sons. That is the story at the crust level, given credence by its direct use of the relationships between John and Edgar (his father) and John and Jacob (his son). But the story is more about the relationship between us and our past, its importance to us as a collective and as individuals. It is about finding our roots, and roots will always take us back "home" where our great-grandfathers were buried. If we cannot do this physically, we do it spiritually or mentally. Wideman is able to do both.

The coincidence of the name of the place to which John and his father undertake the journey that becomes the connecting thread of *Fatheralong* is an interesting one—Promised Land. Historically the name recalls the journey of the Israelites to the Promised Land, the land of their freedom, but the journey was a tortuous one. Promised Land, South Carolina, is where the Wideman clan comes from, so a journey to it (a kind of return home) is both a connecting with roots and finding one's freedom. Although all peoples respect their roots, Africans in particular have a deep and passionate connection with their roots and the land on which their ancestral roots are planted.

There was a time when many African Americans were fascinated with the idea of going back to Africa. There is a sense in which *Fatheralong* evokes that romance of returning home, though the Widemans may not have been part of it, and John certainly was not. But a "connection" with his father and grandfather, both of whom he had become somewhat estranged from, and the "connection" with their ancestral birthplace in Promised Land, was certainly a healing experience. Like the biblical journey, John's was not without pains. However, what made the journey rewarding and healing were the pains (and joys) that came with so many discoveries.

Wideman declares in the closing paragraph of the preface, which he entitles "Common Ground," that "the pieces that follow on fathers, color, roots, time, language are about me, not my 'race.' They are an attempt . . . to break out, displace, replace the paradigm of race. Teach me who I might be, who you might be—without it" (xxv). But how are we expected to believe this? Why is it "common ground"? How can something about color, roots, time, language, and even fathers, for that matter, be an individual experience and not about race? How can replacing the paradigm of race not be about race? Surely Wideman does not mean to be taken seriously, not the Wideman we left at the end of *Philadelphia Fire*, or even the

Wideman of *Brothers and Keepers*. To prove the point we turn to the opening paragraph of the same preface:

> If a certain kind of camera . . . achieved the capacity to record the instantaneous give-and-take between two black people meeting in the street, looking at the artifact this camera produces you would see the shared sense of identity, the bloody secrets linking us and setting us apart, the names . . . black, negro . . . we sometimes answer to but never internalize completely because they are inadequate to describe the sense of common ground we exchange at this moment. (1994, ix)

Further on Wideman affirms, "Americans of African descent share a continent, a gene pool, a history. Who we are is partly determined by this triple heritage" (xi). *Fatheralong* is the story of America's blacks, the search and the pains of discovery, their own.

In all three novels considered here, Wideman presents a self "inhabited by more than one self." In *Fatheralong* we are confronted with the self who refused to go down South with his grandfather, and the self of later years who, realizing the dislocating effect of not connecting with his father, decides to go down South. One of the reasons he did not like to go down South was founded on the memory of it as the place where "they lynched black boys . . . for whistling at white women, where everybody black was crusty black and ate watermelon . . ." (16), and he did not "want to travel back to slavery days . . ." (17), to a place where "we were urban-removed, permitted to settle by white people who controlled what we could buy, where we could buy, how much we had to spend" (23).

For Wideman, as it is for Achebe, whom he quotes in this novel, fathers, grandfathers, and (hi)story are one and the same thing. They make each other; stories make fathers and grandfathers what they are, and fathers and grandfathers make stories (and histories) meaningful. "Father stories are about establishing origins and through them legitimizing claims of ownership, of occupancy and identity" (Wideman 1994, 63). He argues that such stories are "about blood and roots and earth," and should people allow their stories to fade away, they too will diminish, or even worse be lost because their sense of connection, of community, will disappear and each "becomes a solitary actor." History (or story) is also the source of life. It not only connects grandfathers and fathers to their children, giving them their identity, but it also defines their future. This is why it becomes important not only to possess the space and the power to tell one's own story but also to be listened to. Unfortunately, in America, "the power to speak, father to son, is mediated or withheld . . ." (65), because whites own the country and run it whereas blacks are relegated to the margins. The system, Wideman argues, "stands between black fathers and sons, impeding communication, frustrating development, killing or destroying the bodies and minds of young men . . ." (65).

One of the saddest discoveries for Wideman—which he discusses at length in the novel—is the historical condemnation of the African race to a status that leaves Africans debased or invisible.

> The African, once "discovered," was abruptly situated during Renaissance in an evolving paradigm of race: first as *different*, then *other*, then *inferior* . . . With the added advantage of being beasts of burden, not only to perform the heavy-duty work of empire building in New World colonies, but also to bear the psychic weight of guilt and punishment for man's dualism, his warring impulses. (1994, 80)

Organized religion contributed to this historical distortion. Achebe had said it long ago, and so does Armah, that God was not one of the white man's discoveries. Early in life Wideman realized that "the faces of God, of Jesus were white faces with silky flowing hair and flowing beards" (1994, 54). And because God was white, the white man became his son and representative on earth, with all the powers given unto him. "To be white is to be connected to the Great White Father, the ultimate source of power, privilege, and legitimacy" (Wideman 1994, 82). For those who cannot claim to be white, their case is closed, Wideman suggests. Relegation to the dark spots of history or even invisibility confronts Wideman, again sadly, in his discovery that Promised Land does not exist on most maps (1994, 94). He thinks this is a good thing because that distortion of history can create or further awareness of "the inadequacy of maps we don't make ourselves, teach us how to . . . reimagine connections others have forgotten or hidden" (94–95), like the pictures of blacks on display at the

South Carolina Historical Museum: images, faces without names, without identity (1994, 146).

Fatheralong can be defined as a novel with many climaxes, as many as there are in the shocking discoveries for John. Most significant of all is his encounter with the white history professor, Bowie Lomax. To find out information about their family they had to go to a white man the age of his father. Wideman remembers that "because of his color, my father was denied the prospects, the possibilities that had enriched the career and life of the white man below me" (1994, 114). Above all, he discovers that:

> In this room there was no denying the solid, banal, everyday business-as-usual role slavery played in America's past. Meticulously, unashamedly, the perpetrators had preserved evidence of their crimes . . . these documents also confirmed how much the present, my father's life, mine, yours, are still being determined by the presumption of white over black inscribed in them. (116)

It is at this point that Wideman realizes that his suppression of the essential black man in him, the one prone to violence, was only skin deep. Denied opportunities, denied speech, and lynched for protesting injustice, as it happened to Anthony Crawford, blacks were pushed to the brink of endurance. The natural human instinct is to fight back. Wideman, who has consciously avoided violence, discovers on this trip to Promised Land that violence may well be inevitable unless the perverse history of the African American is put right. In her discussion of the trip to Promised Land, Tracie Guzzio aptly notes:

> It is also a redemptive quest for Wideman, who, as a young boy, had not wanted to visit his father's family in the South, the place where they "lynched black boys like Emmet Till" . . . Wideman now sees an opportunity to learn about his past—the history of his people—and to repair his relationship with his father. He discovers in the course of this journey the importance of "father stories"—stories that strengthen ties to the past and establish identity and manhood in the wake of racism; stories that have been historically denied the African American father and son. (2006, 187)

Conclusion

In reading Ayi Kwei Armah and John Edgar Wideman we pointed out that they traveled along different historical routes but arrived at the same destination. Obviously their paths must have crossed many times along the road. We pointed out the coincidences of birth and growing up or schooling in America. Armah's knowledge of America is relevant to the extent that two of his novels are partly set there. Ast, the co-protagonist of *Osiris Rising*, is an African American. Three of his characters studied in America before returning to Africa.

Both Armah and Wideman engaged in the search for a lost past, through which the present and future social order can be constructed. Without this reconnection the future is bleak. The authors blame their own people for failing to preserve their life-giving culture. Although this may be inevitable for African Americans, Africans have no excuse. Armah argues that this failure to keep the roots alive has come about because Africans accepted the tag of inferiority and further enslaved themselves because of greed and a lust for power. Both authors canvass for a return to African roots, but not necessarily the kind of return to Africa advocated in the 1960s. It is not what Armah suggests in Ast's character or her journey to Africa either. In fact, her journey is more like Wideman's to South Carolina.

While Wideman attaches great value to community and connectedness, he tacitly believes in the power of the individual, acting alone, even invisibly, to bring about change. Armah had tested that method and found it to be inadequate. Their decisions are also a product of their histories or social contexts. As Wideman demonstrates through one of his characters in *Fatheralong*, the individual activist without the force of a mass behind him is considered harmless until he harms a white man. What is important ultimately are the conclusions Armah and Wideman make about history and its role in the lives of a people, in particular the African people. They argue that Africa and Africans have not been treated fairly in the histories that have been invented by the West and that the knowledge of African history is absolutely important to Africans wherever they are. They challenge their readers with historical facts and dare them to investigate their veracity. They argue that community—the African way, which recognizes individual excellence but not in a competitive sense, as opposed to the individuality of the West—is to be preferred because that is what defines our humanity. These writers have significantly invoked history because literature gains more power and relevance through history, especially when that literature is committed to social change. Above all, they confront the politics of race and racism, which manifests in the denial, abuse, exploitation, and underdevelopment of the African, by taking us on a trip through the experience of personal, national, and racial histories. The ultimate aim is to raise the consciousness that will bring about not just change but a revolutionary transformation.

12

Special Report

The Michael J. C. Echeruo Valedictory Symposium

MAIK NWOSU AND OBI NWAKANMA

The Michael J. C. Echeruo Valedictory Symposium was held at Syracuse University, New York, on October 15, 2010 to mark Professor Echeruo's formal retirement from the academy. A broad range of scholars, writers, and university administrators—Echeruo's colleagues—came to Syracuse for the event.

The symposium began with a welcome message by Professor Gregg Lambert, Director of the Humanities Center at Syracuse University. He noted that the symposium was cosponsored by the Department of English and Textual Studies and the dean's office (College of Arts and Sciences), and recalled that planning for the symposium began in the office of Catherine Newton, who was dean from 2000 to 2008.

In her welcome address, Professor Newton said that, as a paleontologist, she could not think of beginning something without exploring a bit of history. The symposium, she said, was born in a special way. It began "two and a half years ago" when she spoke with Echeruo about who his colleagues were and how he imagined his work and intellectual life. It was a thrilling meeting, very Echeruoan. She welcomed the assembly with joy and described Echeruo's works—such as *The Conditioned Imagination from Shakespeare to Conrad, Joyce Cary and the Novel of Africa*, the *Igbo–English Dictionary*, and the critical edition of *The Tempest*—as stirring. She praised the exceptional range, breadth, and depth in Echeruo's scholarship and intellectual life, and his academic leadership and mentoring of academic leaders, especially the way he combined these qualities in a fully unitary way. She referenced Echeruo's tenure at Imo State University, which gave him the chance to define the mission and culture of an institution, and pointed out that there was no one better than Echeruo to do this. She recalled with gratitude conversations with Echeruo on issues that then faced the College of Arts and Sciences when she was the dean—such as how to do justice to strengthening departments when the intellectual world was no longer departmentalized and how to understand what English as an academic discipline was or could be. She expressed her gratitude for the three or four interventions by Echeruo, which helped her to better understand some issues. On a personal note, she recalled attending the postcommencement lunch for Echeruo's nephew and how the experience made her reflect on what she could mean, as an academic, in the intellectual life of not only her family but also the children of her two brothers. It is in the context of Echeruo's quiet brilliance and mentoring that the symposium was held. Finally, Dean Newton introduced Professor Abiola Irele, who was scheduled to give the opening address, as an academic whose leadership has been crucially important in defining the direction of the fields that Echeruo is associated with.

Beginning his address, Professor Abiola Irele (former Professor of African, French, and Comparative Literature at The Ohio State University; former editor of *Research in African Literatures*; former Visiting Professor of African and African American Studies at Harvard University; recently the Provost of the College of Humanities, Kwara State University, Ilorin; and currently Professor of French and Comparative Literature, Kwara State University, Ilorin) thanked Dean Newton for her introduction and said that he had wonderful memories of Syracuse because of a previous visit, probably in the 1970s. He recalled an occasion long ago, at University College, Ibadan, when Echeruo spoke on Beckett's *Waiting for Godot* and he was startled by the depth of Echeruo's insight. He has, however, never agreed with Echeruo letting Conrad off the hook (in *The Conditioned Imagination from Shakespeare to Conrad*), but said that Echeruo brings to the argument a very sharp intellectual acumen. Echeruo has done very good work in both African and English literature (including

Shakespeare). Irele described Shakespeare as an "African" writer and said that there is no play more "African" than Shakespeare's *Macbeth.* At this point, Irele told a story, about finding Wole Soyinka's *Ibadan* in the anthropology section (instead of the autobiography section) of Blackwell's, the most famous bookshop at Oxford. The incident reminded him of Soyinka's account of his having to give his series of lectures at Cambridge (later published as *Myth, Literature, and the African World*) in the anthropology department. There was a certain reluctance at the time to accept the validity of African literature because of a general misapprehension about the nature of African literature. It was a question of valuation, of Western literature being taken as a measure of the imaginative function, and one that did not require a demonstration of justification. This was a conditioned response rather than a reflective attitude. The assumption was that African literature was not only incomprehensible but also without value.

Irele recalled the statement by Saul Bellow—"Show me the Zulu equivalent of Tolstoy"—and noted that, interestingly, Saul Bellow was later joined by Wole Soyinka and Naguib Mahfouz as Nobel laureates. These sorts of responses, he pointed out, have also been made with reference to women's literature, responses that highlight the question of power relations that the canon raises. Much of the denigration of non-Western or African literature specifically is sometimes due to plain ignorance. Africa is represented as incapable of cultural achievement. All these factors set the ambiguous situation of African and related literatures in the Western academy, along with the attendant consequences—such as the increasing scarcity of texts and that African literature is subordinated to the theoretical category called "postcolonial" literature. There is also a sense in which trends or fashionable modes in academic literary theory, such as structuralism, have been imposed on African literature as dogmas. There is the tendency to dissociate literature from experience in these traditions of literary criticism. Irele made a case for the distinctive and autonomous character of African literature, including the need for us to reflect on the significance of this uniqueness. To appreciate the significance of African literature, we need to consider the three categories that account for the African literary experience: oral tradition and the lyric (and the value systems embodied by these forms), the written literature in the languages wholly or partially indigenous to Africa, and the new literature in European languages. From a formal point of view, orality provides a fundamental common ground of the three categories, for it functions as a reference for all three as a sort of intertext. This literature continues to demonstrate the continuity of our imaginative forms.

Irele then discussed the two levels of articulation—the historical thematic and the formal poetic—in these categories of literature. Talking about African literature, he clarified, is inclusive of North African Islamic literature. For the literature in European languages, there is the question of transposing the oral tradition into a new modern register of expression, a development that is very clear in South African writing. This new literature has been invested with a new purpose of reflecting the acute awareness we Africans have of a radical discontinuity of our history, of having been plunged into a new mode of existence with all the consequences that this entails. The colonial situation has been the determining context of social transformation and cultural change, it is the historical setting for the dilemma of modernity in Africa. Irele noted contradictions between the humanist claims of Western civilization and the reality of the African and black situation in the world. Consequently, there was an early recognition of the failure of the Enlightenment project from the African black point of view particularly. In the documentation of the African experience, we have witnessed the indictment of Western civilization. This indictment is one of the major aspects of Chinua Achebe's *Things Fall Apart*, an example of counterdiscourse in African literature. This counterdiscourse highlights the promotion of an alternative vision of the world rooted in local knowledge, and this is why Irele has always been a defender of Négritude. A strong emphasis on the collective experience in African literature attests to an earnest effort by writers to chart a new direction, the utopian—the notion of commitment, the potential of literature for the elaboration of values, the statement it makes of its function for the creation of a new social and moral order. Implicit in its aesthetic function has been the emancipatory value in the confrontation of Africa with its ambiguous history. There is a real sense in which African literature provides a specific testimony of a distinctive collective experience.

Dean Newton introduced the moderator of the first panel, Professor Emmanuel Obiechina, a distinguished scholar and an authority on the novel of Africa, one of Echeruo's principal interests. Introducing the members of the first panel—Professor Biodun Jeyifo, Professor Kenneth Harrow, Professor Lokangaka Losambe, and Professor Chukwuma Azuonye—Professor Obiechina described their job as the exploration of African literature from the seminal stage to the present time. African literature, he noted, has grown over the years to the point that it is now accepted in the intellectual sanctuaries of the world.

Professor Biodun Jeyifo, Professor of African and African American Studies and of Comparative Literature at Harvard University, began his talk, entitled "Between Postcolonialism and Globalization," with a set of posed and implied questions: Have we moved decisively in literary and cultural studies from postcolonialism to globalization? Is the moment of postcolonial studies over? Is the sign of this shift seen in the progressive rise of *world literature* as the fastest growing new field in literary and cultural studies? The present reality, he noted, referring to the advice that he half-jokingly gave a graduate student recently, may be to keep the term "postcolonial studies" and emphasize "postcoloniality" as one's particular specialization. The term "postcoloniality" operates like the term "world" in world literature. At the very least, he said, postcoloniality is the forerunner of globalization in the field of literary and cultural studies. He pointed out the resemblance between postcoloniality and globalization. Both constructs are rooted in the common theoretical presupposition that a scholarly field of study is as much constructed by language and mind as by anything in the world. The two concepts are constructed in defiance of untidy things out there in the world that might be resistant to a field of knowledge constructed in pure thought. Postcolonial studies and globalization focus on this perennial question of the relational roles of the minds of scholars, their students, and the world to the constitution of teaching programs and research agendas of fields of study. He saluted

Echeruo at this point as one of the finest scholars that Nigeria, and Africa, has produced.

To its credit, Jeyifo continued, postcolonial studies as an academic field has always been open to constant critical review and projection. It remains to be seen whether globalization will also be open to this practice. Jeyifo then posed some more questions: What has postcolonial studies taught us about the African experience of the language and literature connection? What does globalization portend for the present and the future? Postcolonialism lasted for more than two centuries, starting from the American revolt against Britain in the eighteenth century through the Latin American and anticolonial independence movements in the early nineteenth century to the decolonizing movements in the twentieth century of Southeast Asia, Africa, and the Caribbean. "Globalization" as a temporal phase has barely begun, though the term has been around for more than a century. "Globalization," as the term is currently used, dates from around the 1980s when neoliberalism seemed hegemonic in nearly every corner of the world and there was a move from the discourse of emerging nations to the discourse of emerging markets. Jeyifo pointed out that his focus in his talk is more on postcolonialism and globalization as fields of study with research and curricular programs than as historical processes. It is probably more accurate to say that we are still in an interregnum in which the two fields are in a relation of contention and interrelation.

At the present time, noted Jeyifo, world literature is the best example of globalization in the field of literary and cultural studies. Differences between the diverse regions of the world are not ignored in world literature but they are not given the same sort of interpretive muscularity that comes from paying close attention to the inequality and volatility around the world, in which languages and national traditions live in relations of exchange and inequality. For postcolonialism, local, national, and regional realities and traditions matter greatly, and it is only on the basis of a solid grounding in these relations and traditions that solidarity with other parts of the world are expressed and can be sustained. Globalization emphasizes cosmopolitanism without borders, a so-called unhomely worldliness that sees the local in the global and the global in the local. Radical postcolonial studies has given tremendous encouragement to Afrophone literature or writing in African languages without taking the extreme stance of Ngugi wa Thiong'o, whereas globalization has more or less strongly given a sense of English or Portuguese (or some other European languages) as no longer alien to Africa (as African languages). The language question has taken a sublated form. Instead of tirelessly being invested in the dichotomy between Afrophone and Europhone, we should focus on the language problem as a contradiction internal to neocolonialism and the threat that globalization poses to us in Africa. All languages—whether Afrophone or Europhone—are badly taught in Africa, and this affects writing. The humane, radical, and transformative currents of globalization can only be unlocked (or the shift from postcolonialism to globalization be actualized) with the sound defeat of neoliberalism.

Professor Kenneth Harrow, Distinguished Professor of African Literature and Cinema at Michigan State University, began his presentation by explaining that his paper was drawn from a chapter in a book he is writing on "trash." The book is devoted to African cinema and rethinking our approach to African culture. He said he is interested in looking from the point of view of matter or the material and in reversing our notion of the idea as dominant. He then posed a series of questions: What would an understanding of African culture look like if it is seen from below? What is the site of the "below" from which to view the larger, more powerful, better educated, wealthier—or the dominant—features of the social order? He used the term "trash" to describe that "below." Trash is the location of the desire to shape a new structure of what we take to be real. Jacques Rancière calls this the "partition (or distribution) of the sensible"—that is, an ordered way of seeing and describing the world. There is one question for trash, which has to be addressed before any other if we are going to relate the trope to African cinema: the "distribution of the sensible" in relation to African cinema—a cinema of art and a cinema of polity. The first trap for trash arises when African cinema or art is judged to be inadequately serious when addressing social issues. This is the trap of art for art's sake, which sets art against politics in a binary fashion. The second trap is when African cinema is judged to be adequately serious or successful in raising social issues but fails to meet aesthetic standards; it is taken as a second-rate cinema that must resort to special pleading in order to be taken seriously as art or cinema. In the first case, African cinema is measured against the standards of high culture, which defines itself against trash, commercial, porno, or amateur cinema. In the second case, trashy cinema is equated with subjective, asocial, introspective films. Both (evaluations) determine an outcome in which African cinema maintains its marginal status. Both are now tedious ways of framing the division of African cinema.

Harrow argued that we need a new distribution of the sensible. Special pleading implies inferior art, raises the question of whose standards constitute "international norms" and whether there is such a thing as an African film practicing African aesthetics. The work of Senegalese, Malian, and Burkinabe directors would typically be cited (by critics for whom Africa remains a site of otherness) as examples of this style of "authentic African cinema practice" despite the programmatic prescriptiveness of these injunctions. More important, art for art's sake in international norms become code words for Western aesthetic values and dominant cinematic practices. The concern over politics and the commercial world of cinema was structured around anticolonial arguments that yielded with time to postcolonial theorizing, which eventually had to deal with the tricky question of what to do with films (such as those of Nollywood) that proved indifferent to agendas seeking to convey truth serums to African audiences. Art and politics remain dueling partners, but they are becoming increasingly sidelined by the overwhelming problem of the financing of serious African filmmaking and by the competing commercial success of Nollywood. Commodification as a key issue for a postmodern economy rose to prominence and found its definitions in terms supplied by the vocabulary of globalization and its accompanying neoliberal agendas. Harrow counseled that we have to stop looking at the world from the high point down (the notion of "high culture") but from the bottom up—from trash. There is a dynamic culture that we must access by moving to a vision that takes us beyond the binary of high and low art but seeks to find that which has been discarded as unworthy of cultural studies, perhaps starting from Onitsha Market Literature and ending with Nollywood as the location of a new, dynamic, and successful creativity. Notably, these elements (the melodramatic, the personal, and the sentimental) have always been there in African cinema.

In his paper "Olaudah Equiano, Michael Echeruo, and the Politics of Remembering," Professor Lokangaka Losambe, the Frederick M. and Fannie C. P. Corse Professor of English at the University of Vermont, acknowledged Echeruo's influence on his Congolese and African generation of writers and critics. Losambe situated Echeruo's incisive vision and analysis, as is evident in *Joyce Cary and the Novel of Africa* and *The Conditioned Imagination from Shakespeare to Conrad*, at the beginning of postcolonial studies. But Echeruo's physical location at the time (in Ibadan, Nigeria) possibly limited his influence. He then connected Echeruo's critical practice to Olaudah Equiano (author of the slave narrative *The Interesting Narrative of the Life of Olaudah Equiano*, 1789) and the postcolonial corrective tradition. In Losambe's view, Echeruo is one of those African scholars to truly engage the Western mind—in a manner comparable to Equiano.

Professor Chukwuma Azuonye, Professor of Africana Studies at the University of Massachusetts, Boston, began his critical discourse on Echeruo's poetry by describing him as "one of the most powerful voices among the first-generation African writers and critics writing in English." He noted that Echeruo won the first prize at the first All-Africa poetry prize organized by Mbari in 1962 and still has an unpublished poetry collection entitled *Khaki No Be Leather*. Azuonye analyzed what he identified as the three phases in Echeruo's poetry—the movement from the ivory tower to the public square (or a deschooling from the canons of Euromodernism). Echeruo finds his voice in the third phase. Azuonye demonstrates this interpretation by the deconstruction of a poem, "Sophia," that "has posed problems for critics." His close reading of the poem highlighted the "deeper Africanisms" beneath what some critics have described as the "abstract style" or "modernist bricolage and defamiliarization phraseology" in Echeruo's poetry.

The second panel featured four speakers—Professor Anthonia Kalu, Professor Ernest Emenyonu, Professor Tejumola Olaniyan, and Professor Micere M. Githae Mugo—in a session moderated by Professor Silvio

Torres-Saillant of the Department of English and Textual Studies, Syracuse University.

Professor Torres-Saillant began by establishing the basic framework of the discussion and by introducing the panelists, whom he called "notable and admired colleagues." First, he introduced Professor Kalu, Professor of English and chair of the African and African American Studies Program at The Ohio State University in Columbus, Ohio. Professor Kalu's talk was entitled "Images of Women and the African Novel."

The next presentation, by Professor Ernest Emenyonu (chair, Department of Africana Studies, University of Michigan-Flint and editor of *African Literature Today*), was also in many ways an extension of the conversation about the literary moment that Echeruo occupies. His evolving biographical work on the Nigerian novelist Cyprian Ekwensi, "Unspoken Echoes from the Heart: The Cyprian Ekwensi No One Else Knew," was the focus of his discussion. As Emenyonu noted in his preface to his discussion, "one might wonder what Cyprian Ekwensi is doing in a valedictory symposium on M. J. C. Echeruo. Perhaps more than he realizes it, Echeruo has played an incomparable mediatory and interventionist role between generations in the theory and criticism of African literatures." Tracing the fundamental and inexorable link of the work of the writer and critic to memory, remembrance, and continuity (the key theme of Echeruo's 1979 Ahiajioku lecture "Ahamefula"), Emenyonu attempted to connect the lecture to his own presentation with regard to Cyprian Ekwensi. All biography, needless to say, speaks to the act of memory and memorializing—"not forgetting what I stand for," in Emenyonu's own words.

Emenyonu's direct biographical exposition and anecdotal strategies aimed to explore and fully situate critical questions about the situation of Ekwensi's literary legacies. He recalled his first meeting with Ekwensi in 1968 when he was still a doctoral student at the University of Wisconsin-Madison, while Ekwensi, in the company of the novelist Chinua Achebe and the poet Gabriel Okara, was a war emissary on a diplomatic mission for the now defunct secessionist Republic of Biafra during the Nigerian civil war. That first encounter led, on a return from the United States at the end of the war, to a visit with Ekwensi at his homes, first in Enugu and then at Nkwelle Ezunaka, where Emenyonu spent a week of archival work on Ekwensi. As Emenyonu testified, "Cyprian Ekwensi had stacks and stacks of files on practically every critic who had said anything negative on him." Ekwensi felt himself a much misunderstood and misrepresented writer. The basic premise of Ekwensi's deep personal reaction against critics of his works was his rejection of a broad negative categorization of all his creative output. He fought against the use of one example of his books, Emenyonu noted, as the basis for determining the quality of his entire output, as was exemplified by one critic, Professor Bernth Lindfors, who declared that Ekwensi's entire writing was "a failure." The second apparently was his rejection of the selection and validation of the "Ibadan school" of writers by Ulli Beier in the 1960s as representative of the Nigerian canon. But he rarely voiced his exceptions publicly, choosing rather to keep notes and make his annotated comments on these critical statements and views in newspaper cuttings, personal notes, and diaries. His work is without doubt a biographer's trove, which at his death Ekwensi entrusted to Emenyonu.

Emenyonu tried to situate Ekwensi's method of critical engagement, using various means—letters, notes, annotations, and diaries with which he responded privately to these critical assertions made about his work. Emenyonu used three examples from the Ekwensi collection to register the tenor of Ekwensi's reaction to his critics. The first example is a more public one—perhaps Ekwensi's first and possibly only public reaction to a critic of his novel. The background is worth summarizing. At the publication of Ekwensi's novel *Jagua Nana* in the 1960s, a group of filmmakers proposed to make it into a film. But the Nigerian government refused to grant permission on the basis that the subject of the novel turned into film was too racy. An undergraduate at the University of Ibadan had read the novel, burned his copy, and afterward wrote to the *Morning Post* urging every Nigerian to burn their copy of *Jagua Nana*. Ekwensi fired a bruising letter to the university undergraduate, a bitter letter that highlights his deep emotional anguish over "ignorant" critics.

However, it does seem that Ekwensi's last effort at preserving his own story—the story of Ekwensi that no one else knew—is mired in a new current of controversy. Emenyonu revealed the dimension of this controversy in the conclusion of his presentation, throwing up the crucial question that summarizes his paper: By what means is the legacy of the African writer and Africa's heritage of letters preserved? Who has the rights to determine a place for the unpublished manuscripts and papers of an African writer of the stature of Cyprian Ekwensi? This question is especially vital in the case of a writer like Ekwensi, whose conscious archival and documentary strategies aimed clearly at preserving his literary legacy in ways that would offer definitive insight into both his work as a writer and his perceptive, even if subjective, response to his critics through his notes and diaries. It is a question that was complicated by Emenyonu's revelation of a brewing scandal following the unauthorized sale of a copy of the manuscript of Ekwensi's unpublished autobiography, *In My Time*, by the critic Charles Larson to the Harry Ransom Center, a humanities research library and museum at the University of Texas at Austin. Emenyonu's account detailed his own indirect involvement in the unfolding drama and the reactions of the Ekwensi family and Charles Larson in letters exchanged on the subject of Ekwensi's manuscript. Emenyonu concluded with a rhetorical question: "Is this what African literature has come to, fifty years after?"

Professor Tejumola Olaniyan (the Louise Durham Mead Professor of English at the University of Wisconsin-Madison) continued thereafter to extend the discourse on African modernist culture and ideas, albeit in a different direction. Professor Olaniyan, who earned his doctorate in English from Cornell University after studying at the University of Ife, also noted that although he did not come under the direct tutelage of Echeruo at either Nsukka or Ibadan, he had nonetheless come under the grip of his ideas early on, like many in his generation of students in Nigerian and other universities in the Anglophone world. Echeruo's important essay "The Dramatic Limits of Igbo Ritual" and his seminal book *Victorian Lagos* were two hallmark examples for Olaniyan of how his encounters with Echeruo's scholarship and ideas helped to shape his own intellectual and scholarly quest. His presentation on what he described as "garrison architecture" referenced the work done by Echeruo on the evolution of urban culture in West Africa as its point of departure. "At the time I came across the book (*Victorian Lagos*) it seemed odd to me that a literary critic would go to the archives and do that kind of work. The book was published in

1977, and I do not know any other critic who has done that kind of work. Later on when I began work on political cartooning in Africa, and I had to go back to the archives using some of the newspapers that he used, it was like a kind of authorization in fact to do the work."

Having established an intellectual debt to Echeruo, Olaniyan proceeded to his own analysis on the situation of the built space in the production of modern African imagination. His argument is based on a perception of architecture "not only as a system of verbal signs" but also, in a more holistic manner, as the lived space—"where we live" and presumably where the social and emotional interplay of forces shape the reality of the African artist. From Chinua Achebe's portrayal of African architecture at the turn of the twentieth century in his novels to Chimamanda Adichie's more contemporary portrayal, "what you would get," said Olaniyan, "is a portable, very suggestive look into the profound transformations in the ways and modes of African living, of course (seen) through literature." The very texture of modern African literature with its acute engagement with the social reality of postcolonial society has also created a highly determined form of "status distinction" or an awareness of class and social differences and "the myriad of ways they are produced, reproduced, and subverted." Olaniyan drew from what he discerns as the highly political character of modern African literature as well as from aesthetic theory to contextualize how these shifts in Africa's modern landscape and the production of its distinct social categories affect and condition the imaginative life of the African writer.

As contemporary African writing becomes more cosmopolitan, with some of the producers of that literature crossing many metropolitan boundaries and increasingly producing their writing beyond traditional African locales, the African city—the domain of the contemporary African imagination—has grown to become "most unwelcoming." Olaniyan made clear that the transformation of the African space dates back to the rapid urbanization and the growing metropolis in Africa from the nineteenth century; however, shifts in the cultural forms of late capitalism have also led to "citification," with the increasing diversity and complexity of the African urban environment marked by its "fetish for property." The contemporary African city is thus characterized by what Olaniyan described as "garrison architecture" with its fortified or fortress conditions, which is the product of the "era of globalization." Garrison architecture is that "colorful feature" of the urban African landscape enclosed by walls—usually residential houses enclosed by high walls spiked at the top with broken bottles and barbed wires.

In situating or constructing a deeper history of this phenomenon, Olaniyan made a distinct analysis of the difference between the era of the precolonial walled cities in Africa such as Meroe, Kano, Benin, or Great Zimbabwe and the new architecture of modern African cities with their fortress architecture frequently socially normalized by the visual pageantry of Nollywood. Precolonial walled cities and palaces signified a more critical use and purpose of the built space—either as monuments or sites of the ceremonial, of refuge, or of industry. In all that, the city was a protective zone of community and a grand tribute to the public imagination rather than the individual's desire for security and surveillance. From his reading of the works of African writers—such as Wole Soyinka's preface to his satirical play *Opera Wonyosi*, Nadine Gordimer's short story "Once Upon a Time," Alan Paton's 1945 essay "Who Is Really to Blame for the Crime Wave in South Africa?," or Chimamanda Adichie's *Purple Hibiscus*—Olaniyan pointed out that contemporary African cities like Capetown, Johannesburg, Lagos, or Enugu, with their garrison architecture, reflect the production of a more complex social crisis; it is the reflection of a degenerative social condition marked by a wide gap of inequality; it is "abnormal, functionally disordered, and parasitic"—or what Olaniyan described as "paracapitalism." Paracapitalism is fundamentally oligarchic and characterized by reverse expectations, growth without development, progressive degradation of the quality of life, and above all the absence of adequate surveillance structures and systems.

Because the built space itself is the domain of social performance, one of the great tasks of literature is to represent characters in that space of performance honestly and with visual authority. "Part of creating memorable characters is showing where and how they live," Olaniyan noted. Part of Olaniyan's project lays out an architecture of the literature itself or what he calls "architecture and its literary inscriptions." Modern African literature, to put it simply, makes visible the complex contradictions of evolving

African society, which is characterized by the shifts and transformations in our visible reality—the new urban reality of modern Africa—whose architecture in that sense reifies its material as well as spiritual conditions. It is the writer's or artist's inner and outer worlds projected.

The critic and emeritus professor of African Literature at the University of Austin, Texas, Professor Bernth Lindfors, who was originally billed to speak next, was unable to attend the symposium. The moderator then invited Professor Irele, who gave a summary of Lindfors's prepared paper "Deciphering the Past"—a quantitative or statistical look at fifty years of African literature.

Then came the Kenyan writer Micere M. Githae Mugo (Professor of African and African American Studies at Syracuse University), to respond to the presentations made by this distinguished panel of speakers. Professor Mugo began by first paying a personal tribute to Echeruo and properly situating Echeruo's place in the academy during the last fifty years of African literature. First, she drew attention to Aime Cesaire's reminder to the black elite of the double bind in which African intellectuals exists from their double location within a heritage of traditions, with Africa on the one hand and the West on the other. As a result, "we have a schizophrenic relationship with ourselves," Mugo observed. However, she noted, Echeruo has managed to locate himself in both worlds, "in what we have inherited in the colonial classroom, but has not allowed himself to be swallowed by that tradition. He manages to locate himself in both traditions without being schizophrenic. And I think that is an achievement." In Mugo's assessment, Echeruo transcends the double bind. Echeruo's unity of being, it must thus be said, permits him a unique perspective as a scholar of modern African literature and culture and a stable basis for interrogating its place in the context of modernity. Mugo elaborated on another important dimension of Echeruo's career: his collegial leadership and mentorship. This is the substance of Echeruo's investments in the intellectual tradition—his legacy of sustaining the tradition of inquiry, debate, and dissent within the academy, a tradition that is increasingly lost to a new generation of scholars. "I want to suggest that we are too afraid to engage and disagree with each other," Mugo said, while also noting the necessity for continuing the tradition of robust debate emblematized by scholars such as Echeruo, who could agree to disagree. As for Echeruo, "he can be quite provocative, especially when he has a different point of view," Professor Mugo testified.

Mugo's talk segued into the importance of locating the agency of women in the discourse of African literature and criticism. She observed the critical aspects of Kalu's presentation on women in African literature as constituting "new sites" of knowledge; Emenyonu's discussion on Ekwensi as raising important questions about the legacies of colonialism; and Olaniyan's discourse on African literature and architecture as opening up exciting new possibilities of discourse in African literature and aesthetics.

References ▣ Notes on Contributors ▣ Index

References

Abani, Chris. 2006. *Becoming Abigail: A Novella*. New York: Akashic Books.

———. 2004. *Graceland*. New York. Farrar, Straus and Giroux.

———. 2009. *Song for Night: A Novella*. Brooklyn, NY: Akashic Books.

———. 2007. *The Virgin of Flames*. New York: Penguin.

Abdullahi, Denja. 1999. *A Volcano of Voices*. Edited by Steve Shaba. Lagos: Association of Nigerian Authors.

Achebe, Chinua. 2008. "Achebe Discusses Africa 50 Years after 'Things Fall Apart.'" Interview by Jeffrey Brown. *PBS Newshour*, May 2.

———. 1982 (1975). "The African Writer and the Biafran Cause." In Achebe, *Morning Yet on Creation Day*, 78–84.

———. 1994. "The Art of Fiction." Interview by Jerome Brooks. *The Paris Review* (Winter): 139. http://www.theparisreview.org/interviews/1720/the-art-of-fiction-no-139-chinua-achebe.

———. 2010. *The Education of a British-Protected Child*. New York: Knopf.

———. 1972. *Girls at War and Other Stories*. New York: Doubleday.

———. 2000. *Home and Exile*. New York: Oxford University Press.

———. 1988. *Hopes and Impediments: Selected Essays, 1965–1987*. Oxford: Heinemann.

———. 1988. "An Image of Africa: Racism in Conrad's *Heart of Darkness*." In Achebe, *Hopes and Impediments*, 1–20.

———. 1982 (1975). *Morning Yet on Creation Day*. London: Heinemann.

———. 2013. "The Song of Ourselves." *New Statesman*, March 22, http://www.newstatesman.com/books/2013/03/song-ourselves.

———. 2012. *There Was a Country: A Personal Narrative of Biafra*. New York: Penguin.

———. 1994. *Things Fall Apart*. New York: Doubleday.

Adedeji, J. A. 1968. "The Place of Drama in Yoruba Religious Observance." *Odu* 3, no. 1: 88–94.

Adeoti, Gbemisola. 2005. "The Re-Making of Africa: Ayi Kwei Armah and the Narrative of an (Alter)-native Route to Development." *Africa Media Review* 13, no. 2: 1–15.

Adepitan, Titi. 2006. "Issues in Recent African Writing." *African Literature Today* 2: 124–28.

Adesanmi, Pius. 2011. *You're Not a Country, Africa: A Personal History of the African Present*. Parklands, South Africa: Penguin Books.

Adesokan, Akin. 2004. *Roots in the Sky*. Lagos: Festac Books.

Adewale, Toyin. 2000. "Introduction." In *25 New Nigerian Poets*, edited by Toyin Adewale, iii–v. Berkeley, CA: Ishmael Reed Publishing.

Adichie, Chimamanda Ngozi. 2008. "African 'Authenticity' and the Biafran Experience." *Transition* 99: 42–53.

———. 2009a. "The American Embassy." In Adichie, *The Thing around Your Neck*, 127–40.

———. 2009b. "The Danger of a Single Story." TED, October 29.

———. 1998. *For Love of Biafra*. Ibadan: Spectrum Books.

———. 2006. *Half of a Yellow Sun*. New York: Alfred A. Knopf.

———. 2009c. "I Am a Happy Feminist." Interview by R. Krithika. *The Hindu*, August 14.

———. 2003. *Purple Hibiscus*. New York: Anchor Books.

———. 2009d. *The Thing around Your Neck*. New York: Alfred A. Knopf.

———. 2006b. "Truth and Lies." *The Guardian*, September 16.

Adorno, Theodor. 1974. *Minima Moralia: Reflections from Damaged Life*. Translated by E.F.N. Jephcott. London: Verso.

Afigbo, Adiele A. E. 1979. "Salute to a Colleague." In *Ahiajoku Lecture*, 3–5. Owerri, Nigeria: Culture Division, Ministry of Information, Culture, Youth, and Sports.

Aidoo, Ama Ata. 1997. *The Girl Who Can and Other Stories*. Oxford: Heinemann.

———. 1995 (1970). *No Sweetness Here and Other Stories*. New York: The Feminist Press.

Aiyejina, Funso. 1988. "Recent Nigerian Poetry in English: An Alter-Native Tradition." In Ogunbiyi, *Perspectives on Nigerian Literature*, 112–28.

Ajibade, Kunle. 2003. *Jailed For Life: A Reporter's Prison Notes*. Ibadan: Heinemann.

Ajima, Maria. 2000. *Poems of Sanity*. Lagos: Mace Books.

Akhuemokhan, Sophie. 2009. "The Ankh & Maat: Symbols of Successful Revolution in Ayi Kwei Armah's *Osiris Rising*." *African Literature Today* 27: 65–74.

Akubuiro, Henry. 2005. "Interview with E. Usman Shehu." *The Sunday Sun*, December 15, 50.

Ali, Ayaan Hirsi. 2007. *Infidel*. NY: Free Press.

Alu, N. Alu. 2001. "Echoes of Commitment in Modern African Poetry." In *Studies in Language and Literature*, edited by Macpherson Nkem Azuike, 198–203. Jos: Mazlink.

Amadi, Elechi. 1982. *Ethics in Nigerian Culture*. Ibadan: Heinemann.

———. 1969. *The Great Ponds*. London: Heinemann.

Amali, Idri. 2001. Generals without War. Lagos: Malthouse Press.

Amankulor, J. Ndukaku. 1993. "English-Language Drama and Theater." In *A History of Twentieth-Century African Literatures*, edited by Oyekan Owomoyela, 138–72. Lincoln: University of Nebraska Press.

Amuta, Chidi. 1988. "Literature of the Nigerian Civil War." In Ogunbiyi, *Perspectives on Nigerian Literature*, 85–92.

———. 1992. "Portraits of the Contemporary African Artist in Armah's Novels." In Wright, *Critical Perspectives on Ayi Kwei Armah*, 13–21.

———. 1989. *The Theory of African Literature*. London: Zed Books.

Andrade, Susan Z. 2001. "Adichie's Genealogies: National and Feminine Novels." *Research in African Literatures* 42, no. 2: 91–101.

Andres, Philippe. 1998. *La nouvelle*. Paris: Ellipses.

Anozie, Sunday O. 1984. "Negritude, Structuralism, Deconstruction." In *Black Literature and Literary Theory*, edited by Henry Louis Gates Jr., 105–25. London: Routledge.

Anyanwu, Chris. 2002. *The Days of Terror*. Ibadan: Spectrum Books.

Anyidoho, Kofi. 1997. "Prison as Exile/Exile as Prison: Circumstances, Metaphor, and a Paradox of Modern African Literature." In *The Word Behind the Bars and the Paradox of Exile*, edited by Kofi Anyidoho, 1–17. Evanston, IL: Northwestern University Press.

Apollon, Willy. 1996. "Introduction II." In Apollon and Feldstein, *Lacan, Politics, Aesthetics*, xix–xxvii.

———. 1996. "A Lasting Heresy, the Failure of Political Desire." In Apollon and Feldstein, *Lacan, Politics, Aesthetics*, 31–44.

Apollon, Willy, and Richard Feldstein, eds. 1996. *Lacan, Politics, and Aesthetics*. Albany: State University of New York Press.

Appiah, Kwame Anthony. 2006. *Cosmopolitanism: Ethics in a World of Strangers*. New York: W. W. Norton.

———. 1992. *In My Father's House: Africa in the Philosophy of Culture.* New York: Oxford University Press.

Aririesike, Jude. 2009. "Re: Rebranding Nigeria Image Project: We All Must Support and Contribute." *Online Nigeria,* April 16, http://www.onlinenigeria.com/articles/ad.asp?blurb=723.

Aristotle. 1996. *Poetics.* Translated by Malcolm Heath. London: Penguin Books. Ann Arbor: The University of Michigan Press.

Armah, Ayi Kwei. 1969. *The Beautyful Ones Are Not Yet Born.* London: Heinemann.

———. 1969. *Fragments.* London: Heinemann.

———. 1979. *The Healers: An Historical Novel.* London: Heinemann.

———. 1995. *Osiris Rising: A Novel of Africa Past, Present, and Future.* Popenguine, Senegal: Per Ankh.

———. 1979. *Two Thousand Seasons.* London: Heinemann.

———. 1969. *Why Are We So Blest?* London: Heinemann.

Ashcroft, Bill, Gareth Griffiths, and Helen Tiffin. 1989. *The Empire Writes Back: Theory and Practice in Post-Colonial Literatures.* London: Routledge.

Atta, Sefi. 2005. *Everything Good Will Come.* Lagos: Farafina; Northhampton, MA: Interlink Books.

Azikiwe, Nnamdi. 1970. *My Odyssey: An Autobiography.* Ibadan: Spectrum Books.

Azodo, Ada Uzoamaka. 1999. "(Re)defining Africa's Limits: A Comparison of the Novel and the Short Story." In *Migrating Words and Worlds: Pan-Africanism Updated,* edited by Anthony E. Hurley et al., 295–306. Trenton, NJ: Africa World Press.

Azuonye, Chukwuma. 2009. "The African Roots of Michael Echeruo's Poetry: A Close Reading of 'Sophia.'" Africana Studies Faculty Publication Series 9, 1–29. Boston: University of Massachusetts. http://scholarworks.umb.edu/africana_faculty_pubs/9/.

———. 1987. "Interview with Michael J. C. Echeruo." *Nsukka Journal of the Humanities* 1 (June): 161–80.

Bâ, Amadou Hampaté. 1999. *The Fortunes of Wangrin.* Translated by Aina Pavolini Taylor. Bloomington: Indiana University Press.

Bair, Deirdre. 2003. *Jung: A Biography.* Boston: Little, Brown.

Bajaj, Vikas. 2005. "Hopping the Subway?: Jump on the Web First." *The New York Times,* August 1.

Bak, Abuk. 2008. "Beyond Abeeda: Surviving Ten Years of Slavery in Sudan." In Jesse and Kasten, *Enslaved,* 39–60.

Bakhtin, M. Mikhail. 1981a. *The Dialogic Imagination: Four Essays.* Edited by Michael Holquist. Translated by Caryl Emerson and Michael Holquist. Austin: University of Texas Press.

———. 1981b. "Discourse in the Novel." In *Dialogic Imagination,* 259–422.

———. 1981c. "Epic and Novel." In *Dialogic Imagination,* 3–40.

Banda, Fareda. 2005. *Women, Law, and Human Rights: An African Perspective.* Oxford, UK: Hart Publishing.

Barber, Karin. 2007. *The Anthropology of Texts, Persons, and Publics.* Cambridge: Cambridge University Press.

Barbre, Joy Webster, et al., eds. 1989. *Interpreting Women's Lives: Feminist Theory and Personal Narratives.* Bloomington: Indiana University Press.

Baron-Cohen, Simon. 2011. *Zero Degrees of Empathy.* London: Allen Lane.

Bashir, Halima, and Damien Lewis. 2008. *Tears of the Desert: A Memoir of Survival in Darfur.* NY: One World Books.

Bennet, Tony. 2005. "Texts in History: The Determinations of Readings and Their Texts." In *Post-Structuralism and the Question of History,* edited by Derek Attridge, Geoff Bannington, and Robert Young, 63–81. Cambridge: Cambridge University Press.

Benstock, Shari, ed. 1988. *The Private Self: Theory and Practice of Women's Autobiographical Writings.* Chapel Hill: University of North Carolina Press.

Bhabha, Homi K. 1994. *The Location of Culture.* London: Routledge.

Blevins, Jacob. 2008. "Introduction." In *Dialogism and Lyric Self-Fashioning: Bakhtin and the Voices of a Genre,* edited by Jacob Blevins, 11–22. Selinsgrove, PA: Susquehanna University Press.

Bray, Rosemary L. 1990. "The Whole City Seen the Fire." *The New York Times,* September 30, http://www.nytimes.com/books/98/10/04/specials/wideman-philadelphia.html.

Braziel, Jana Evans, and Anita Mannur, eds. 2003. *Theorizing Diaspora.* Malden, MA: Blackwell.

Buell, Lawrence. 2000. "What We Talk about When We Talk about Ethics." In *The Turn to Ethics,* edited by Marjorie Garber et al., 1–14. New York: Routledge.

Bunch, Charlotte. 1990. "Women's Rights as Human Rights: Toward a Re-Vision of Human Rights." *Human Rights Quarterly* 12, no. 4: 486–98.

Burleson, Blake W. 2005. *Jung in Africa.* New York: Continuum.

Butler, Judith. 2005. *Giving an Account of Oneself.* New York: Fordham University Press.

Casanova, Pascale. 2004. *The World Republic of Letters.* Translated by M. B. Debevoise. Cambridge, MA: Harvard University Press.

Casmier, Stephen. 2006. "The Funky Novels of John Edgar Wideman: Odor and Ideology in *Reuben, Philadelphia Fire,* and *The Cattle Killing.*" In TuSmith, *Critical Essays on John Edgar Wideman,* 191–204.

Certeau, Michel de. 1988. *The Practice of Everyday Life.* Translated by Steven Rendall. Berkeley: University of California Press.

Chambers, Douglas B. 2014. *The Igbo Diaspora in the Era of the Slave Trade: Introductory History.* Foreword by Chima J. Korieh. Glassboro, NJ: Goldline and Jacobs Publishing.

———. 2005. *Murder at Montpelier: Igbo Africans in Virginia.* Jackson: University Press of Mississippi.

Chamoiseau, Patrick. 1998. *Texaco.* Translated by Rose-Myriam Réjouis and Val Vinokurov. New York: Vintage-Random.

Chinweizu. 1975. *The West and the Rest of Us: White Predators, Black Slavers, and the African Elite.* New York: Random House.

Chinweizu, Onwuchekwa Jemie, and Ihechukwu Madubuike. 1985. *Toward the Decolonization of African Literature.* London: Kegan Paul Intl.; 1983 ed., Howard University Press; 1980 ed., Fourth Dimension.

Chuku, Gloria, ed. 2013. *The Igbo Intellectual Tradition: Creative Conflict in African and African Diasporic Thought.* New York: Palgrave Macmillan.

Chukukere, Gloria. 1998. "An Appraisal of Feminism in the Socio-Political Development of Nigeria." In *Sisterhood, Feminism, and Power: From Africa to the Diaspora,* edited by Obioma Nnaemeka, 133–48. Trenton, NJ: Africa World Press.

Chukwuma, Helen. 1989. "Two Decades of the Short Story in West Africa." *WAACLALS Journal* 1: 1–14.

Cixous, Helene. 1998. "Where Is She in Language?" Translated by Meg Bortin. In *Philosophy and Sex,* edited by Robert B. Baker, et al., 311–17. Amherst, NY: Prometheus Books.

Clark-Bekederemo, John Pepper. 1965. "Poetry of the Urhobo Dance Udje." *Nigeria Magazine* 87: 282–87.

Coetzee, J. M. 1999. *Waiting for the Barbarians.* New York: Penguin.

Conrad, Joseph. 2006. *Heart of Darkness.* Edited by Paul B. Armstrong. New York: W. W. Norton.

Curtin, Philip. 1964. *The Image of Africa: British Ideas and Action, 1780–1850.* Madison: The University of Wisconsin Press.

Daly, Brenda. 1998. "I Stand Here Naked, and Best Dressed in Theory: Feminist Re-fashionings of Academic Discourse." In Kuribayashi and Tharp, *Creating Safe Space*, 11–26.

Damrosch, David. 2003. *What Is World Literature?* Princeton, NJ: Princeton University Press.

Dangaremgba, Tsitsi. 2006. *The Book of Not*. Oxfordshire: Ayebia Clarke Publishing.

———. 1988. *Nervous Conditions*. New York: Seal Press.

Dawood, Yusuf K. 2000. *Return to Paradise*. Nairobi: East African Educational Publishers.

Daymond, Margaret J. 2002. "Complementary Oral and Written Narrative Conventions: Sindiwe Magona's Autobiography and Short Story Sequence, 'Women at Work.'" *Journal of Southern African Studies* 28, no. 2: 331–46.

De Lauretis, Teresa. 1984. Alice Doesn't: Feminism, Semiotics, Cinema. Bloomington: Indiana University Press.

De Waal, Frans. 2009. *The Age of Empathy: Nature's Lessons for a Kinder Society*. New York: Harmony Books.

Derrida, Jacques. 1998. "Geopsychoanalysis: '. . . and the Rest of the World.'" Translated by Donald Nicholson-Smith. In *The Psychoanalysis of Race*, edited by Christopher Lane, 65–90. New York: Columbia University Press.

———. 1995. "Unsealing ('the Old New Language')." Translated by Peggy Kamuf and others. In *Points . . . Interviews, 1974–1994*, edited by Elisabeth Weber, 115–31. Stanford, CA: Stanford University Press.

Diop, Cheikh Anta. 1996 *Towards the African Renaissance: Essays in Culture and Development, 1946–1960*. Translalted by Egbuna P. Modum. London: Karnak House.

Dirie, Waris, and Cathleen Miller. 2001. *Desert Flower: The Extraordinary Life of a Desert Nomad*. New York: Vintage Books.

Dovey, Teresa. 1988. *The Novels of J. M. Coetzee: Lacanian Allegories*. Johannesburg: Ad. Donker.

Eagleton, Terry. 2003. *After Theory*. New York: Basic Books.

Echeruo, Michael J. C. 1989. "After Derrida." Review of Rand Bishop's *African Literature, African Critics: The Formation of Critical Standards, 1947–1966*. *Yearbook of Comparative and General Literature* 38: 186–88.

———. 2004. "Christopher Okigbo, *Poetry Magazine*, and 'Lament of the Silent Sisters.'" *Research in African Literatures* 35, no. 3: 8–25.

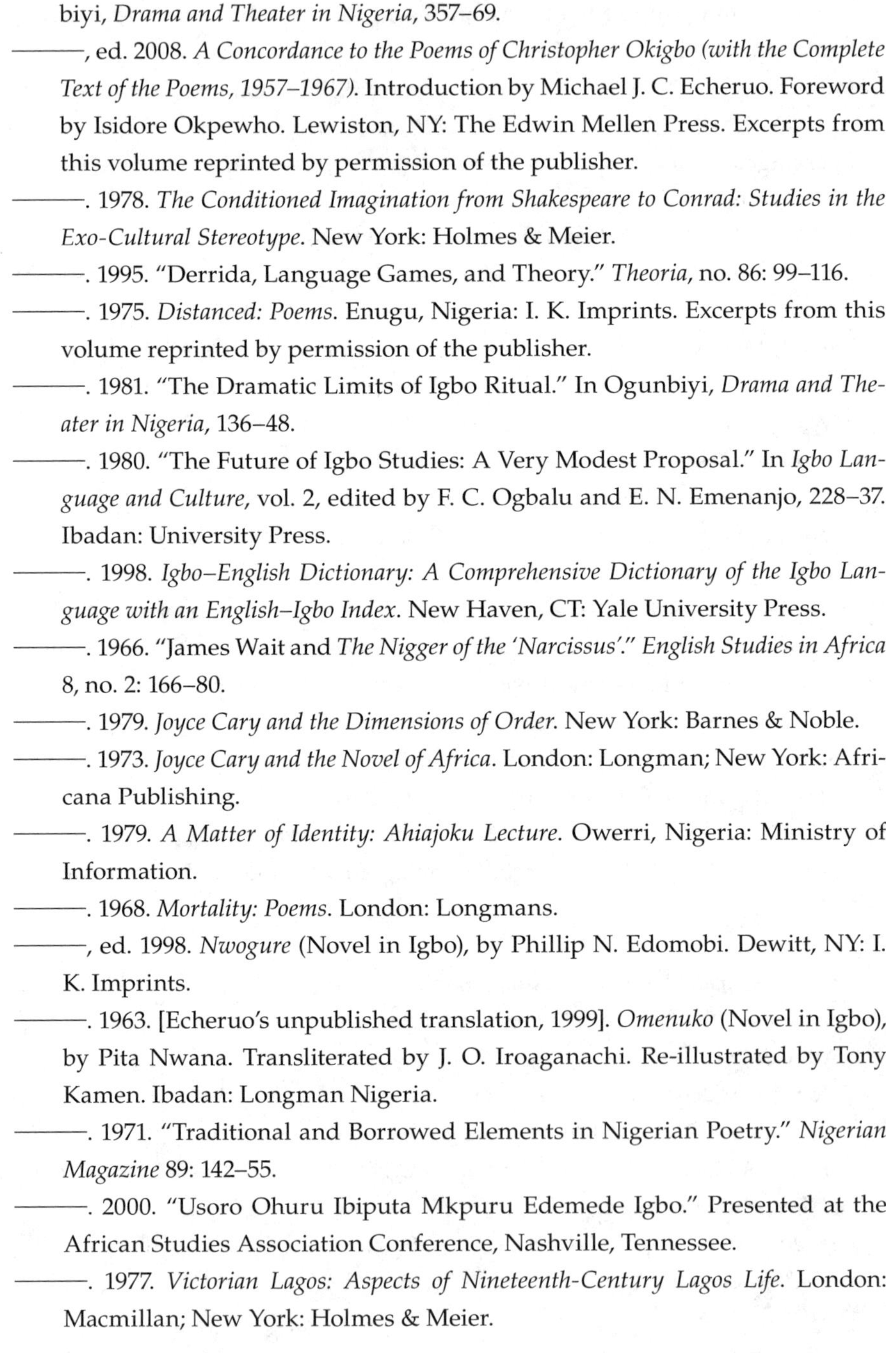

———. 1981. "Concert and Theater in Late Nineteenth-Century Lagos." In Ogunbiyi, *Drama and Theater in Nigeria*, 357–69.

———, ed. 2008. *A Concordance to the Poems of Christopher Okigbo (with the Complete Text of the Poems, 1957–1967)*. Introduction by Michael J. C. Echeruo. Foreword by Isidore Okpewho. Lewiston, NY: The Edwin Mellen Press. Excerpts from this volume reprinted by permission of the publisher.

———. 1978. *The Conditioned Imagination from Shakespeare to Conrad: Studies in the Exo-Cultural Stereotype*. New York: Holmes & Meier.

———. 1995. "Derrida, Language Games, and Theory." *Theoria*, no. 86: 99–116.

———. 1975. *Distanced: Poems*. Enugu, Nigeria: I. K. Imprints. Excerpts from this volume reprinted by permission of the publisher.

———. 1981. "The Dramatic Limits of Igbo Ritual." In Ogunbiyi, *Drama and Theater in Nigeria*, 136–48.

———. 1980. "The Future of Igbo Studies: A Very Modest Proposal." In *Igbo Language and Culture*, vol. 2, edited by F. C. Ogbalu and E. N. Emenanjo, 228–37. Ibadan: University Press.

———. 1998. *Igbo–English Dictionary: A Comprehensive Dictionary of the Igbo Language with an English–Igbo Index*. New Haven, CT: Yale University Press.

———. 1966. "James Wait and *The Nigger of the 'Narcissus'*." *English Studies in Africa* 8, no. 2: 166–80.

———. 1979. *Joyce Cary and the Dimensions of Order*. New York: Barnes & Noble.

———. 1973. *Joyce Cary and the Novel of Africa*. London: Longman; New York: Africana Publishing.

———. 1979. *A Matter of Identity: Ahiajoku Lecture*. Owerri, Nigeria: Ministry of Information.

———. 1968. *Mortality: Poems*. London: Longmans.

———, ed. 1998. *Nwogure* (Novel in Igbo), by Phillip N. Edomobi. Dewitt, NY: I. K. Imprints.

———. 1963. [Echeruo's unpublished translation, 1999]. *Omenuko* (Novel in Igbo), by Pita Nwana. Transliterated by J. O. Iroaganachi. Re-illustrated by Tony Kamen. Ibadan: Longman Nigeria.

———. 1971. "Traditional and Borrowed Elements in Nigerian Poetry." *Nigerian Magazine* 89: 142–55.

———. 2000. "Usoro Ohuru Ibiputa Mkpuru Edemede Igbo." Presented at the African Studies Association Conference, Nashville, Tennessee.

———. 1977. *Victorian Lagos: Aspects of Nineteenth-Century Lagos Life*. London: Macmillan; New York: Holmes & Meier.

Echeruo, Michael J. C., and Emmanuel N. Obiechina, eds. 1971. *Igbo Traditional Life, Culture, and Literature*. Lagos: Conch Magazine.

Effiong, Phillip. 1970. "Lt.-Col. Effiong Announces Surrender of Biafra." January 12, http://www.dawodu.com/effiong1.htm.

Eliot, T. S. 2001. "Tradition and the Individual Talent." In *The Norton Anthology of Theory and Criticism*, edited by Vincent B. Leitch et al., 1092–98. New York: W. W. Norton.

Ene, M. O. 2000. "Echeruo's Igbo–English Dictionary: Advancing Igbo Linguistic Legacy." Kwenu.com, http://pirate.shu.edu/~enemauri/publications/echeruo_review.htm.

Equiano, Olaudah. 2001 (1789). *The Interesting Narrative of the Life of Olaudah, or Gustavus Vassa, the African, Written by Himself*. Edited by Werner Sollors. New York: W. W. Norton.

———. 2003. *Interesting Narrative and Other Writings*. Edited by Vincent Carretta. New York: Penguin Group.

Evans, Dylan. 1999. "From Kantian Ethics to Mystical Experience: An Exploration of Jouissance." In *Key Concepts of Lacanian Psychoanalysis*, edited by Dany Nobus, 1–28. NY: Other Press.

Eze, Chielozona. 2007. "The Pitfalls of Cultural Consciousness." *Philosophia Africana* 10, no. 1: 37–47.

Ezeanah, Chiedu. 2005. *The Twilight Trilogy*. Ibadan: Kraft Books.

Falade, Solange. 1971. "Women of Dakar and the Surrounding Urban Area." Translated by H. M. Wright. In *Women in Tropical Africa*, edited by Denise Paulme, 217–29. Berkeley: University of California Press.

Fanon, Frantz. 1965. *The Wretched of the Earth*. Translated by Constance Farrington. New York: Grove Atlantic; 1967 ed., Penguin.

Fischer, Ernst. 1970. *The Necessity of Art*. Translated by Anna Bostock. New York: Penguin Books.

Foucault, Michel. 1997. *Ethics: Subjectivity and Truth: Essential Works of Foucault, 1954–1984*, vol. 1. Edited by Paul Rabinow. Translated by Robert Hurley. New York: The New Press.

Fox-Genovese, Elizabeth. 1988. "My Statue, My Self: Autobiographical Writings of Afro-American Women." In *The Private Self: Theory and Practice of Women's Autobiographical Writings*, edited by Shari Benstock, 63–89. Chapel Hill: The University of North Carolina Press.

Frank, Katherine. 1987. "Women without Men: The Feminist Novel in Africa." *African Literature Today* 15: 14–34.

Fraser, Robert. 1980. *The Novels of Ayi Kwei Armah*. London: Heinemann.

Freud, Sigmund. 1997. *Dora: An Analysis of a Case of Hysteria*. Introduction by Philip Rieff. New York: A Touchstone Book.

———. 1965. *The Interpretation of Dreams*. Translated by James Strachey. New York: Avon Books.

———. 1966. *On the History of the Psycho-Analytic Movement*. Revised and edited by James Strachey. Biographical introduction by Peter Gay. Translated by Joan Rievere. New York: W. W. Norton.

Friedman, Thomas L. 2005. *The World Is Flat: A Brief History of the Twenty-first Century*. New York: Farrar, Straus and Giroux.

Fyfe, W. Hamilton. 1940. *Aristotle's Art of Poetry: A Greek View of Poetry and Drama*. Oxford: Clarendon Press.

Gakwandi, Shatto. 1977. *The Novel and Contemporary Experience in Africa*. London: Heinemann & Africana Publishing House.

Garuba, Harry. 1988. "Introduction." In *Voices from the Fringe: An ANA Anthology of New Nigerian Poetry*, edited by Harry Garuba. Lagos: Malthouse Press.

———. 2005. "The Unbearable Lightness of Being: Re-figuring Trends in Recent Nigerian Poetry." *English in Africa* 32, no. 1: 51–72.

Gengenbach, Heidi. 1994. "Truth-Telling and the Politics of Women's Life History Research in Africa: A Reply to Kirk Hoppe." *The International Journal of African Historical Studies* 27, no. 3: 619–27.

Gide, André. 2001 (1935). *If It Die . . . : An Autobiography*. Translated by Dorothy Bussy. New York: Vintage.

———. 1986. (1929). *Travels in the Congo*. Translated by Dorothy Bussy. New York: Penguin Books.

Gikandi, Simon. 2001. "Chinua Achebe and the Invention of African Culture." *Research in African Literature* 32, no. 3: 3–8.

———. 1992. "History and Character in The Healers." In Wright, *Critical Perspectives on Ayi Kwei Armah*, 315–23.

Gilbert, Sandra M., and Susan Guber. 1987. *No Man's Land: The Place of the Woman Writer in the Twentieth Century*, vol. 1, *The War of the Words*. New Haven, CT: Yale University Press.

Godenne, Rene. 1995. *La nouvelle*. Paris: Honoré Champion Editeur.

Goldberg, Elizabeth Swanson. 2007. *Beyond Terror: Gender, Narrative, Human Rights*. New Brunswick, NJ: Rutgers University Press.

Golley, Nawar al-Hassan. 2003. *Reading Arab Women's Autobiographies: Shahrazad Tells Her Story*. Austin: University of Texas Press.

Gordimer, Nadine. 1995. *Writing and Being*. Cambridge, MA: Harvard University Press.

Gourevitch, Philip. 2010. "Alms Dealers." *The New Yorker*, October 11, 102–9.

Grahame, Iain. 1980. *Amin and Uganda: Personal Memoir*. London: Granada.

Graves, Robert. 1934. *I, Claudius*. New York: Harrison Smith and Robert Haas.

Gregg, Gary S. 1998. "Culture, Personality, and the Multiplicity of Identity: Evidence from North African Life Narratives." *Ethos: Communicating Multiple Identities in Muslim Communities* 26, no. 2: 120–52.

Gregory, Robert. 1993. *Quest for Equality: Asian Politics in East Africa, 1900–1967*. New Delhi: Orient Longman.

Grigg, Russell. 1999. "From the Mechanism of Psychosis to Universal Condition of the Symptom: On Foreclosure." In *Key Concepts of Lacanian Psychoanalysis*, edited by Dany Nobus, 48–74. New York: Other Press.

Gundan, Farai. 2014. "The 10 Most Powerful Men in Africa 2014, #2: Chinedu Echeruo, Nigeria, Tech Entrepreneur & Founder of HopStop.com and Tripology.com." Forbes.com, January 31, http://www.forbes.com/sites/faraigundan/2014/01/31/the-10-most-powerful-men-in-africa-2014/.

Gupta, Anirudha. 1975. "India and the Asians in East Africa." In Twaddle, *Expulsion of a Minority*, 125–39.

Guzzio, Tracie. 2006. "All My Father's Texts." In TuSmith, *Critical Essays on John Edgar Wideman*, 175–89.

Gwyn, David. 1977. *Idi Amin: Death-Light of Africa*. Boston: Little, Brown.

Habila, Helon. 2004. *Waiting for an Angel*. New York: W. W. Norton.

Haggard, H. Rider. 1951. *Three Adventure Novels: She, King Solomon's Mines, Allan Quatermain. Each Complete and Unabridged*. New York: Dover.

Hall, Stuart. 2003. "Cultural Identity and Diaspora." In Braziel and Mannur, *Theorizing Diaspora*, 233–46.

Halliwell, Stephen. 1998. *Aristotle's Poetics*. Chicago: The University of Chicago Press.

Harlow, Barbara. 1986. "From the Women's Prison: Third World Women's Narratives of Prison." *Feminist Studies* 2, no. 3: 501–24.

Hawley, John C. 2008a. "Biafra and Heritage and Symbol: Adichie, Mbachu, and Iweala." *Research in African Literatures* 39, 2: 15–26.

———. 2008b. "Introduction: Unrecorded Lives." In *India in Africa, Africa in India: Indian Ocean Cosmopolitanisms*, edited by John C. Hawley, 1–15. Bloomington: Indiana University Press.

Head, Bessie. 1995. *The Cardinals*. Edited by M. J. Daymond. Essex, UK: Heinemann.

———. 1992. *The Collector of Treasures*. London: Heinemann.

Hewett, Heather. 2005. "Coming of Age: Chimamanda Ngozi Adichie and the Voice of the Third Generation." *English in Africa* 32, no. 1: 73–97.

Hill, Rick. 2011. "Meditations on Fanon: A Review Essay on John Edgar Wideman's *Fanon: A Novel*." *The Journal of Pan African Studies* 4, no. 7: 134–36.

Hirsch, Marianne. 2008. "The Generation of Postmemory." *Poetics Today* 29, no. 1: 103–28.

———. 1983. "Spiritual Bildung: The Beautiful Soul as Paradigm." In *The Voyage In: Fictions of Female Development*, edited by Marianne Hirsch, 23–48. Hanover, NH: University Press of New England.

Holquist, Michael. 1990. *Dialogism: Bakhtin and His World*. New York: Routledge.

hooks, bell. "Writing Autobiography." In Smith and Watson, *Women, Autobiography, Theory*, 429–32.

Hoppe, Kirk. 1993. "Whose Life Is It, Anyway?: Issues of Representation in the Life Narrative Texts of African Women." *The International Journal of African Historical Studies* 26, no. 3: 623–36.

Horvitz, Deborah M. 2000. *Literary Trauma: Sadism, Memory, and Sexual Violence in American Women's Fiction*. Albany: State University of New York Press.

House, Humphrey. 1967. *Aristotle's Poetics: A Course of Eight Lectures*. London: Rupert Hart-Davis.

Hron, Madelaine. 2008. "*Ora na-azu nwa*: The Figure of the Child in Third-Generation Nigerian Novels." *Research in African Literatures* 39, no. 2: 27–48.

Ifowodo, Ogaga. 1998. *Homeland and Other Poems*. Ibadan: Kraft Books. Excerpts from this volume reprinted by permission of the publisher.

Igwe, Dimgba. 1987. "Ayi Kwei Armah's Celebration of Silence: An Interview." *Sunday Concord*, April 12, 12.

Ikheloa, Ikhide. 2010. "Chinua Achebe: Lecturing the West in the Past Tense." 234 Next.com, March 7, http://234next.com/csp/cms/sites/Next/ArtsandCulture/Books/5536033-183/story.csp.

Imam, Ayesha M. 2005. "Women's Reproductive and Sexual Rights and the Offense of *Zina* in Muslim Laws in Nigeria." In *Where Human Rights Begin: Health, Sexuality, and Women in the New Millenium*, edited by Wendy Chavkin and Ellen Chesler, 65–94. New Brunswick, NJ: Rutgers University Press.

Inyama, Nnadozie. 1992. "The 'Rebel Girl' in West African Literature: Variations on a Folklore Theme." In *Power and Powerlessness of Women in West African*

Orality, edited by Raoul Granqvist and Nnadozie Inyama, 109–21. Umea Papers in English 15. Umea: Printing Office of Umea University.

Irobi, Esiaba. 1988. *Cotyledons*. Lagos: Update Communications.

Isegawa, Moses. 2000. *Abyssinian Chronicles*. New York: Alfred A. Knopf; 2001 ed., New York: Vintage-Random House.

Ishiguro, Kazuo. 1988. *The Remains of the Day*. New York: Vintage.

Isizoh, Chidi Denis, comp. 2002. "Bibliography on African Traditional Religion." Afrikaworld.net, January 19, http://www.afrikaworld.net/afrel/atr_bibliography.htm.

Iwuanyanwu, Obi ("Obiwu"). 1993. "Ben Obumselu: The Responsible Critic." *The Guardian* (Nigeria), June 19, 19.

———. 2011. "In the Name of the Father: Lacanian Reading of Four White South African Writers." PhD diss., Syracuse University.

Iyer, Pico. 1993. "The Empire Writes Back." *Time International*, February 8, 46–51.

Johnson, Joyce. 1985. "Metaphor, Myth, and Meaning in Bessie Head's *A Question of Power*." *World Literature Written in English* 25, no. 2: 198–211.

Julien Eileen. 1983. "Of Traditional Tales and Short Stories in African Literature." *Presence Africaine* 125: 146–65.

Kaminsky, Alice. 1974. "On Literary Realism." In *The Theory of the Novel: New Essays*, edited by John Halperin, 213–32. New York: Oxford University Press.

Keck, Margaret, and Kathryn Sikkink. 1998. *Activists beyond Borders: Advocacy Networks in International Politics*. Ithaca, NY: Cornell University Press.

Kibera, Leonard. 1979. "Pessimism and the African Novelist: Ayi Kwei Armah's *The Beautyful Ones Are Not Yet Born*." *Journal of Commonwealth Literature* 14, no. 1: 64–72.

Killam, G. D. 1981. "Review of Michael J. C. Echeruo's *Victorian Lagos: Aspects of Nineteenth-Century Lagos Life*." *Research in African Literatures* 12, no. 1: 126–29.

Kuribayashi, Tomoko, and Julie Tharp, eds. 1998. *Creating Safe Space: Violence and Women's Writing*. Albany: State University of New York Press.

Kyemba, Henry. 1977. *A State of Blood: The Inside Story of Idi Amin*. New York: Grosset & Dunlap.

Lacan, Jacques. 1977. *Écrits: A Selection*. Translated by Alan Sheridan. New York: W. W. Norton.

———. 2006. *Écrits: The First Complete Edition in English*. Translated by Bruce Fink in collaboration with Heloise Fink and Russell Grigg. New York: W. W. Norton.

———. 1991b. *The Ego in Freud's Theory and in the Technique of Psychoanalysis, 1954–1955: The Seminar of Jacques Lacan,* Book 2. Edited by Jacques-Alain Miller. Translated by Sylvana Tomaselli. Notes by John Forrester. New York: W. W. Norton.

———. 1997b. *The Ethics of Psychoanalysis, 1959–1960: The Seminar of Jacques Lacan,* Book 7. Edited by Jacques-Alain Miller. Translation and notes by Dennis Porter. New York: W. W. Norton.

———. 1981. *The Four Fundamental Concepts of Psychoanalysis: The Seminar of Jacques Lacan,* Book 11. Edited by Jacques-Alain Miller. Translated by Alan Sheridan. New York: W. W. Norton.

———. 1991a. *Freud's Papers on Technique, 1953–1954: The Seminar of Jacques Lacan,* Book 1. Edited by Jacques-Alain Miller. Translated and notes by John Forrester. New York: W. W. Norton.

———. 2008. *My Teaching.* Preface by Jacques-Alain Miller. Translated by David Macey. London: Verso.

———. 2006. "On My Antecedents." In *Écrits: The First Complete Edition in English,* 51–57.

———. 1997a. *The Psychoses, 1955–1956: The Seminar of Jacques Lacan,* Book 3. Edited by Jacques-Alain Miller. Translated by Russell Grigg. New York: W. W. Norton.

———. 1990. *Television: A Challenge to the Psychoanalytic Establishment.* Edited by Joan Copjec. New York: W. W. Norton.

———. 2006 (1958). "The Youth of Gide, or the Letter and Desire: On a Book by Jean Delay and Another by Jean Schlumberger." In *Écrits: The First Complete Edition in English,* 623–44.

Landy, H. V. 1975. "Is There Anything as a National Literature?" *The Muse* 7 (May): 47–54.

Lauter, Estella. 1993. "Re-enfranchising Art." In *Aesthetics in Feminist Perspective,* edited by Hilda Hein, 21–34. Bloomington: Indiana University Press.

Levinas, Emmanuel. 1985. *Ethics and Infinity: Conversations with Phillip Nemo.* Translated by Richard Cohen. Pittsburgh, PA: Duquesne University Press.

Lindfors, Bernth. 1992. "Armah's Histories." In Wright, *Critical Perspectives on Ayi Kwei Armah,* 267–77.

———. 1974. "Interview with Michael J. C. Echeruo." In *Dem-Say: Interviews with Eight Nigerian Writers,* edited by Bernth Lindfors , 5–15. Austin: African and Afro-American Studies and Research Center, the University of Texas at Austin.

Longinus. 1962. "On the Sublime." In *English Critical Texts,* edited by D. J. Enright and Ernst de Chickera, 393–95. London: Oxford University Press.

Maduakor, Obi. 1986. "Violence as Poetic Focus: Nigerian Poetry and the Biafran Experience." *Nsukka Studies in African Literature* 4: 53–70.

Mahfouz, Naguib. 1986. *Children of the Alley.* Translated by Peter Theroux. New York: Anchor.

———. 2001. *Naguib Mahfouz at Sidi Gaber: Reflections of a Nobel Laureate, 1994–2001.* Cairo: The American University in Cairo Press.

———. 1991. *Palace of Desire.* Translated by William Maynard Hutchins, Lorne M. Kenny, and Olive E. Kenny. Cairo: The American University in Cairo Press.

———. 1989. *Palace Walk.* Translated by William Maynard Hutchins and Olive E. Kenny. Cairo: The American University in Cairo Press.

———. 1992. *Sugar Street.* Translated by William Maynard Hutchins and Angele Botros Samaan. Cairo: The American University in Cairo Press.

Maier, Karl. 2000. *This House Has Fallen: Nigeria in Crisis.* London: Penguin.

Makuchi, Juliana, and Nfah Abbenyi. 1997. *Gender in African Women's Writing.* Bloomington: Indiana University Press.

Marini, Marcelle. 1992. *Jacques Lacan: The French Context.* Translated by Anne Tomiche. New Brunswick, NJ: Rutgers University Press.

Marx, Karl. 1978. "The German Ideology, Part 1." In *Marx-Engel Reader,* edited by Robert C. Tucker, 146–200. New York: W. W. Norton.

McDowell, Lesley. 2008. "Tears of the Desert: One Woman's True Story of Surviving the Horrors of Darfur." *The Scotsman,* August 8.

McGann, J. Jerome. 1988. *Social Values and Poetic Acts: The Historical Judgment of Literary Work.* Cambridge, MA: Harvard University Press.

Miller, Jacques-Alain. 2002. *The Tenderness of Terrorists and Other Letters Written by Jacques-Alain Miller to an Enlightened Public.* Translated by Barbara P. Fulks. Boston, MA: The Wooster Press.

Miller, Judith. 1991. *Album Jacques Lacan: Visages de mon père.* Paris: Seuil.

Mutua, Makau W. 2008. "Human Rights in Africa: The Limited Promise of Liberalism." *African Studies Review* 51, no. 1: 17–39.

———. 2001. "Savages, Victims, and Saviors: The Metaphor of Human Rights." *Harvard International Law Journal* 42, no. 1: 201–45.

Nanji, Shenaaz. 2008. *Child of Dandelions.* Asheville, NC: Front Street.

Nazareth, Peter. 1991. *The General Is Up.* Toronto: TSAR.

———. 1972. *In a Brown Mantle.* Nairobi: East African Literature Bureau.

———. 1981. "Practical Problems and Technical Solutions in Writing My Two Novels." *Callaloo* 11, no. 13: 56–62.

Nazer, Mende, and Damien Lewis. 2003. *Slave: My True Story*. New York: Public Affairs.

Nduka, Uche. 1985. *The Bremen Poems*. Bremen: New Leaf Press.

———. 1997. *Chiaroscuro*. Bremen: Yeti Press.

———. 1988. *Flower Child*. Lagos: Update Communications.

Niles, John D. 2010. *Homo Narrans: The Poetics and Anthropology of Oral Literature*. Philadelphia: University of Pennsylvania Press.

Njogu, Kimani. 2004. *Reading Poetry as Dialogue: An East African Literary Tradition*. Nairobi: Jomo Kenyatta Foundation.

Nnolim, Charles. 1979. "Dialectic as Form: Pejorism in the Novels of Ayi Kwei Armah." *African Literature Today* 10: 207–23.

Nölleke, Brigitte. 2013. "Solange Faladé (1925–2004)." *Women Psychoanalysts in France*, August 8.

Novak, Amy. 2008. "Who Speaks? Who Listens?: The Problem of Address in Two Nigeria Trauma Novels." *Studies in the Novel* 40, nos. 1–2: 31–51.

Nussbaum, Martha. 1990. *Love's Knowledge: Essays on Philosophy and Literature*. New York: Oxford University Press.

———. 2001. *Upheavals of Thought: The Intelligence of Emotions*. New York: Cambridge University Press.

Nwadike, Inno Uzoma. 2000. "Achebe Missed It." *The News*, March 27, 45–47.

Nwapa, Flora. 1992 (1980). *Wives at War and Other Stories*. Trenton, NJ: Africa World Press.

Nwoga, Donatus I. 1994. "From Dialectal Dichotomy to Igbo Standard Development." In *The Gong and the Flute: African Literary Development and Celebration*, edited by Kalu Ogbaa, 103–17. Westport, CT: Greenwood Press.

Nwosu, Maik. 2002. *Invisible Chapters*. Lagos: Hybun Books.

———. 1998. *Suns of Kush*. Lagos: Malthouse Press. Excerpts from this volume reprinted by permission of the publisher.

Nzekwu, Onuora. 1959. "Carnival in Opobo." *Nigeria Magazine* 63: [n.p.].

———. 1981. "Masquerade." In Ogunbiyi, *Drama and Theater in Nigeria*, 131–35.

Obafemi, Olu. 1992. *Nigerian Writers on the Nigerian Civil War*. Ilorin, Nigeria: J. Olu Olatiregun.

Obiechina, Emmanuel. 1985. "Preface." In *African Creations*, edited by Emmanuel Obiechina, vii–viii. Enugu, Nigeria: Fourth Dimension.

Obiwu. 1993. "Ben Obumselu: The Responsible Critic." *The Guardian*, June 19, 19.

———. 2002. "Emeka Echeruo: Even the Stars . . . !" USAfricaonline.com, July 13, http://www.usafricaonline.com/echeruo.obiwu.html.

———. 1996. *Igbos of Northern Nigeria*. Lagos: Torch.

———. 2007. "The Pan-African Brotherhood of Langston Hughes and Nnamdi Azikiwe." *Dialectical Anthropology* 31: 143–65.

Ocaya-Lakidi, Dent. 1975. "Black Attitudes to the Brown and White Colonizers of East Africa." In Twaddle, *Expulsion of a Minority*, 81–97.

O'Connor, Frank. 1962. *The Lonely Voice: A Study of the Short Story*. New York: The World Publishing Company.

Ogbaa, Kalu. 1989. "An African Critic on African Literary Criticism: An Interview with Ben Obumselu." *The Literary Half-Yearly* 30, no. 2: 82–104.

———, ed. 1994. *The Gong and the Flute: African Literary Development and Celebration*. Westport, CT.: Greenwood Press.

Ogunba, Oyin. 1966. "Theater in Nigeria." *Presence Africaine* 30, no. 58: 65–88.

Ogunbiyi, Yemi, ed. 1981. *Drama and Theater in Nigeria: A Critical Source Book*. Foreword by Stanley Macebuh. Lagos: Nigeria Magazine.

———, ed. 1988. *Perspectives on Nigerian Literature: 1700 to the Present*, vol. 1. Lagos: Guardian Books.

Ojaide, Tanure, and Joseph Obi. 2002. *Culture, Society, and Politics in Modern African Literature: Texts and Contexts*. Durham, NC: Carolina Academic Press.

Okpanachi, M. Idris. 2007. *The Eaters of the Living*. Ibadan: Kraft Books.

Okpewho, Isidore. 1992. *African Oral Literature: Backgrounds, Character, and Continuity*. Bloomington: Indiana University Press.

———. 1994. "The Dignity of Intellectual Labor: A Fiftieth Birthday Tribute." In Ogbaa, *The Gong and the Flute*, 185–92. (Originally published in 1988 as "Michael J. C. Echeruo: The Dignity of Intellectual Labor" In Ogunbiyi, *Perspectives on Nigerian Literature*, 142–51.)

———. 1979. *Epic in Africa: Toward a Poetics of the Oral Performance*. New York: Columbia University Press.

———, ed. 1990. *The Oral Performance in Africa*. Ibadan: Spectrum Books.

Ola, Virginia U. 1986. "Women's Role in Bessie Head's Ideal World." *ARIEL* 17, no. 4: [n.p.].

Orwell, George. 1980 (1949). *1984*. London: Heinemann.

Osundare, Niyi. 2005. "Soyinka and the Generation After." *Nigerian Newsday Weekly*, April 8, 21.

Otiono, Nduka, and Odo Diego Okenyodo, eds. 2006. *Camouflage: Best of Contemporary Writing from Nigeria*. Yenagoa, Nigeria: Treasure Books.

Ouolouguem, Yambo. 1984. *Bound to Violence*. Translated by Ralph Manheim. London: Heinemann.

Pereen, Esther. 2008. *Intersubjectivities and Popular Culture: Bakhtin and Beyond*. Stanford, CA: Stanford University Press.

Personal Narrative Group. 1989. "Origins." In Barbre et al., *Interpreting Women's Lives*, 3–15.

Polkey, Pauline, ed. 1999. *Women's Lives into Print: The Theory, Practice, and Writing of Feminist Auto/Biography*. New York: Palgrave Macmillan.

Rabaté, Jean-Michel. 2000. "Construing Lacan." In Rabaté, *Lacan in America*, xvii–xlii.

———, ed. 2000. *Lacan in America*. New York: Other Press.

Radhakrishnan, R. 2003. "Ethnicity in an Age of Diaspora." In Braziel and Mannur, *Theorizing Diaspora*, 119–131. Malden, MA: Blackwell.

Reiss, Timothy J. 2004. "Mapping Identities: Literature, Nationalism, Colonialism." In *Debating World Literature*, edited by Christopher Pendergast, 110–47. New York: Verso.

Roark, Chris. 2002. "John Edgar Wideman." In *African American Autobiographers: A Sourcebook*, edited by Emmanuel S. Nelson, 379–85. Westport, CT: Greenwood Press.

Roazen, Paul. 2000. "What Is Wrong with French Psychoanalysis?: Observations on Lacan's First Seminar." In Rabaté, *Lacan in America*, 41–60.

Roscoe, Adrian. 1971. *Mother Is Gold: A Study of West African Literature*. Cambridge: Cambridge University Press.

Roudinesco, Elisabeth. 1997. *Jacques Lacan: Outline of a Life, History of a System of Thought*. Translated by Barbara Bray. New York: Columbia University Press.

———. 1990. *Jacques Lacan & Co.: A History of Psychoanalysis in France, 1925–1985*. Translated by Jeffrey Mehlman. Chicago: University of Chicago Press.

Sage, Jesse, and Liora Kasten, eds. 2008. *Enslaved: True Stories of Modern-Day Slavery*. NY: Palgrave Macmillan.

Said, Edward. 1994. *Culture and Imperialism*. New York: Vintage Books.

Sartre, Jean-Paul. 1988. *What Is Literature and Other Essays*. Cambridge, MA: Harvard University Press.

Scarry, Elaine. 1985. *The Body in Pain: The Making and Unmaking of the World*. Oxford: Oxford University Press.

Schaffer, Kay, and Sidonie Smith. 2004. *Human Rights and Narrated Lives: The Ethics of Recognition*. New York: Palgrave Macmillan.

Schneiderman, Stuart. 1983. *Jacques Lacan: The Death of an Intellectual Hero*. Cambridge, MA: Harvard University Press.

Sekoni, Ropo. 1990. "The Narrator, Narrative-Pattern, and Audience Experience of Oral Narrative Performance." In *Oral Performance in Africa*, edited by Isidore Okpewho, 139–59. Ibadan: Spectrum.

Shaba, Steve, ed. 1999. *A Volcano of Voices: Poems*. Lagos: Association of Nigerian Authors.

Shaw, Valery. 1983. *The Short Story: A Critical Introduction*. London: Longman.

Shehu, Emman Usman. 1988. *Questions for Big Brother*. Lagos: Update Communications.

Siddiqi, Jameela. 2001. *The Feast of the Nine Virgins*. London: Bogle-L'Ouverture.

Slaughter, Joseph R. 2007. *Human Rights, Inc.: The World Novel, Narrative Form, and International Law*. New York: Fordham University Press.

Smith, Mary F. 1954. *Baba of Karo: A Woman of the Muslim Hausa*. London: Faber and Faber.

Smith, Sidonie, and Julia Watson, eds. 1998. *Women, Autobiography, Theory: A Reader*. Madison: University of Wisconsin Press.

Sollors, Werner. 2001. "Introduction." In Equiano, *The Interesting Narrative of the Life of Olaudah Equiano*, ix–xxxi.

"South African, Nigerian Win Mbari Literary Prizes." 1963. *Fighting Talk* (January): 4.

Soyinka, Wole. 1994 (1988). *Art, Dialogue, and Outrage: Essays on Literature and Culture*. Introduction by Biodun Jeyifo. New York: Pantheon Books.

———. 1982. *Collected Plays 1*. London: Oxford University Press.

———. 2000. "Demystifying the Imperial Will." Speech Given at the Conference on "Preventing the Breakdown of Democracy in Nigeria: Strategies for a Living Constitution," Colin Powell Center, City University of New York, March 23–24. Facebook.com, https://m.facebook.com/note.php?note_id=10151164397359712&refid=17.

———. 1981. "Towards a True Theater." In Ogunbiyi, *Drama and Theater in Nigeria*, 457–61.

———. 1975. "The Writer in a Modern African State." In *When the Man Died: Views, Reviews, and Interviews on Wole Soyinka's Controversial Book*, edited by John Agetua, 25–30. Benin, Nigeria: John Agetua. Reprint 1994, in Soyinka, *Art, Dialogue, and Outrage*, 15–20.

Spender, Dale. 1989. *Women in Isolation*. Townsville, Australia: James Cook University of North Queensland.

Stanley, Liz. 1999. "How Do We Know about Past Lives?: Methodological and Epistemological Matters Involving Prince Philip, the Russian Revolution,

Emily Wilding Davison, My Mum and the Absent Sue." In Polkey, *Lives into Print*, 3–21.

Stratton, Florence. 1994. *African Literature and the Politics of Gender*. London: Routledge.

Strehle, Susan. 2011. "Producing Exile: Diasporic Vision in Adichie's *Half of a Yellow Sun*." *MFS Modern Fiction Studies* 57, no. 4: 650–72.

Suetonius. 1989. *The Twelve Caesars*. Translated by Robert Graves. London: Penguin.

Taiwo, Olufemi. 2001. "Prophets without Honor: African Apostles of Modernity in the Nineteenth Century." *West African Review* 3, no. 1: 11–15. http://www.westafricareview.com/war/vol3.1/3.1war.htm.

Taylor, Charles. 1994. "The Politics of Recognition." In *Multiculturalism*, edited by Amy Gutman, 25–73. Princeton, NJ: Princeton University Press.

Tejani, Bahadur. 1971. *Day After Tomorrow*. Nairobi: East African Literature Bureau.

Thiong'o, Ngugi wa. 1986. *Decolonizing the Mind: The Politics of Language in African Literature*. London: Heinemann.

———. 1977. *Petals of Blood*. New York: E. P. Dutton.

———. 1964. *Weep Not, Child*. Oxford: Heinemann.

Tinker, Hugh. 1975. "Indians Abroad: Emigration, Restriction, and Rejection." In Twaddle, *Expulsion of a Minority*, 15–29.

Tripp, Aili Mari. 2009. "Introduction." In *African Women's Movements: Changing Political Landscapes*, edited by Aili Mari Tripp, Isabel Casimiro, Joy Kwesiga, and Alice Mungwa, 1–24. Cambridge: Cambridge University Press.

TuSmith, et al., eds. 2006. *Critical Essays on John Edgar Wideman*. Knoxville: The University of Tennessee Press.

Tuttle, Kate. 2010. "Transition." *Encyclopedia of Africa*, vol. 2, edited by Kwame Anthony Appiah and Henry Louis Gates Jr., 492. New York: Oxford University Press.

Tutuola, Amos. 1994 (1952). *The Palm-wine Drinkard and My Life in the Bush of Ghosts*. New York: Grove Press.

Twaddle, Michael. 1975. "Was the Expulsion Inevitable?" In *Expulsion of a Minority: Essays on Ugandan Asians*, edited by Michael Twaddle, 1–14. London: Athlone Press.

Twain, Mark. 1995. *A Connecticut Yankee in King Arthur's Court*. New York: Barnes and Noble.

Uchechukwu, Chinedu. 2001. "Echeruo na Eceruo: Kedu nke ka Mma . . . ?" *Kwenu* 1, no. 8: 16–22.

Uka, Kalu. 2002. "Creation and Creativity: Theatre Practice in Nigeria." *The Guardian*, May 16, http://nigeriaworld.com/news/source/2002/jun/headlines/06122-newshtml.

Umeh, Okechukwu. 1988. "Cataclysm of Orthodoxy: Religion in Echeruo's 'To God and O'Brien' Poems." *Awka Journal of Education* 1, no. 1: 203–8.

Uwakweh, Pauline Ada. 1995. "Debunking Patriarchy: The Liberational Quality of Voicing in Tsitsi Dangarembga's *Nervous Conditions*." *Research in African Literatures* 26, no. 1: 75–84.

Van der Merwe, Chris, and Pumla Gobodo-Madikizela. 2007. *Narrating Our Healing: Perspectives on Working through Trauma*. Newcastle: Cambridge Scholars Publishing.

Vickroy, Laurie. 2002. *Trauma and Survival in Contemporary Fiction*. Charlottesville: University of Virginia Press.

Wainaina, Binyavanga. 2005. "How to Write about Africa: Instructions for Beginners." *Granta* 92: 91–95.

Wali, Obi. 1963. "The Dead End of African Literature." *Transition* 10: 13–15.

Waliaula, K. Walibora. 2009. "Prison, Poetry, and Polyphony in Abdilatif Abdalla's Sauti ya Dhiki." *Research in African Literatures* 40, no. 3: 129–48.

Walker, Alice. 1982. *The Color Purple*. Orlando, FL: Harcourt.

Waller, Margaret. 1989. "Interview with Julia Kristeva." In *Intertextuality and Contemporary American Fiction*, edited by Patrick O'Donnell and Robert Davis, 280–93. Baltimore: The Johns Hopkins University Press.

Webb, Hugh. 1980. "The African Historical Novel and the Way Forward." *African Literature Today* 11: 24–38.

Wendkos, Paul. 1987. *Blood Vows: The Story of a Mafia Wife*. New York, NY: MTV.

Wesling, Donald. 2003. *Bakhtin and the Social Moorings of Poetry*. Lewisburg, PA: Bucknell University Press.

White, Hayden. 1999. *Figural Realism: Studies in the Mimesis Effect*. Baltimore: The John Hopkins University Press.

Wideman, John Edgar. 2005. *Brothers and Keepers*. Boston: Houghton Mifflin.

———. 1994. *Fatheralong*. New York: Pantheon Books.

———. 1985. "The Language of Home." *The New York Times*, January 13.

———. 1990. *Philadelphia Fire*. New York: Henry Holt.

Wilentz, Gay. 2000. *Healing Narratives: Women Writers Curing Cultural Dis-Ease.* New Brunswick, NJ: Rutgers University Press.

Williamson, Kay, ed. 1972. *Igbo-English Dictionary: Based on the Onitsha Dialect.* Compiled by G. W. Pearman. Revised and expanded by C. N. Madunagu et al. Benin, Nigeria: Ethiop Publishers.

Wren, Robert M. 1979. "Review of Michael J. C. Echeruo's *The Conditioned Imagination from Shakespeare to Conrad.* New York: Holmes and Meier, 1978. 135pp." *Research in African Literatures* 10, no. 3: 458–60.

———. 1991. *Those Magical Years: The Making of Nigerian Literature at Ibadan, 1948–1966.* Boulder, CO: Lynne Rienner; Washington, DC: Three Continents Press.

Wright, Derek, ed. 1992. *Critical Perspectives on Ayi Kwei Armah.* New York: Three Crowns.

Wright, Marcia. 1989. "Personal Narratives, Dynasties, and Women's Campaigns: Two Examples from Africa." In Barbre et al., *Interpreting Women's Lives,* 155–71.

y Gasset, José Ortega. 1968. *The Dehumanization of Art and Other Essays on Art, Culture, and Literature.* Princeton, NJ: Princeton University Press.

Notes on Contributors

GLEN BUSH is a Distinguished Professor of Literature and Humanities at Heartland Community College in Normal, Illinois. While a Fulbright Scholar attached to the University of Jos, in Jos, Nigeria (1991–93), he published a book and several essays on American literature for non-American students. He has also worked closely with the Nigerian scholar and poet Obiwu and the late Professor Francis Ngwaba on several literary projects. Currently, Professor Bush is finishing a series of articles on twentieth-century American literature and has begun work on his third novel, tentatively entitled *The Misadventures of a Drifter.* Bush has published academic articles in the United States, Nigeria, South Africa, India, and Australia on American, British, and African literature.

BOJANA COULIBALY is a lecturer and researcher in African postcolonial literature. She holds a PhD in African literature from the University of Tours and an MA in English from the University of Orleans. She has taught African short fiction, African literature and film, and political thought in African literature in the Department of African, Middle Eastern, and South Asian Languages and Literatures, Rutgers University, as well as American and African American literature in the Department of English, University of Orleans, France. Her research focuses on postcolonial African Anglophone and Francophone literature, genre studies, trauma, and war literature.

SULE E. EGYA is an associate professor in the Department of English, Ibrahim Badamasi Babangida University, Lapai, Nigeria. From 2009 to 2011 he was an Alexander von Humboldt Fellow and resident scholar at the Institute of Asian and African Studies, Humboldt University, Berlin. His research interests include the intersection of literature and politics in Africa, feminism, cultural studies, and ecocriticism. He has published numerous journal articles. He is the author of *Poetics of Rage: A Reading of Remi Raji's Poetry, The Writings of Zaynab Alkali,* and *In*

Their Voices and Visions: Conversations with New Nigerian Writers. He is also a creative writer. His first novel, *Sterile Sky* (winner of the Commonwealth Book Prize for African region, long-listed for the Nigeria Prize for Literature, and short-listed for the Commonwealth Prize), was published by Pearson Education in the African Writers Series in 2012. His poetry volumes include *What the Sea Told Me* (winner of the ANA Gabriel Okara Prize), *Naked Sun,* and *Knifing Tongues.*

CHIELOZONA EZE is an associate professor of English and African literatures at Northeastern Illinois University, Chicago. He is the author of *Postcolonial Imagination and Moral Representations in African Literature and Culture.* He is completing a book manuscript on African feminism and human rights.

HEATHER HEWETT has published in numerous scholarly journals, including *WSQ: Women's Studies Quarterly, English in Africa, MELUS, The Scholar and Feminist Online,* and *Women's Review of Books,* and has published articles in anthologies such as *Expressions of the Body: Representations in African Text and Image* (2009 and *Teaching Human Rights and Literature* (forthcoming, MLA). She is an associate professor of English and Women's, Gender, and Sexuality Studies at the State University of New York at New Paltz, where she teaches courses in literature, women's and gender studies, and nonfiction writing.

DUL JOHNSON is a filmmaker, creative writer, and literary and film scholar. He started his career as a drama director at the Nigerian Television Authority in Jos. He produced many documentaries for the Nigerian Film Corporation, Jos, including *For the Good of All* (1997) and *Of Rocks and Jos* (1999). He variously taught scriptwriting, producing, and directing at the Television College, Jos, and literature at the University of Jos (1995–2004). He also taught film scriptwriting and directing at the National Film Institute, Jos, where he became director of academic planning (2004–2006). He has run workshops on film, television, and radio production, and has been a juror at numerous film festivals throughout Nigeria. Johnson has won national and international awards for his films and dramas, including *There Is Nothing Wrong with My Uncle* (distributed by the Royal Anthropological Institute of Britain), *The Widow's Might,* and *Basket of Water.* In 2010, he won the International Writers Program Fellowship to Brown University. He is the author of two short story collections, *Why Women Won't Make It to Heaven* and *Shadows and Ashes,* and a political biography, *Ugba Uyeh, the Living Legend* (2012). He currently teaches at Bingham University, Karu.

OBI NWAKANMA is an assistant professor of English at the University of Central Florida, Orlando, Florida. He earned an MFA (Poetry) at Washington University in St. Louis, Missouri, and a PhD in English at Saint Louis University, St. Louis, Missouri. He has worked as a journalist for the *Vanguard* newspapers in Lagos, Nigeria, *Newsweek* (New York), and the *Neue Zurcher Zeitung* (Zurich). He was awarded the ANA/Cadbury prize for poetry (1996) and the Walter J. Ong Prize for Distinguished Achievement (2008). His biography of the modernist poet Christopher Okigbo, *Thirsting for Sunlight*, was published by James Currey (Oxford, UK) to wide acclaim in 2010. He has also published *The Horsemen & Other Poems* (2007), and his latest collection of poems, *Birthcry* (2013), was short-listed for the Nigeria Prize for Literature in 2013. Nwakanma taught creative writing and literature as an assistant professor at Truman State University, Kirksville, Missouri, and at various places including Fontbonne University, Harris Stowe State University, Saint Louis University, and Washington University in St. Louis, Missouri, before coming to the English department at the University of Central Florida, where he currently teaches creative writing, transnational literatures, and the black diaspora.

MAIK NWOSU is an associate professor of African and world literature at the University of Denver, Colorado. He worked as a journalist (and received the Nigeria Media Merit Award for Journalist of the Year) before moving to Syracuse University, New York, for a PhD in English and Textual Studies. His research areas include African, African diaspora, postcolonial, and world literatures; fiction, nonfiction, and poetry; and semiotics and critical theory. Nwosu's poetry collection, *Suns of Kush*, was awarded the Association of Nigerian Authors/Cadbury Poetry Prize in 1995. His novels, *Invisible Chapters* and *Alpha Song*, received the Association of Nigerian Authors Prose Prize and the Association of Nigerian Authors/Spectrum Prose Prize in 1999 and 2002, respectively. Nwosu is a fellow of the Akademie Schloss Solitude, Stuttgart, Germany, and of the Civitella Ranieri Center in Umbertide, Italy, as well as a member of the Phi Beta Delta Honor Society for International Scholars. Nwosu's essays have appeared in several journals, including *Research in African Literatures*, *Journal of Postcolonial Writing*, and *Semiotica: Journal of the International Association for Semiotic Studies*. His book, *Markets of Memories: Between the Postcolonial and the Transnational* (2011), explores the traveling sign in the context of cultural-ideological intersections.

OBIWU is a Nigerian American scholar and writer who has published widely and taught at universities in Nigeria and the United States. He received his PhD in English from Syracuse University, where he wrote his dissertation on Lacanian analytics. His book *Igbos of Northern Nigeria* (1996) laid the foundation for contemporary studies on the Igbo diaspora. His essay "The Ecopoetics of Christopher Okigbo and Ezra Pound" won the 2009 Donatus Nwoga Prize for Literary Criticism in Poetry. His studies on the poetry of Chinua Achebe, Nnamdi Azikiwe, and Langston Hughes have been popularly anthologized and referenced. His second collection of poems, *Tigress at Full Moon*, was ranked twentieth on Amazon's 100 poetry best-seller list of February 2012. Obiwu is a fellow of the International School of Theory in the Humanities, Santiago de Compostela, Spain; a fellow of the Presidential Leadership Institute, Central State University, Wilberforce, Ohio; and a multiple winner of the Faculty Excellence Award at Central State University, where he teaches English and creative writing. He was a recipient of the 2007 Resolution Recognition (No. 07-4-12-31) from the Greene County Board of Commissioners of Ohio.

RASHNA B. SINGH currently teaches at Colorado College as a visiting professor in the English department and the Race and Ethnic Studies Program. She received her BA honors degree from the University of Calcutta, her MA from Mount Holyoke College, and her PhD from the University of Massachusetts at Amherst. Singh is the author of *The Imperishable Empire: British Fiction on India* (1977) and *Goodly Is Our Heritage: Children's Literature, Empire, and the Certitude of Character* (2004). She has published book chapters in *Kipling and Beyond: Patriotism, Globalisation, and Postcolonialism* (2010) and *Things Fall Apart, 1958–2008* (2011). She has also contributed to *Asian American Playwrights: A Biobibliographical Critical Sourcebook* and the *Encyclopedia of the Jewish Diaspora: Origins, Experiences, and Culture.* Singh is the author of many scholarly articles and conference papers on the literature of the British Empire, postcolonial literatures, and multicultural and pedagogical issues. In 2003 Singh received a National Endowment for the Humanities Grant to participate in a summer institute at Oxford University. Singh was one of two professors in the state awarded the Massachusetts Council for International Education Lectureship in 1998.

KANCHANA UGBABE is Professor of English at the University of Jos, Nigeria. Her areas of research and publication include feminism, women's writing, and creative writing. *Soulmates* (2011) is her collection of short stories.

Index